ISAIAH

Readings

ISAIAH

Peter D. Miscall

SHEFFIELD PHOENIX PRESS

2006

For Ruth, Fran and Irene
faithful friends are a
sturdy treasure

Copyright © Sheffield Phoenix Press, 2006

First published by Sheffield Academic Press, 1993

Published by Sheffield Phoenix Press
Department of Biblical Studies, University of Sheffield
Sheffield S10 2TN

www.sheffieldphoenix.com

A CIP catalogue record for this book
is available from the British Library

Typeset by Vikatan Publishing Solutions, Chennai, India

Printed by Lightning Source

ISBN 13-digit 978-1-905048-44-1 (hardback)
ISBN 10-digit 1-905048-44-0 (hardback)

ISBN 13-digit 978-1-905048-45-8 (paperback)
ISBN 10-digit 1-905048-45-9 (paperback)

Contents

Preface

When Sheffield Phoenix Press first said that they were going to republish my Isaiah commentary from 1993, I considered reworking it but decided not to because of time constraints. It is being republished in its original form with this preface looking back on the last 12 years of Isaiah study, particularly on my own work and how it relates to this commentary. As I reread my own book in full – something not done in almost eight years – I was pleased with my decision not to rewrite it. The book stands on its own as a contribution to the reading of Isaiah. Rewriting it would have changed it, to the positive in some ways but to the negative in too many others. I found myself thinking, 'Did I really say that?', both with pleasure and chagrin and with more of the former than the latter. And I am a different reader of the Bible, particularly of Isaiah, than the early 90s author of *Isaiah* and I am convinced that I would have lost much of the original even if I tried to change only its writing style. I have since developed, expanded and deepened many of the insights of *Isaiah*, but I have not left them behind.

Since 1993 I have produced two more works on Isaiah. *Isaiah 34–35: A Nightmare/A Dream* (1999) is a close and intense reading of the poem, with two opposed frames, in Isaiah 34–35.[1] Poetic analysis, discussion of relevant modes of interpretation and the poem's relation to the rest of Isaiah are at the heart of the work. *Isaiah* already contains all three focuses in brief while the subsequent work develops them in both extent and detail. In *Isaiah* I also deal consistently with the poet's exploration, throughout the Isaiah scroll, of the intertwining of a wide variety of contrasts or opposites, such as good (justice and righteousness) and evil (sin and rebellion), salvation and destruction, light and dark, and wet and dry. There is not a set valuation for the

---

1. Peter D. Miscall, *Isaiah 34-35: A Nightmare/A Dream* (JSOT-Sup, 281; Sheffield: Sheffield Academic Press, 1999).

poles of the latter oppositions. Light, for example, can be the beneficial effects of the sun for sight, warmth and life but it can also be the sun's desiccating, life-robbing heat. And water can be a source of life or of death, as in a flood. *Isaiah 34–35* concentrates on one example of the interplay of oppositions such as destruction and restoration; righteousness and sin; the domestic and the wild; and Israelite and non-Israelite. The book is easily the most detailed, attentive reading of a biblical text that I have yet produced and a fulfillment of a promise in *Isaiah*. 'This [*Isaiah*] is not a detailed poetic analysis of Isaiah, particularly in matters of parallelism and meter; such analyses also belong in other works... concerned with the close reading of selected passages' (9).

Reading Isaiah: Poetry and Vision (2001) is a more general application, in terms of both content and writing style, of central insights of *Isaiah* to a way of reading Isaiah as a grand poetic drama.[1] The presentation in *Reading Isaiah* moves back and forth through Isaiah and is not a sequential commentary; it is more a 'how to read' than a developed reading. The organizing topics of each chapter of the book are already present and developed in *Isaiah*: the book of Isaiah as a single work, themes, imagery, active and speaking characters, and the Lord's Holy Mountain. The latter is a central symbol of what is the good for Isaiah: a way of following the Lord, a moral, spiritual state and a place. *Reading Isaiah* is a logical development of *Isaiah* in my own scholarly development. Anyone reading both books will be immediately struck by the similarity of content and the difference of presentation.

Isaiah also fits a particular stage in the often contentious and ongoing debates about the best way to read Isaiah: the traditional three Isaiahs and the modifications of that division, the wide range of redactional theories and proposals to read Isaiah as a single work. Redactional theories often seek a middle ground between the other two. I remain committed to reading Isaiah as one work and now prefer to call it a scroll—as a first move away from the notions of unity and coherency that so often attend the word 'book'. Presuppositions of certain types of unity of content and coherency of style fuel the traditional division into three Isaiahs and most redactional theories. Reading Isaiah as one

1.   Peter D. Quinn-Miscall, *Reading Isaiah: Poetry and Vision* (Louisville: Westminster John Knox Press, 2001).

work, one scroll, faces the daunting task of dealing with the wide variety of poetic style, themes, terminology and such; the variety weaves its way throughout the book. In *Isaiah* and my subsequent work, I do not regard such reading as seeking to harmonize, to gloss over or in any way to explain away the variety and the complexities of the Isaianic text.

Since *Isaiah* I have expanded the notion of Isaiah's encyclopedic quality, the drive to have as much variety as possible in areas such as literary style, imagery, terminology and theme and in the ways that these various aspects are combined and interwoven in the text. Isaiah wants to say many different things about God, Israel and the rest of the world and how they interact in the past, present, and future, even if those varied ideas clash and contradict one another, and he wants to say it in many different ways, even if the styles and images clash and mutate in often bewildering fashion. *Isaiah* is my first thoroughgoing encounter with the full range of Isaiah's diversity and my first try at reading the scroll with sustained attention to poetic and dramatic categories.

In *Isaiah* I eschew lengthy involvement in the historical issues of the history of ancient Israel and Judah and the peoples surrounding them and of the historical process of the actual composition and writing of the scroll. I have seen no need since to change that focus in any significant fashion. In *Isaiah* and my continuing work I find myself aligned with those who question and usually reject historical reconstructions of all sorts that are based solely on the biblical text with no significant extra-biblical evidence.

Historical knowledge, for example, what we know of the ancient nations Israel, Assyria and Babylon from beyond the biblical text, certainly aids and enriches our grasp of their characterizations in Isaiah; but these entities are, first and foremost, characters within Isaiah's grand drama. To concentrate on them in Isaiah as historical entities with their own actual historical stories is to miss too much of the poetic and dramatic qualities of Isaiah's poem. Babylon, for example, is both King (Isaiah 13) and Lady (Isaiah 47). The ancient city-state may linger somewhere in the background but it is not centrally present in the Isaianic scroll. In *Isaiah* and afterwards I have worked to expand and develop the particularities and the disparate aspects of the characterizations of the personages and peoples who appear within Isaiah. Each, for example, Isaiah, Israel and Assyria, plays different roles within the work and the roles can change as we move through the scroll.

The eighth-century prophet Isaiah appears at a few select points in the first part of the scroll of Isaiah and in the narrative of King Hezekiah in 2 Kings 18–20; the latter, with some changes, is incorporated into Isaiah 36–39. Isaiah the prophet is a personage in the scroll, figuring in detail one way of understanding a prophet and prophetic speech. What this depiction is, what it is to be a prophet, has been a focus of my study from *Isaiah* on. My readings of the Servant and of other prophetic characters in the latter part of the scroll accord with this concern: What do they say and do within the scroll? Who are they in that grand work? What is it to be a servant or a messenger of the Lord? However, whether the prophet Isaiah was an actual historical personage or only a legendary figure tied to Hezekiah is an open question since these biblical texts are the only material that we have about him.

As to the composition of the scroll, I do not doubt that the Isaiah scroll, composed sometime in the first century or two of the postexilic period, includes a great deal of earlier material, preserved in both written and oral form, but I do not think that we can reconstruct, solely from the evidence of this one scroll, what this earlier material was and how it was incorporated into the scroll. All the stylistic, thematic, and verbal diversity that is cited as evidence for the various source and redactional theories is a description of Isaiah and is the stuff that my readings of Isaiah address. The challenge is to describe and read the scroll of Isaiah as it stands, not to dismantle it into more manageable parts. *Isaiah* is my first full meeting of that challenge.[1]

The writing style of *Isaiah* is terse and bare with minimal use of expansions and examples; even explanatory adjectives are at a premium. I no longer attempt to write in such a brusque manner. However, a bare style does leave open possibilities in my book, many of which would likely be lost if I had rewritten the work in a fuller and more expansive manner. I am still satisfied with what I accomplished in *Isaiah* and can present it as originally written.

One significant aspect of my subsequent work that is not in *Isaiah* is the frequent and consistent use of passages from Isaiah

---

1.   For similar comments on the use of the prophetic texts, including Jeremiah, Ezekiel and The Twelve, to reconstruct the history of Israel or the history of the prophetic scrolls, see Edgar W. Conrad, *Reading The Latter Prophets: Toward a New Canonical Criticism* (JSOTSup, 376; London/New York: T. & T. Clark, 2003).

to support and to exemplify my assertions and particular readings. Citing only chapter-and-verse as I do in *Isaiah* does not always clarify and often obscures the point that I am trying to make. I now see the need for ample use of passages in translation with some discussion of the underlying Hebrew text when appropriate. Usually the translations are my own and tend towards the literal end of the translation spectrum. This allows me to show specific aspects of the text that might be missed in another translation and those aspects can concern overall content, terminology, wordplay, and poetic structure. With a poetic text such as Isaiah, the presentation of the text on the page is a significant part of a translation.

In addition, including passages allows me to discuss the necessary relationship of translation and interpretation. Since translation is not an objective, value-free process, a translator cannot translate a text without first reading and interpreting it. And I find that wrestling with different ways of rendering the same passage can give me added insight into the original Hebrew text. Interpretive insight occurs in the interplay of interpretation and translation. To display this interplay I often incorporate one or more translations of the one passage, at times including different renderings of my own. And, as with my reading in general, the goal is to reveal the possibilities and richness of the text and of the reading process, not to produce the one best and most faithful translation.

If, or perhaps better when, I return to write about Isaiah, I will want to work with a combination of all three approaches and focuses. Melding the sequential ordering of *Isaiah* and its attention to the ever-changing diversity of the book with the intensive reading of *Isaiah 34–35* can produce a poetic, dramatic reading of Isaiah like that in *Reading Isaiah* but much more attuned to the overall movement of the scroll from the initial call to hear to the closing view of burning corpses. *Isaiah* provides solid groundwork for such an ambitious project. And *Isaiah* marks a decisive turn in my critical career when I found myself interested far more in reading the Hebrew Bible, here Isaiah, than in debating the story of its composition or of the historical reliability of its references to people and events. Rereading *Isaiah* has only further fueled that interest for me.

Peter D. Miscall

Sigla And Abbreviations

!	When used after a chapter-and-verse citation, this indicates that the passage cited is in tension with or in opposition to the text under discussion.
*	A Hebrew term so marked is the verbal root and not the form in the text; I use this mainly when comparing different parts of speech from the same root.
at	'At' when followed by a chapter-and-verse indicates that the topic is dealt with at greater length at that point.

AnBib	Analecta biblica
BibOr	Biblica et orientalia
CBQ	*Catholic Biblical Quarterly*
HTR	*Harvard Theological Review*
JBL	*Journal of Biblical Literature*
JSNTSup	*Journal for the Study of the New Testament*, Supplement Series
JSOT	*Journal for the Study of the Old Testament*
MT	Masoretic Text
NIV	New International Version
NRSV	New Revised Standard Version
RB	*Revue biblique*
REB	Revised English Bible
RSV	Revised Standard Version
Sem	*Semitica*
SJT	*Scottish Journal of Theology*
TynBul	*Tyndale Bulletin*
VT	*Vetus Testamentum*
WBC	Word Biblical Commentary
ZAW	*Zeitschrift für die alttestamentliche Wissenschaft*

Introduction

This is a reading of the text of Isaiah both as a whole and in its parts and, as much as possible, according to the order of the book. The commentary is meant to enrich and add to the reader's understanding and appreciation of the book of Isaiah and not to replace it; I do not present this commentary as the one and only way to read Isaiah. This is not a detailed treatise on the textual and philological details that form the parameters for a reading. These details should be discussed in another work dedicated to those purposes.[1] Nor is this a reconstruction of the history of Israel. That history with its peoples, characters and events is discussed only when it is incorporated into the book of Isaiah and when reference to it is necessary for a full reading of Isaiah. Further, this is not a detailed poetic analysis of Isaiah, particularly in matters of parallelism and meter; such analyses also belong in other works, especially articles and books concerned with the close reading of selected passages. Finally, as a commentary, this work is not self-contained; it assumes and requires that its reader has the book of Isaiah at hand and consults it consistently.

It has long been noted that Isaiah covers an extensive period of history and that the book breaks into clearly defined sections. Since the rise of historical criticism in the seventeenth and eighteenth centuries, the study of Isaiah has been based on the assumption that the distinct parts of the book are to be understood as contemporary with and referring to different stages of Israel's history. The stages go from the rise of the Assyrian Empire in the last half of the eighth century BCE to the first century of the Persian Empire in the sixth and fifth centuries BCE.

---

1. J.D.W. Watts (*Isaiah 1–33* [WBC, 24; Waco, TX: Word Books, 1985]; *Isaiah 34–66* [WBC, 25; Waco, TX: Word Books, 1987]) thoroughly and clearly deals with philological and textual details and problems, and he includes extensive bibliography.

This assumption led first to the division of the book into two parts, chs. 1–39 and 40–66. In the late nineteenth century Bernhard Duhm refined this into the hypothesis of the three Isaiahs, chs. 1–39 (First Isaiah), 40–55 (Second or Deutero-Isaiah) and 56–66 (Third or Trito-Isaiah), based on the rough movement from threats of Assyrian and Babylonian invasion to their accomplishment, especially in the sixth century Exile, and to the promises and accomplishment of return and finally of rebuilding. Even conservative commentators such as Keil and Delitzsch take this change of historical scene into account when they ascribe the entire book to the eighth-century prophet announced in chs. 1, 6–8 and 36–39 and regard chs. 40–66 as his prediction of the sixth-century return from the Exile.

Within these divisions of Isaiah, there have been many proposed subdivisions and then subdivisions within the subdivisions. Within Isaiah 1–39, chs. 1–12, 13–23 (The Oracles against the Nations) and 24–27 (The Isaianic Apocalypse) are excellent examples since these sections are further broken into ever shorter passages.[1] There has been little concern for the flow or structure of the whole book or even of the main divisions. Indeed in most commentaries, two different scholars in two books or parts comment on chs. 1–39 and 40–66.[2]

However, in the last two decades there have been attempts, in rhetorical and redaction-critical studies, to look at the structure of Isaiah in its major parts and as a whole. The scholars still regard the parts of Isaiah as referring to different stages in Israel's history. However, the book was edited and re-edited at points during this history to update it and give it a continuing relevance. Rémi Lack, writing in 1973, is perhaps the earliest and

---

1. See S. Erlandsson (*The Burden of Babylon: A Study of Isaiah 13.2–14.23* [Lund: Gleerup, 1970], pp. 43-63) for a review of the many proposed divisions of chs. 13–23.

2. *The Interpreter's Bible*, V (Nashville: Abingdon Press, 1956), is an example. Scott and Muilenburg respectively deal with chs. 1–39 and 40–66. Their introductions, pp. 151–64 and 381–418, discuss the division and subdivision of the book in greater detail. In the Old Testament Library, Kaiser and Westermann similarly divide the duties; Kaiser divides his work on chs. 1–39 into two commentaries on 1–12 and 13–39.

the most thorough; he analyses the imagery, *la symbolique*, of Isaiah as a main redactional device.[1]

More recently John D.W. Watts,[2] in his two-volume commentary on Isaiah, has argued that Isaiah is a unified work, a Vision, composed in the mid-fifth century BCE. He specifies 435 BCE in the reign of Artaxerxes I. The book of Isaiah is addressed to a divided community struggling to find its identity as a small province in a powerful world empire. The message and vision of the book stretch back to the traditions about the great eighth-century prophet, Isaiah of Jerusalem. However, Watts maintains the historical bias. Isaiah 1–39, although composed in the fifth century, are read as an accurate and chronological portrayal of historical events of the pre-exilic period.

Edgar W. Conrad's *Reading Isaiah* is the first significant work that approaches Isaiah both as a unified work and as a work to be read on its own terms and not as a poetic rendering of Israel's history. Isaiah 6–39 is the vision of Isaiah of Jerusalem which was lost on its original audience who were 'deaf' and 'blind'; the vision is given a new setting for its reception with chs. 1–5 and 40–66. They provide a setting when Judah is still threatened by Babylonian power and dreams of its demise. Since Isaiah terms itself a vision, this implies 'that its language is not used primarily for descriptive or mimetic purposes'. Although the whole book of Isaiah provides a new setting for a reading of the old vision, it is not attempting to describe an actual world, present or past. It presents 'a world that never was but that is filled with the possibility of what might be. To enter into that world does not require a journey into the past but contemplation of a future.'[3]

---

1. R. Lack, *La symbolique du livre d'Isaïe* (AnBib, 59; Rome: Biblical Institute Press, 1973).

2. See p. 15 n. 1.

3. E.W. Conrad, *Reading Isaiah* (Overtures to Biblical Theology; Minneapolis: Fortress Press, 1991), p. 161.

There are also a growing number of studies of selected sections and motifs within Isaiah;[1] they offer close readings of passages and are concerned with the literary and poetic character of the text of Isaiah. They pay attention to poetic features such as parallelism, balance and figurative language. Stephen A. Geller responds in the affirmative to the question contained in his title 'Were the Prophets Poets?'. Finally, I note Barry Webb's 'Zion in Transformation' which regards Isaiah as a whole and briefly traces the changes that the concepts of Zion and the remnant undergo in the book.[2]

With Watts and Conrad I share the assumption of a unified work composed in the postexilic period, probably in the fifth century. However, I do not enter into further debate about date, authorship or the process of composition. I assume that the postexilic author(s) used much existing material, written and oral, some perhaps deriving from the eighth century, but I am not attempting to isolate any of that material, particularly 'original prophetic speeches'. We have too little independent information about pre- or postexilic Israel to reconstruct a historical setting or process of writing except in the most general respects. I am offering an interpretation of Isaiah; I am not trying to prove a historical hypothesis. I recognize the distinct parts of the book and their movement through Assyrian, Babylonian and Persian periods of history. However, I am not using Isaiah as a source to reconstruct the history of these periods.

I speak of Isaiah as a vision in the sense of a text that presents something to be seen and imagined rather than just thought and conceptualized. Therefore, I devote attention to the imagery and other poetic features of Isaiah. In addition, I use 'vision' in the broader sense of the realm of the imagination. Isaiah presents a

---

1.   Excellent examples are D.J.A. Clines, *I, He, We and They: A Literary Approach to Isaiah 53* (JSOTSup, 1; Sheffield: JSOT Press, 1976); J.C. Exum, 'Of Broken Pots, Fluttering Birds, and Visions in the Night: Extended Simile and Poetic Technique in Isaiah', *CBQ* 43 (1981), pp. 331-52; S.A. Geller 'A Poetic Analysis of Isaiah 40.1-2', *HTR* 77 (1984), pp. 413-20; J.F.A. Sawyer, 'Daughter of Zion and Servant of the Lord in Isaiah: A Comparison', *JSOT* 44 (1989), pp. 89-107.

2.   B.G. Webb, 'Zion in Transformation: A Literacy Approach to Isaiah' in D.J.A. Clines, S.E. Fowl and S.E. Porter (eds.), *The Bible in Three Dimensions* (JSOTSup, 87; Sheffield: JSOT Press, 1990), pp. 65-84.

panorama of God and world and, against this backdrop, he envisions a way of life that is God's way and an ideal community that dwells on God's holy mountain. In Conrad's words, however, this is 'a world that never was but that is filled with the possibility of what might be'.

In addition, this is a vision of a community, of an ideal way of life, and not an attempt to codify or legislate specific behavior that characterizes that mode of life. Isaiah decisively distinguishes righteous from wicked behavior. Even though he gives more specific examples of the latter, there is no doubt in Isaiah about the distinction. On the other hand, the distinction, in the text of Isaiah, is between ways of acting, that is, following the Lord's ways or following one's own ways, and not between righteous and wicked groups who can be definitively equated with actual political, religious and social groups existing in postexilic Israel.

Isaiah 1–39 are a postexilic representation and interpretation of the pre-exilic period. They tell us much more about the fears and hopes of people of this later time than they do about the people and events of the later eighth and early seventh centuries. In the same vein, I regard Isaiah 40–66 as a later representation and interpretation of the return from exile and of the early days of the postexilic era. I do not read them as contemporary compositions from this early postexilic period. The book of Isaiah draws intricate analogies between these past eras, late eighth and mid-sixth centuries, so that what happened in the days of Isaiah (the eighth-century prophet), Ahaz and Hezekiah had much in common with sixth-century Israel facing and fearing both return from exile and the daunting project of rebuilding the community.

Put simply, chs. 1–39 contain the full message of the book of Isaiah. From the point of view of chs. 40–66, set in the sixth century, it was all said 'back then'. This is argued explicitly by the Lord when he refers to his powers of prediction, for example in 41.25-29. The exile was predicted and brought into being by the Lord. In spite of this fullness, the people back then missed or deliberately refused the message; they were deaf and blind. Chapters 40–66 repeat the message stressing even more that it is the Lord's word. Will people now, as they return from exile, see, hear and accept the vision? Despite the restatement and the evidence of prediction and fulfillment, there are people who reject the prophet's message.

At the same time and on another level, Isaiah, the fifth-century prophet-poet-author, draws analogies between these past times and his fifth-century situation. I treat this in the commentary on chs. 40–66. As people in the eighth to seventh and in the mid-sixth centuries resisted and rejected the message, whether of hope or of judgment, people in the fifth century question and reject Isaiah's vision. These latest people are most deaf and blind since they can learn from the experiences of two past eras.

Time

The entire book of Isaiah envisions the past in ways that speak to the present and leap into the future. However, such a statement is too simple. Isaiah is at once an interpretation, a vision, of the past, the present and the future. This melding and overlaying of times and of sections of the book are a significant part of what I understand a vision to be. It is an overlaying since the times and the parts of Isaiah do not become identical or indistinguishable. For example, there is a plot in Isaiah in which divine goodness is repaid with rebellion and sin. This leads to judgment by invasion, destruction and exile, but a remnant is left. The grimness is partially offset by the promise and hope of deliverance and ultimate victory. But this plot does not resolve itself into a simple narrative of past goodness and past sin, present (or past) judgment and future (or present) hope. Divine benefit, sin, judgment and promise are all past, present and future. Isaiah is monotonous, repetitive reading if one reads it just for the themes; the story of the book of Isaiah is already there in the first four chapters.

The melding of time can be exemplified by a brief discussion of the Hebrew verb system and its translation. Isaiah opens with a familiar call:

(1.2)Hear, O Heavens; give ear, O Earth for the Lord speaks: 'Children I rear and raise but they rebel against me.
(3)The ox knows its owner and the ass, the manger of its Lord; Israel does not know; my people do not understand'.

In Hebrew all of the verbs from 'speaks' on are in the perfect form which refers to an action as in some sense completed or complete; the completion can refer to a characteristic action that is habitual or ongoing. Many English translations, for example NRSV, use a past tense in v. 2—'has spoken', 'reared', 'brought up' and 'rebelled'—and a present tense in v. 3—'knows', 'does not know' and 'do not understand'. My translation emphasizes the immediacy and temporal inclusiveness of what is seen and heard; Isaiah's vision spans past, present and future. There is plot sequence here. Rebellion follows the rearing; the punishment of 1.4-9 follows the rebellion; this is followed by a promise of restoration in 1.26-27. But the overall plot can begin at any point in time. Whenever the Lord raises children, they rebel, are punished and then restored.

Isaiah 2 opens with 'the word (or thing) that Isaiah envisions' for 'the latter days', the future (2.1-2). He gives a present vision of that future.

(2) The mountain of the house of the Lord is set at the head of the
        mountains and is raised above the hills.
All nations stream to it (3) and many peoples come...from Zion goes
        forth teaching and the word of the Lord from Jerusalem.
(4) He/it judges between the nations and arbitrates for many peoples.
        They beat their swords into plows and their spears into
        pruning hooks; nation does not lift the sword against
        nation, and they no longer learn the art of war.

Much of the impact of Isaiah as a vision is lost in English translations which consistently put sin and judgment in the past and present with hope and promise situated in the present and looking to the future. Isaiah sees it all at once and now. In the commentary, my translations of isolated sections and my comments usually read Isaiah with this present emphasis.

The Isaianic Community

The postexilic community was concerned with their identity and self-understanding. Their existence as a people was threatened by the consequences of the catastrophe of exile and loss of national independence. Judah was a small province in the Persian Empire which stretched from eastern Europe to the borders of India. There were other Jewish communities, and perhaps provinces, in close proximity to Judah, for example in Samaria and Transjordan, and far away, for example in Egypt and Babylon. Isaiah presents a vision for this community, a particular way for this people to understand themselves, their God and their world; the vision spans past, present and future. Questions of the historical reference and accuracy of the vision are another matter; I am not asking these questions.

The community is open and inclusive (ch. 56). Restored Jerusalem is a city without stone walls, an unwalled garden and a mountain to which others may flow (2.2-4; chs. 60–62). The Lord protects his people with a canopy (4.5-6), a cover[1] and hovers over them like a flock of birds (31.4-5). He is not a fortified wall. In ch. 66, he speaks against the temple as a symbol of enclosure and exclusion. Within the community, the people have just and compassionate leaders who do what past kings claimed they would do. This is messianic, that is, royal, ideology. The society is structured around peace, justice, care for the poor and oppressed, and around proper worship of the Lord and trust in his word and ways. True worship, symbolized by proper fasting, is going out of oneself to care for others in the community (ch. 58).

The Drama

In Isaiah, the community is called Israel, the people of God, the remnant, the servants of the Lord, etc. They are distinguished from others: God, the nations and even other groups within Israel; however, these distinctions are not hard-and-fast. The divisions within humanity and within Israel are a constant theme in Isaiah, and he portrays many relationships between the groups formed by these divisions. The book concerns the heavens and the earth, all nations and peoples, humanity and all flesh. We cannot resolve Isaiah into a simple narrative nor can we resolve it into a morality tale of good versus evil with Israel good and the nations evil. The story of sin, judgment (2.9-22) and restoration applies to all (2.2-4).

Israel as a people participates in this story (1.2-9; 4.2-6) and, at the same time, Israel is comprised of wicked and righteous, oppressors and oppressed (1.19-23, 27-28; 3.13-15). The distinction between good and evil that is at points applied to Israel over against the nations can be applied to Israel itself. Combined with my comments on righteous versus wicked behavior, this is an important point. There is no doubt in Isaiah about the radical separation of good and evil. What is in doubt, indeed, what is denied, is the equation of these absolute categories with actual human groups, whether defined in religious or political terms.

Isaiah presents his vision as a quasi-drama. The book is dominated by dramatic speeches; even the narrative sections in chs. 6–8 and 36–39 provide settings for further speeches. The characters

---

1. 37.35 with Watts, *Isaiah 34–66*, p. 40.

are not presented as distinct and historical individuals; they are constructs in the grand poetic work of Isaiah. Israel, for example, is masculine singular (1.4), masculine plural (1.5-7) and feminine singular (1.21-26). The latter text is addressed to Jerusalem which stands on its own as a woman and, as the capital city, is a metonym for Israel. Israel is judged and condemned, desolate and devastated, and comforted and redeemed. Finally, Israel, as a name, is generally the people of God; however, at points in the book, it is the northern kingdom, whose capital is Samaria, which was destroyed in 722 BCE (7.1-9; 9.8-12; 28.1-4).

Generally male, God at times is female, whether as a woman and mother (42.14; 45.10; 66.9-13) or as Mother Nature (35.1-7; 41.18-19). God is powerful, judging and even savage; chs. 34 and 63.1-6 contain some of the most gory descriptions of God in the Bible. He is also mild, forgiving and comforting. God is described in human, animate and even inanimate terms. He is a bull (1.24), a lion and birds (31.4-5), a gem (28.5), light and fire (10.17) and the sun and the moon (60.19-20).

Assyria is proud and rebellious (ch. 10). He is cut down and sent back 'on the way by which you came' (37.29). Babylon is proud and arrogant. The king assaults the throne of God (14.1-21) and Lady Babylon considers herself God (ch. 47). Like Israel, Babylon is male and female. Like Assyria, Babylon is cut down and destroyed. All humans who are proud and arrogant are cut down and cast in the dust (2.9-21). But a remnant returns; a remnant of Israel and of other nations such as Moab (chs. 15–16), Egypt (ch. 19) and Tyre (ch. 23). Indeed Egypt, Assyria and Israel are God's people, creation and heritage (19.24-25).

Isaiah's character portrayals are fluid. Israel and the nations are separate nations that become indistinguishable when put into the category of humanity or all flesh. They can share the same characteristics and fates. They can be proud and sinful; judged and destroyed; saved, with only a remnant left. The lines which separate the characters blur and blend and therefore the identity of Israel envisioned in Isaiah is blurred. Israel cannot be clearly separated from the nations, particularly in religious or moral terms; Israel is not righteous and the nations, wicked. In Isaiah a final and ultimate distinction between the righteous and the wicked is a vision; it is something to be hoped and waited for, rather than a reality to be lived and experienced. It is only a hope that someday 'they will go out and gaze upon the corpses of the people who rebel against me' (66.24).

Prophet and Poet

Isaiah, the prophet and poet of the community, envisions it through and over against the past. There is a dramatic movement in the book in which elements of the past, for example kingship and prophecy as represented in chs. 1–39, are transformed and transferred to others. In chs. 40–66, the question revolves more around what the role and function of king and prophet are than around the person who fills and performs them. The past provides images and patterns for understanding these roles. Chapters 1–39 are therefore read in themselves and then re-read in chs. 40–66 through the lens of exile and return. The past is also the tradition represented in other parts of the Hebrew Bible; I will note some of the many parallels, but only enough to give a sense of Isaiah's place in the Hebrew Bible. I do not comment on the parallels at length. In contemporary criticism, such parallels belong to the phenomenon called intertextuality.[1] Transformation is one of the main concepts I use in discussing the relationships with the past and other writings since transformation includes both preservation and change.

Watts sees in Isaiah a major transformation in God's rule of the world. In the past God's impact on the world came through the independent nations of Israel and Judah and through their kings, especially the Davidic dynasty in Judah. However, in the eighth century and later, God changed his ways and worked in the world through the great empires of Assyria, Babylon and Persia. Cyrus is now the Lord's shepherd and messiah (44.28–45.1). A large part of the burden of Isaiah is to get Israel to accept this change and to give up their dreams of political independence and imperial power. This is one of Watts's main bearings on my reading of Isaiah.

Intertextuality also involves self-definition over against other peoples and cultures, especially their religious and mythic writings. I mainly have in mind Baal in Syria-Palestine and the solar gods, Aten and Amun-Re, in Egypt; the consistent use of light imagery in the book is one example of the latter. Isaiah has to cast his vision in ways that take into account not only Israel's traditions and writings, for us the Hebrew Bible, but also the

---

1. P.D. Miscall, 'Isaiah: New Heavens, New Earth, New Book', in D.N. Fewell (ed.), *Reading Between Texts* (Louisville: Westminster Press, 1992), pp. 41-56.

writings of other cultures. He incorporates them into his vision and, at the same time, displaces them, pushes them aside, so that there is room for his work to stand both with them and separate from them. One strategy, especially in relation to other religions, is to turn their gods and myths into poetic images that are used for Isaiah's visions and not for the worship of Baal or Amun-Re.[1]

In reading Isaiah as a poem, a prophetic vision, we deal with its words, with its poetry. Words, their effect and their staying power, are a central theme in Isaiah. The Rabshakeh asks Hezekiah what we can ask this book: 'Is a mere word of the lips counsel and strength for war?' (36.5). Can this book and its words go forth into the world and stand forever? (2.3; 40.8). As prophet, Isaiah describes, in a sweeping vision, God's ways in the world and with humanity in the past, the present and the future. The vision is meant to move and to motivate its readers. They should trust in the Lord and in his ways as depicted in Isaiah and live their lives and structure their society accordingly.

As poet, Isaiah with only his words wants to change the world; he wants to move Israel and all others who read the book to act to bring about this change. However, if the prophet-poet is so strong and effective, does his book not then risk becoming an idol which has been made by human hands (see 44.9-20)?[2] Isaiah's diversity and encyclopedic style, especially in regard to the characterization of God, are part of the attempt to prevent this; he includes so much and places it all in intricate relationships to make his book too complicated to reduce to the simplistic status of an idol.[3] I say more about this in my treatment of the last half of the book when I deal with the issue of resistance and debate reflected within Isaiah.

In dealing with Isaiah's poetry I comment on literary features, but since this commentary presumes that many of its readers are looking at English translations and not at the Hebrew text of

1.   N. Frye, *The Great Code: The Bible and Literature* (New York: Harcourt Brace Jovanovich, 1982), p. 92.
2.   M. Dick ('Prophetic *Poiesis* and the Verbal Icon', *CBQ* 46 [1984], pp. 226-46) develops the point in regard to Isaiah 40–55 and cites pertinent texts to support the point. I extend his argument to the entire book of Isaiah.
3.   P.D.Miscall, 'Isaiah: The Labyrinth of Images', *Sem* 54 (1991), pp. 103-21.

Isaiah, this treatment is restricted, as much as possible, to the features apparent in translation. Although I have consulted many translations of Isaiah, I presume the translation and wording of the NRSV for purposes of convenience and consistency; I indicate and explain when I depart from this particular translation.

Isaiah has a universal cast. God has created the heavens and the earth and all the creatures and plants in them and on them. An aspect of the universal cast is Isaiah's encyclopedic style in his use of words, images, concepts, etc. I point out key examples of this in the commentary; at this point I acknowledge my debt to Rémi Lack's *La symbolique du livre d'Isaïe* for his detailed analyses of conceptual and imagistic schemes in Isaiah such as the antitheses of high and low, full and empty, space and time and the motifs of the cycles of human and vegetable life. The inclusiveness extends to a wide variety of literary styles and types. Form criticism has analyzed many different forms or genres within Isaiah; I am indebted to this type of work but I read the varied forms as an integral part of the book, not as evidence to take passages out of their context.

The Structure of Isaiah

Although there is agreement that Isaiah has obvious sections within it, there are a number of ways to divide the book on a large scale and to relate the sections to one another. Structure refers to this process of dividing and relating. Since I see the book of Isaiah as addressing many issues on many fronts, I see the structure as multi-level and subject to different divisions at the same time. I do not break the book down into one set of divisions that are related to each other in only one way.

For example, ch. 1 introduces the book and forms an inclusion with 65–66; this frames 2–64. At the same time it introduces 1–39 since 36–39 narrate the scene(s) of ch. 1; this frames 2–35 while 2 and 34–35 pair glorious dreams with horrific nightmares. Chapter 1 introduces 1–12 by forming an inclusion with the hymn in 12; this marks off 2–11 which begin and end with a messianic vision of justice and peace. Chapter 13, as 1 and 2, begins with a superscription and develops the desolation depicted in 2.9-22. Finally, ch. 1 introduces 1–5 which set the stage for the appearance of the prophet in 6, for the advance of the Assyrian army, for the attack of the cosmic army of 13, and for the rest of the book. The structure of Isaiah is multiple, shifting and dynamic.

Although I often note their occurrence, I do not generally use the frequent formulas and phrases, such as 'thus says the Lord', 'saying of the Lord', 'in that day', as structuring devices. Nor do I make much of the distinction between poetic speeches, prose speeches and prose comments, usually introduced by 'in that day'. Isaiah's prose has such a balanced, poetic quality to it that recent translations print a larger portion of the book in poetic form than past ones.[1]

For practical purposes I start with the traditional division into chs. 1–39 and 40–66. Chapters 1–39 are set in the years of approximately 735 to 700 BCE, that is from the beginning of the Syro-Ephraimite crisis in Ahaz's reign to Sennacherib's invasion during Hezekiah's. Considerable detail of the period, for example proper names, is presented. Historical nations and their kings are named: Judah, Israel (7.1), Damascus (17.1), Assyria (20.1; 36–37), Egypt (36.6) and Babylon (ch. 39). Judean officials are named in 8.1-3, 22.15-25 and 36.1-37.2. The dominant picture is of rebellion and punishment punctuated and partially offset by scenes and pronouncements of peace and restoration (1.24-27; 2.2-4; 4.2-6).

Chapters 40–66 are set in the time of exile and return, but it is impossible to be more specific. The style of these chapters and the scenes depicted in them are more consistently visionary and metaphorical than in chs. 1–39. Chapters 40–66 are a dream set in a nightmare time, and they are a dream troubled by reality. Names used are traditional and symbolic rather than personal and individual. For example, Jacob, Israel, Sarah, Abraham and Moses refer to the people or to traditional figures, not to historical individuals of the postexilic period. Cyrus, who is referred to by name in 44.28 and 45.1, could be an exception, but his nation, Persia, is not named. In Daniel 1, Ezra 1 and 2 Chronicles 36, he is called 'the king of Persia'. In Isaiah he is a figure somewhere between history and vision. Merodach-baladan, king of Babylon, sent envoys to Hezekiah (39.1). In chs. 40–55, it is not the historical kingdom of Babylon but 'the virgin daughter Babylon,

---

1.   The *Biblia hebraica stuttgartensia* of 1966/67 already does this with the Hebrew text. Compare the RSV and the NRSV since they are based, respectively, on the older and newer editions of the *Biblia hebraica;* the presentations of 22.15-23, 30.19-33 and 44.9-20 are instructive.

daughter of the Chaldeans' (47.1). Cyrus has no nation and Babylon has no king.

Isaiah: Prophet, Poet, Author

The book of Isaiah is a work composed in the postexilic period. I designate the assumed author(s) as Isaiah. The name 'Isaiah' is shorthand for the book as a whole and for its message, views and vision. In the relevant parts of chs. 1–39, I use 'Isaiah' to designate the eighth-century prophet as a character in the book. I will keep the two designations distinct in my discussions. Within the book, others speak. When they are designated by name or title, for example, the Lord, a king or the people, I will use the designation in my comments. However, frequently and throughout the book a person speaks who is over against the others; I designate this speaker as the prophet or the poet without attempting further identification. Even in chs. 1–39 I say prophet or poet, although it may be Isaiah the eighth-century prophet who is speaking within the book. Throughout we must keep in mind that what a character within the book says, even if it is the Lord or the prophet, may differ from what Isaiah, the author of the book, says through that speech.

From the perspective of a whole book, we must remember that Isaiah's vision of God, community and world is not the only one. I note the narrative work in Genesis–2 Kings and the prophetic book of Ezekiel as alternative interpretations. Isaiah's vision is in competition with these and others; many are questioning and rejecting it and the competition and rejection manifest themselves in the text. Although the debate is implicit in chs. 1–39, we will encounter it in explicit form in chs. 40–66.

Cross-References

Isaiah is characterized by diversity and repetition at every level; it is easy to understand why so many have resorted to disintegrative strategies to deal with these features. Reading Isaiah as one book can be a daunting venture. I already noted that reading solely at a thematic level is monotonous, and therefore, I augment a thematic reading with significant attention to literary features such as imagery, repetition at all textual levels, antitheses, wordplay and puns. A major part of the experience of reading Isaiah is the constant moving back-and-forth through the text to find where he says the same or the opposite thing; where he uses similar or opposed imagery; where he employs similar terminology and phraseology; and to examine the parallel passages to determine whether they agree with one another, build on one another or stand in tension with one another.

My commentary is peppered with cross-references to other passages, sometimes with and sometimes without indication of what the parallel passage conveys and of what the overall allusion may entail. I do not claim to be exhaustive in citing parallels. What counts as a parallel is a matter of interpretation and it would be presumptuous for me to claim that I have identified all the parallel texts. One reader's parallels may not exist for another. I offer my perspective on Isaiah and my experience of reading it; my readers will certainly differ in how they react to this perspective and experience. Finally, I do not want to give the impression that reading and appreciating Isaiah is a mechanical matter of looking up words and allusions. Cross-referencing is a way into Isaiah; it is not a map to guide us infallibly through the labyrinth that the text is.

Hebrew

References to the Hebrew text (MT) will be kept to a minimum. However, in the case of a number of Hebrew terms that occur frequently and throughout the book, I will indicate their use with an English transliteration; this is the most efficient way to display the repetition of key words that is a major feature of Isaiah and a major thread that binds the whole together. Generally I will discuss a particular word or related group of words at one point in the text and then cross-reference this discussion. Occasionally I will note when Isaiah employs a different word, perhaps for the only time, since such use can be evidence of a thematic shift or change. The transliteration will usually be the basic noun or verb so that a reader with little knowledge of Hebrew can recognize the repetition; seldom will I transliterate the actual form in the Hebrew text since prefixes and suffixes can obscure the fundamental noun or verb. When I do, it is to illustrate a pun or word play.

In Hebrew in the vast majority of instances, a root has three consonants, for example ṣdq, that take on verbal, nominal or other meanings through the system of vowels and prefixes-suffixes. For example, ṣādēq is 'to be righteous, innocent'; ṣedeq and ṣᵉdāqâ are 'righteousness'; and ṣaddîq is 'righteous one'. Further the verb can have different forms with different meanings. For example, the causative form hiṣdîq is 'to declare innocent, to acquit'. This linguistic feature of Hebrew allows Isaiah a latitude in repetition and word play that is often impossible to capture in translation; my use of Hebrew transliterations provides limited examples of the feature.

Isaiah 1–39

Chapter One

Chapter 1 is an introduction to the book of Isaiah as a whole and in its various parts. My comments on it are partly introductory since I set the framework for my treatment of the other chapters of Isaiah and lay out many of the specifics that I will be discussing.

The superscription presents a vision envisioned in the last half of the eighth century BCE. What is seen includes words to be heard; this is succinctly stated in 2.1—the word that Isaiah envisioned. Seeing and hearing permeate the book and enclose it; 66 concludes the book with the sound of battle (v. 6), a question of hearing and seeing (v. 8) and a going forth to look on corpses (v. 24). However, since we are commenting on Isaiah in English translation, we are more or less restricted to hearing the message, the content; we cannot hear the actual Hebrew, the words and sounds themselves. At points I comment on the Hebrew poetry and its general effect, but I do not give lengthy examples.

The address to heavens and earth open a space for the vision that includes the entire universe. The heavens contain the sun, moon, stars and the heavenly armies; the earth contains seas and land and all the nations upon those lands; beneath this earth is the underworld of death—Sheol and the Pit (5.13-15; 14.12-15). God dwells in the heavens and it is his manifestations and words that are seen and heard by humans on the earth.

The Lord raises and brings up children; the family metaphor refers to the creation of Israel as a people. The two verbs are the first part of the ubiquitous opposition of high and low. But the children rebel and turn against the Holy One. Verses 3-4 are a catalogue of terms for sin (see 59.13). Isaiah uses a large number of terms and phrases for sin and sinners. The main ones are in vv. 2-4; I discuss the Hebrew words here but do not distinguish them elsewhere in Isaiah. *rā'a', in v. 4, and its related nouns are translated 'evil', 'evildoers', etc. pāša', in vv. 2 and 28, and the noun *peša'* (24.20), are translated 'rebel-rebellion' (48.8; 66.24) or 'transgress-transgression' (24.20; 43.25-26). *ḥāṭā'*, in v. 4, has several nominal forms, *ḥaṭṭā't* being the most frequent; they are translated with 'sin', 'sinner', 'sinful', etc. *'āwôn*, in v. 4—the verb occurs only in 21.3 and 24.1—is translated 'iniquity', 'guilt' (6.7) and 'penalty' (40.2). The latter three terms occur together in 43.24-27 and 59.12. (For 'forsake' and 'despise', see remarks at the end of ch. 6.)

The people, imaged as a body in v. 5, have been beaten. Their land has been invaded and devastated. Imagery of war, invasions, desolation and ruin pervades the entire book. The distinction between rural (the country) and urban (the city) and their respective imagery is introduced in vv. 7-8; the ox and donkey belong to the first set of imagery. Imagery of burning and fire makes its entrance. The nations, aliens, are invading enemies; we will follow their changing roles.

A remnant, daughter Zion, is left although both alone and surrounded by enemies. (The vineyard makes its first appearance in v. 8.) This image of Zion is narrated in 36–37; transformed and glorious mother Zion is displayed in 66. Zion and Jerusalem are used in parallel in Isaiah and figure the people as a woman. We will trace her fortunes. In v. 9, the people come center stage and speak. They are the remnant and through God's intervention they have avoided the annihilation that befell Sodom and Gomorrah. The prophet cuts them off with a renewed call to hear but they, in their corruption, are equated with the two cities. From Genesis 18–19, the two cities are archetypes for corruption and total destruction.

The Lord is cited. His weariness with the sacrificial system is marked by the list of vv. 11-14. This is the first of many times that Isaiah uses cultic practices and terms, the cultic metaphor, to portray the relation between God and people. God matches Israel's sin since neither will he see or hear. This situation will be transformed by the beginning of 65. The people's hands are filled with the blood of sacrifice and of murder (v. 21). This is one pole of the full–empty antithesis. Change to the other pole is marked by washing, cleansing and removing. 'To remove', vv. 16 and 25, is the causative stem of *sûr, to take away or empty for cleansing and saving (6.7; 10.27; 14.25; 25.8) or for punishing (3.1, 18; 5.5; 18.5). Good is defined as justice, as care for the unprotected such as the widow and the orphan. This introduces the range of juridical metaphors which I discuss in greater depth at 3.13-15.

The theological plot of divine goodness, human rebellion and subsequent judgment is spelled out in principle in vv. 18-20 and with the possibility of an alternative plot. The people can respond to God's past goodness with a willingness to listen and to act. (The verb *šāmaʿ* means to hear, listen to and obey, that is, act upon what is heard. I limit my use of the translations 'obey' and 'obedience' because they have connotations of rigidity and authoritarianism that are not present in Isaiah.) If they do, they eat the good of the land; if they don't, the sword eats them. 'For the mouth of the Lord speaks' continues the oral metaphor.

In vv. 21-26 the prophet addresses Zion, the woman last seen in v. 8. The city was once filled with faithfulness, justice and righteousness. All three nouns belong to Isaiah's vision of the ideal community and all include ideas of attitude and action. The righteous and faithful city is to be just and governed according to God's word, not according to greed and self-interest. The three roots underlying these nouns are frequent and significant in Isaiah in their nominal, verbal and adjectival forms; I comment on them here and will note many of their occurrences throughout the book. *'āmēn* includes ideas of trust, belief, faithfulness, firmness, trustworthiness; *šāpaṭ* entails ideas of justice and rights, judgment including process and punishment, a just and proper mode of life (*mišpāṭ* is the main nominal form); *ṣādaq*, which often is paired with *šāpaṭ*, is close to it in meaning, but has the additional denotations of innocence and righteousness in legal and religious senses. *ṣedeq* and *ṣᵉdāqâ* are nouns whose meanings range from righteousness to deliverance; *ṣaddîq* refers to the innocent or righteous person.

This fullness has been emptied; now the city is filled with murderers. The finest, her silver and wine, are corrupted by being mixed with the worst. The poet quotes the Lord using an elaborate title to draw the people's attention. The Lord pours out his wrath. This is a form of the verb that elsewhere means to comfort (12.1; 40.1; 66.13). Wrath and comfort, judgment and restoration go together in Isaiah; they cannot be easily resolved into a narrative of present wrath and future comfort. The combination is present in the image of smelting, a part of the imagery of fire and burning and a part that combines positive and negative aspects. God picks up on the prophet's image of corruption, defiled silver, and turns it to good use; he will burn away the dross and restore the pure metal.

This will be 'as in the beginning, as at the first'. 'In the beginning [*bāri'šōnâ*]' plays upon the opening of Genesis *bᵉrē'šît*. 'Afterward you will be called . . .' These phrases open a temporal setting for the vision that duplicates the space of the universe intoned with the call to the heavens and the earth. In time, the vision stretches from creation through the entire history of Israel and humanity, past and present, to the future of the new heavens and the new earth in 65–66.

Verses 27-28 remain with Lady Zion and return us to the alternative plots of redemption and destruction (vv. 18-20). NRSV refers to 'those who repent'; REB translates 'her returning people'. Both are correct and reflect the ambiguity of the *šûb* which means to return both in the physical sense of return from exile and dispersion and in the symbolic, spiritual sense of return to the Lord. To repent entails both attitude and action; it is a change of mind and a return to former ways of acting and living.

At the close of the chapter the prophet renews his address to the people. They have been worshipping in sacred groves; oaks and gardens signal rural imagery. Delight and choice are favorite terms of Isaiah and frame the book; the people choose their own ways and delight in abominations (66.3-4). In a stroke of poetic justice, their sin is turned into their punishment since they become a dried and withered oak and garden. (In 66.4 God chooses punishment for them because they chose what he does not delight in.) This is the opposite of the Garden of Eden where trees grow and water abounds (Gen. 2.6-14). It is an intensification of the desolation of Isa. 1.7 and an anticipation of both the demonic land seen in chs. 13 and 34 and the transformation of Jerusalem and the people into a new Eden in 60–62 and 66 (51.3). To say 'without water', introduces the ubiquitous water imagery.

Dryness images desiccation and death. And the dry trees and grass of the waterless garden provide fuel for the fire of v. 7. But the fire has moved into the symbolic, and even mythic, realm of the nightmare of an unending, unquenchable burning which opens and closes the book (66.24; see 34.8-10). Verse 31 turns from direct address to a third person description, from 'you' to 'them', from now to the time of myth.

Figurative Language. Isaiah's poetry, as biblical poetry in general, is marked by constant and intense use of all manner of figurative language. Seldom is anything said or described in what can be called ordinary prose or everyday language. The people are not just the people; they are children, a wounded body, a city, a woman, a whore, impure and pure silver, a tree and a garden. God is a parent, a teacher and a bull (*'ābîr* in v. 24). Within this intense usage, a further although not exact distinction can be made between sections that can be read as metaphorical descriptions of reality, as can most of ch. 1, and sections, like the closing verses of the chapter, that envision a world that is other than our world. These are the mythic, symbolic worlds of the nightmare and the dream, of Death and Life, of Sheol and Eden.

Chapter Two

The first verse re-introduces the vision that is heard and sets off ch. 1 as a multiple introduction to the various ways of segmenting Isaiah. Chapters 2–5, or 1–5, are the first section that we look at. The vision of 2.2-4 is of 'the latter days' (literally, 'the back of the days'). The preposition 'back of', *b^e'ah^arît*, is a form of 'afterwards' of 1.26 and it plays upon *b^erē'šît*, of Gen. 1.1. Isaiah moves us from the beginning of his vision, from creation, to its end, the time after our time. He takes us from the nightmare at the close of ch. 1 to a dream of the future.

The mountain of the house of the Lord is raised on high; it is above the mountains and hills. (The latter are a frequent pair.) 'All the nations stream to it' uses a water image that is reversed in the terrible flood of 8.5-8. The nations come to the mountain of the Lord for instruction and not to destroy the land. The teaching and the word of the Lord come forth from Zion-Jerusalem. (Teaching or instruction is a preferred translation for *tôrâ* since the translation 'law' carries connotations of fixity and finality not present in the Hebrew term.) Teaching and word are presented as quasi-independent entities that go forth on their own and perhaps act on their own. One major embodiment and manifestation of the teaching is the book of Isaiah; it goes forth into the world and it is to have an effect on people.

The vision closes in 2.4 with settling conflicts between the nations. The subject of the actions is not specified and can be the Lord ('he') or his word and instruction ('it'). God's work in the world can be carried on through many instruments; a book, a prophet and his word are three introduced to this point. The judging ushers in a time of total and universal peace which is paired with the vision in 11.1-9. The shoot, the branch, another divine instrument, judges and decides and this action ushers in the return to the paradisiacal times of Genesis 1 when humans and animals all eat grass and not each other.

Chapters 2.2-4 and 11.1-9 are messianic visions, not because they imagine an individual messiah, but because they picture the ideal time using royal ideology such as is found in Psalms 2; 72; 89; 110; 132. The messiah is the anointed (*māšiaḥ*) who is the king (1 Sam. 2.10; 24.7; 2 Sam. 23.1; Pss. 2.2; 20.7; 28.8). The noun occurs once in Isaiah when it is applied to Cyrus (45.1; see 61.1). The kings claimed that they ruled at God's behest, that their power derived directly from him. They would rule huge areas, if not the entire world, and this wide-ranging dominion would allow them to put an end to war and to establish peace. Within their own kingdom, they would establish justice, peace and prosperity; criminals and oppressors, the wicked, would be done away with and the people, the poor and the righteous, would live with none to prey upon them or disturb them. Finally, the power and stability of the dynasty are often connected with the Lord's creation and foundation of the world (1 Sam. 2.8; Ps. 89.1-37); monarchy is given a mythic basis.

In short, Isaiah takes these claims, this royal propaganda and myth, and its images as a major way to speak of his dream of the ideal society, of what life could be like on the Lord's holy mountain. But he separates it from human kings, whether real or ideal, because their rule has resulted in oppression, war and the devastation of the exile. Since kings brought this on, they cannot be the means to remove it. In chs. 1–5, Isaiah uses royal themes and imagery, but does not speak of kings except in the superscription in 1.1.

Many peoples are walking toward the mountain. A voice, with a tinge of envy, invites the house of Jacob to walk in the light of the Lord since, to this point, they have forsaken the proper ways. 'Light of the Lord' refers to elevated Zion and to the teaching coming forth from it, and it anticipates gleaming and glorious Jerusalem in 60–62. (In 2.2, streaming employs a verb that has the second meaning of shining in 60.5; the peoples stream and gleam.)

Israel is filled with foreigners and wealth; the fullness is countered by the emptying in 3.1–4.1. The land is filled with idols and the people bow down to that which their own hands have made. Israelite bowing down, worship, turns into human bowing down, humiliation; Israel is filled with idols and humanity throws them away. Chapter 2 presents a stark statement of the full–empty and high–low contrasts. It opens with the mountain of the Lord rising up and it closes with only the Lord rising. Anything else on high is proud, arrogant and haughty. It is brought down and laid in the dust. Dust is dryness and death; indeed, the Hebrew word for dust can refer to the netherworld.[1] The opening dream is paired with, countered by, this nightmare of wrath, terror and death. The distinction between Israel and the nations collapses into all-inclusive humanity; all are subject to terror and humiliation. Humans are only a breath and nothing is to be thought of them.

Summary. To this point in Isaiah a considerable portion of what will be treated in the rest of the book has been introduced. The plot elements of divine goodness, human sin, judgment and salvation are here. The scene is set—the heavens, the earth and the netherworld. The main cast of characters are introduced: Israel including Zion and Jerusalem; the nations; and humanity, the category that subsumes the previous. Many of the major terms, images, themes and contrasts have appeared with distinctions within the general category, for example: sin (rebellion, ignorance, oppression and violence, pride and arrogance); the good (justice, knowledge and learning, listening and doing, walking in God's ways); life and death; rural and urban; high and low; full and empty; animals (ox, ass, goats, horses and bats); trees (oaks and cedars); fire and light; water and dryness; family, cultic and juridical metaphors. Israel is man and woman. Israel is masculine plural as in 1.4-20, 29-30 and singular as in 2.6-8. (I note this distinction when relevant and not apparent in translation; English has only 'you' while Hebrew distinguishes the second person according to both gender and number.) The rest of Isaiah presents further distinctions and particularizations of the above list.

Chapter Three
'Now look! The Lord, Yahweh of Hosts, is emptying Jerusalem and Judah.' This is a particular construction using *hinnēh*

---

1. N.J. Tromp, *Primitive Conceptions of Death and the Nether World in the Old Testament* (BibOr, 21; Rome: Biblical Institute Press, 1969), pp. 85-89.

(look! see!) with a participle to present an unfolding scene. (For other examples, see 5.26; 8.7; 10.33; 24.1; 54.11; for *sûr*, to empty, see at 1.16.) The glut is gone: the leaders at the start of the chapter and the finery of the noble ladies, the daughters of Zion, at the close including 4.1. The abundance of the finery is marked by the lengthy list in vv. 18-24; the Lord 'takes away' (*sûr*) the fullness. In vv. 25-26 the prophet turns from the ladies to Zion herself. Her warriors have fallen and in mourning she sits upon the ground, anticipating Daughter Babylon in ch. 47.

As a whole the chapter depicts violence, ruin and chaos. Society is overturned. Children rule; everyone oppresses everyone else; people refuse to rule. The anonymity and generality signify the chaos and the anarchy. To some extent the latter are experienced in reading the chapter with its brief oracles and abrupt shifts in content and speaker. This is even more evident in the Hebrew than in English translations which have smoothed over many of the difficulties.

Jerusalem and Judah have stumbled and fallen; their sin is as obvious as that of Sodom. Woe to them; they have done the evil to themselves. The righteous are not with the wicked for the prophet orders a group to tell them that they are good and eat the fruit of their efforts. Good and evil and eating recall the similar distinctions made in 1.15-20. 3.11 recapitulates 3.9, and 3.12 summarizes the chapter. The prophet or the Lord addresses the people directly—'your leaders mislead you'.

Yet there is clear leadership attested in the midst of the chapter. The Lord rises in court as prosecutor and judge and, in agreement with v. 12, lays the ruin of the people, his people, at the feet of their leaders. There is a sense in which the entire people are guilty and are suffering the consequences, but there is also the political reality—first noted in 1.23—that it is the leaders, the nobility, who have corrupted the society. The righteous eat their own fruit while the princes devour the vineyard, and daughter Zion is left alone 'like a booth in a vineyard' (1.8).

The court scene is a major feature of the juridical metaphors employed throughout Isaiah and noted at 1.16-17. Isaiah shares this metaphorical field with the rest of the Hebrew Bible. 'To argue' is *rîb* (1.17, 23). 'Judgment' is *mišpāṭ* which refers to both the process and the outcome, the judgment rendered and the justice thereby effected (at 1.21; 26.9).

Chapter Four

This is the shortest chapter in Isaiah. The first verse fits with the ruin and chaos of ch. 3 and, in addition, forms a transition to the promise of 4.2-6. The seven women who seize one man can provide for themselves, 'only let us be called by your name; take away our disgrace'. The frequent motif of name and naming, especially when it is a new name, was first encountered in 1.26 when Zion is again called 'the righteous city, the faithful city'.

Disgrace and shame are an integral part of the depiction of desolation and ruin (1.29). The women want it taken away. The Lord removes disgrace (25.8) and promises that it will not return (54.4). The verb, to take away, more often means to gather as when the Lord gathers all exiles (11.12). To return the exiles, the dispersed, is one way to remove Zion's disgrace. The women do this 'on that day'. This is the day of the Lord first announced in 2.12. It is a day of judgment and destruction when the Lord alone is exalted (2.11-17; 3.7, 18; 4.1). It is also a day of salvation, restoration and renewal as in ch. 4. Chapters 34 and 35 vividly portray the two contrasting sides of the day of the Lord.

4.2-6 is a short passage but it is a treasure trove of terms, images and themes and it adds detail and variety to what precedes. 'The branch', paralleled by 'the fruit of the land', belongs to the imagery of trees and gardens that permeates Isaiah. It brings to mind 'the shoot from the stump of Jesse, the branch growing from his roots' (11.1). In the latter, 'branch' is a different term, but the imagery is the same. The Lord is a forester. He plants seedlings and watches them sprout and grow; he puts trees in the desert and the wilderness to transform them. This aspect of the imagery is much more frequent in the latter part of Isaiah, especially in chs. 35 and 40–62. He is also a lumberjack who cuts trees down (2.12–16; 10.33).

Plant Imagery. Plant imagery pervades Isaiah and is a facet of his thorough development of images and metaphors; he uses approximately ninety different terms for trees, grass, planting, gardens, etc. He covers the entire life cycle of a plant from planting (5.2; 28.24; 30.23), to growing and flourishing (37.30-32; 41.17-20), to withering and dying (1.30; 34.4; 40.6-8), and to being cut down and used for a fire or for an idol (44.9-20). Dry and rotten wood or plants are burned (1.31; 5.24; 10.16-19) or blown away (41.14-16). Plant imagery is used in contexts of judgment and destruction, of salvation and restoration and of the lonely remnant (1.8; 6.11-13; 10.19). Isaiah does not restrict himself to using a set of imagery for only one meaning or with only one value.

Beauty, glory, pride and splendor all belong to the imagery and terminology of light and visibility and to the pole of height in the high–low antithesis. However, there are opposing values here. Pride is to be on high, to be visible, but set over against the Lord; the proud are brought low. Glory and beauty is height and visibility like that of the Lord's mountain; others see and come (11.10); the lowly and humble are saved and set on high. 'The survivors', 'the remnant', 'the ones left' recall the remnant of 1.8-9; these are the three main terms for remnant in Isaiah. Zion-Jerusalem is herself and stands for Israel. Being named holy, being written among the living—naming and writing down a name (1.26; 4.1; 44.5; 49.16); holy is to be set apart, dedicated (6.13; 35.8; 48.2); the living imply the dead.

The majesty of 4.2-4 implies the horror of the underside; it anticipates the closing scene of the book when those in the city go out to gaze on the corpses of the rebels. The Lord washes away the filth and cleanses the blood (1.15-17) with 'a spirit of judgment and a spirit of burning'. The splendor of restoration requires the destruction, the refining away, of the wicked, the dross. The nightmare and the dream, judgment and salvation, are intertwined and imply each other. This is the first appearance of *rûaḥ* in Isaiah. The word is polysemic and means spirit, wind and breath. It denotes both life and death. *rûaḥ* animates and invigorates (11.2-4; 28.6; 32.15; 42.5; 44.3; 61.1); it burns, desiccates and destroys (4.4; 11.15; 40.7; 49.10); it blows away (17.13; 41.16; 49.10).

'He will create'. Genesis 1 was alluded to in chs. 1 and 2. Create (*bārā'*) is the verb that refers only to divine creating (40.26-28; 41.20; 45.7; 65.17-18). Isaiah 4.5 alludes to Gen. 1.1 and jumps to Exodus. 'The cloud by day and the smoking, gleaming, flaming fire by night' refer to the pillars of cloud and fire that guided the Israelites (Exod. 13.21-22; 14.19-25). The cloud and the fire are a canopy and a booth (Isa. 1.8); they cover and protect but do not surround and fortify. This is a dream of an open pavilion, not a closed city or garrison. The canopy is shade to protect from the blazing heat of the sun; at this point dark and hiding are beneficial and the sun destructive (16.3; 25.4-5; 32.2; 49.2; 51.16). Rain is beneficial (5.6; 30.23) and destructive if a storm (25.4-5; 30.30; 32.2).

Summary. Isaiah's vision, his drama of good and evil, of life and death, of dream and nightmare moves on through repetition and addition. He repeats words, images and themes, and adds others to them. He enriches and develops what he has already written with increasing specificity and with a growing number of categories in each area; I have given examples of this and will continue to do so at relevant points.

Chapter 1 is an impressive, poetic description of a land in ruins with corrupt and useless rulers whose main concern is their own welfare and wealth. The portrait continues in 2.6-8 and 3.1–4.1, and it stands in juxtaposition with dreams and nightmares that describe worlds other than our own. They are not poetic, metaphorical descriptions of a world we can recognize; they move into a symbolic, mythic realm. First is the unquenchable fire which is contrasted with the messianic dream of exalted Zion to which the nations stream. This, in turn, is countered by the horrific day of the Lord during which anything exalted is brought down; people are in the dust, in the underworld. There is a bright side to the day of the Lord, a dream in which death and destruction usher in life and splendor for survivors, the holy remnant. This dream is not messianic for it is based on a new Creation and a new Exodus, not the ideology of the kings.

Chapter Five

The chapter concludes the first section of Isaiah. It is dominated by pronouncements of sin and judgment with no explicit promise of hope. Although it breaks into obvious sections, there are complicated interrelationships within and between these sections.

The prophet opens with a song about his friend and his friend's vineyard. I read the song on two levels since it is both song and parable. Taken on its own, it is a tale of failed efforts with an obvious temporal frame. In the past, the farmer worked diligently but the vineyard did not produce. The farmer is quoted in vv. 3-6. He shifts to the present, 'and now', and calls to the Judahites to decide the issue. He does not wait for an answer and, with a second 'and now', announces that in the immediate future he will return the vineyard to uncultivated ground and even try to conjure the clouds into withholding rain. He or the prophet turns the tables on the audience: they, Israel and Judah, are the vineyard that has failed and that is being trampled; they are the ones who should have established justice and righteousness. This is like Nathan's parable in 2 Samuel 12. They both operate on a human, rhetorical level and want to change their audience by tricking them into recognition and condemnation of their own wrong. The entire book of Isaiah is on this level since it wants to persuade its readers to change.

Taken in the context of the book, the song is a straightforward version of Isaiah's story of divine goodness, human rebellion and the resultant punishment. The Lord is now farmer and vine-dresser, not parent (1.2-7), and the land is a devastated and dry vineyard, 'like a garden without water' (1.30). The people are still called to change through self-recognition and, just as importantly, through recognition of the Lord and his ways. 'Let us walk in the light of the Lord'. One major manifestation of the Lord's word, teaching and light is the book, the vision of Isaiah. The vision portrays a time—past, present and future—of evil, chaos and devastation, but the picture always contains a remnant. Something survives the destruction and it is in this surviving remnant that the prophet bases his hope, his call for change. Those who remain can change and can return to the previous ways of justice and compassion.

The details of the song reveal its close ties with its context. The poem revolves around the verb to do, to yield, *'āśâ*, which occurs six times in vv. 2 and 4 and a seventh time in v. 5. Past doing was not matched by yielding. Now there is removal and breach; hedge and wall are gone. The result is devouring and burning—the verb has both meanings: 1.31; 3.14; 4.4—and trampling (see 1.12). The vineyard is exposed; the land, overrun. Daughter Zion is left 'like a booth in a vineyard' and 'a besieged city'; pastoral (rural) and military (urban) imagery are combined. The farmer built a (watch)tower, but the Lord topples towers and fortified walls (2.15). The princes devour the vineyard (3.14), but the Lord cleanses the remnant with a burning spirit (4.4). The booth is both alone (1.8) and a shelter, a pavilion (4.6). Being without walls means exposure to enemies, and it also means being open to returning inhabitants and to the influx of all others for learning.

Woe! The farmer no longer cares for his vineyard and it returns to wild land: a dry waste (1.7) filled with briers and thorns. All this because Israel is filled with bloodshed and appeals for help. The rest of ch. 5 develops this picture of the corruption within Israel and the devastation befalling it. Central to it are a series of six woe's (*hôy*), laments which regard the people as already dead (1.4, 24; 3.9, 11; the last two employ *'ôy* a near homophone). Landowners build huge estates, dispossess others and, as an ironic remnant, 'live alone in the midst of the land'. Much comes to little and, in a stroke of poetic justice, failure to yield is the punishment. *'ereṣ* can mean (particular) land or (whole) earth. What is done 'in the midst of the land [Judah]' (6.12) anticipates what is done 'in the midst of the earth' whether weal or woe (10.23; 19.24; 24.13). At another point, we will find that *'ereṣ* also means underworld in parallel with the term for dust (14.9; 25.12).

28.23-29 is a parable on agricultural wisdom. There needs to be timing and balance in planting and harvesting; the farmer must beat and thresh but not beat so hard as to destroy. There should be the same timing and balance in other areas of life. Eating and drinking have their time and place, but these people are consumed with drunkenness (11-12a; 22a). This is part of the imagery of satiety: 1.11-15 and 3.18-23.

But, in their self-indulgence, they do not pay attention to the work and the doings of the Lord. ('To do', **pā'al*, is often used in parallel to 'to do', *'āśâ;* the nouns 'deed' and 'work' are *pō'al* [1.31; 5.12] and *ma'ᵃśeh*.) As in the vineyard song, past good has not been properly responded to; therefore, a work of judgment follows. Lack of seeing leads to lack of knowledge which leads to hunger and thirst for the besotted gluttons.

However, it is Sheol, Death, that opens its mouth and eats. In the Canaanite Baal epic, Baal is swallowed by Death whose mouth and throat are a wide, yawning abyss. The Baal myth is part of a fertility cycle. Baal is swallowed, dies, in the fall, a time of withering plants and falling leaves; he arises in the spring when his consort, bloody Anat, slays Death and sows the ground with his blood and parts.[1] Spring is a time of life, sprouting and growth. Isaiah deploys this mythic cycle and its imagery in his portrayal of judgment and restoration and, in the process, turns the myth into poetic imagery and motifs.

Exile is death for this vast mob as they go down to the underworld to join those already there because of the Day of the Lord (2.9-22). Humanity is brought down and the Lord alone exalted in justice which here means punishment. The land is in ruins.

---

1.   M.D. Coogan, *Stories from Ancient Canaan* (Philadelphia: Westminster Press, 1978), pp. 75-115; J.H. Grϕnback, 'Baal's Battle with Yam—A Canaanite Creation Fight', *JSOT* 33 (1985), pp. 27-44.

(*ḥārēb means to be dry, hot, in ruins and occurs in 4.6, 'heat'. It
is a frequent term for the ruins of Israel and Jerusalem.) Flocks
feed there as in their pastures. This is a compound image of ruin
and remnant and is similar to the ironic remnant of the solitary
landowners.

It is bitterly ironic, then, for these same people to want the
Lord to hasten his doing and his plan so that they may know it.
(Plan is based on *yā'aṣ which means to counsel, plan, advise;
the noun counselor is in 1.26 and 3.3.) An army hastens (5.26);
they seize spoil and prey (8.1-3). These people have everything
backwards. They are wise only in their own estimation; they
don't know (1.3). They are supposed to remove evil (1.16); instead
they remove justice. In v. 23, 'acquit', 'innocent' and 'rights' are
all forms of *ṣādēq (at 1.21; introduction) and refer to the juridical process; 'the guilty' or 'wicked' (3.11) are the rāša'. They are
the princes of Zion (1.21-23).

The chapter concludes with two announcements of judgment
and the approach of a superhuman army. The judgments flow
from the accusations of ch. 5 and all of 1–5. 'Therefore' calls
attention to these chapters and, at the same time, focusses on
what is about to be said.[1] The imagery is characteristic: consum-
ing fire, dryness, grass and dust. 24b repeats 1.4 and 2.3; they
reject the teaching and word which go forth. The imagery takes
on a cosmic aspect. The Lord's wrath burns against his people
and mountains quake (64.1). Their corpses are trash in the
streets; this is the trampling of 5.5 and 10.6. This is not enough
for 'his hand is still stretched out'. The 'still' can reach down to
the postexilic time of the book of Isaiah; the community of Isaiah
still see and experience the anger of the Lord (66.15-16).

God raises a signal, a flag, for nations from afar. This is an
uncanny event for these nations come to attack, not to learn. The
advancing army figures the Assyrian army of chs. 7–10 and 36–
37, the cosmic army of ch. 13 and the Babylonian army that is
alluded to but never actually described. The Lord whistles for
the army; it is his instrument, his implement, and not a power in
its own right. (In 7.18-19 the army is mere insects, flies and
bees.) It is superhuman in its speed, indefatigability and power.

1.   W.E. March, 'Lākēn: Its Functions and Meanings', in J.J. Jack-
son and M. Kessler (eds.), *Rhetorical Criticism: Essays in Honor of
James Muilenberg* (Pittsburgh Theological Monograph Series, 1; Pittsburgh: Pickwick Press, 1974), pp. 256-84.

Their roar can be heard; although there is sound, there are no words. They can be seen in their frightful array, but the vision closes with darkness, distress and clouds. The vision reverses 2.2-4; there is now no light to walk in. The incongruity of hearing roaring without words and seeing only darkness forms a fit transition to the message Isaiah receives in ch. 6.

Chapter Six

The chapter opens with the notice of the death of Uzziah, the first king listed in 1.1. This is 742 BCE, but the exact date is not as important as the inference that the vision occurs in the reign of Jotham, the next king in 1.1, whose reign is not otherwise mentioned. Chapter 7 opens in the reign of Ahaz, the son of Jotham, whose death in 715 BCE is noted in 14.28. With this succession of reigns, chs. 1–5 can be regarded as in Uzziah's reign, 6 in Jotham's and 7–14 in Ahaz's; this produces a structuring that overlaps the usual division between 12 and 13. Structuring in Isaiah is multiple and dynamic, not fixed and rigid. In my reading ch. 6 is transitional pointing both back and forward; we will have frequent opportunity to refer back to the chapter in our commentary on the rest of Isaiah.

The chapter is narrated in the first person singular and is the first time the prophet speaks of himself; although it is generally assumed that Isaiah, the eighth-century prophet, is speaking, the speaker does not identify himself by name. The account is interrupted by a narrator with a third person account in ch. 7; the prophet resumes with the first person in 8. In 6, he tells of a vision he had in the temple; this is not a call narrative since there is no hint that this was the prophet's first encounter with the divine.[1] A human king dies and the prophet sees 'the king, the Lord of hosts' (33.22; 41.21). In chs. 6–9, unlike in 1–5, the prophet speaks of human kings and of the great hopes the people have in them and in their promise; however, the book of Isaiah does not present a positive or hopeful picture of them and their rule. Chapters 6–9, indeed, open with the death of a king.

Chapter 6 is a *mise-en-abîme* of Isaiah. The prophet sees and hears; the Lord is on high; the temple and the earth are filled with the Lord's robe, glory and with smoke. The Lord is holy, a leitmotif of the preceding (1.4; 4.3; 5.16, 19, 24). Seraphim is a

1.   Watts, *Isaiah 1–33*, pp. 70-73.

play on 'fiery ones'; the same root (*śārap*) is in 1.7; to refine
(*ṣārap*) in 1.25 is a homophone; and the burning coal (*riṣpâ*) of
6.6 uses the consonants of the latter. The prophet and the people
are unclean and sinful. Cleanness and innocence are achieved by
burning and refining both the prophet and the people; in the
process, the guilt, the dross, is removed.

The prophet is sent with a word. This sets in motion a series of
sendings: his word, both destructive and saving (9.7; 55.11),
Assyria (10.6), disease (10.16), his servant and messenger (42.19;
48.16; 61.1) and the remnant (66.19). The message, however, is
contradictory; it alludes to the children of 1.2-3. The people hear
and see without understanding and knowledge which is not to
hear and see; they are blind and deaf. They are to remain this
way for if they were to see and hear, they might return, repent
and be healed.

There is a time limit for this condition, and it is the fulfillment of the previous visions of the destruction of the land. Cities
will be without inhabitant (5.9) and the land will be desolate
(1.7; 5.9). The Lord calls an army from afar (5.26) and, as an
effect of the invasion, puts the people afar. At a future time, he
will 'gather the dispersed from the four corners of the earth'
(11.12); they will return from far away (43.6; 49.12). The land,
which may be filled with the Lord's glory, is empty of humans.
Because this people forsake God, the land is forsaken (7.16). The
ten acres that produced so little (5.10) are reduced by a factor of
one hundred and the tenth that remains is burned again. But
still a stump, a holy seed, is left.

The play on 'afar' and 'forsake' yields good examples of the
multiple meanings that Isaiah can give to a word, concept and
image. At points, 'far' occurs in opposition to 'near' (13.5-6; 33.13;
57.19); I will note other examples of the play on 'far' and on 'near'
as the reading progresses. 'Forsake' is *ʿāzab*, one of a number of
verbs for abandon, reject, despise. People should not reject the
Lord or his word (1.4; 5.24; 30.12; 58.2) but should reject evil and
idols (7.15-16; 31.7; 55.7). If they violate this, they will be rejected
and abandoned. (In 6.12 'emptiness' is a form of the verb.) I will
pay attention to this play on forsake and abandon with some
notice of this particular verb.

Chapter Seven
Chapters 7 and 8 are placed against the background of the Syro-
Ephraimite War. (See 2 Kgs 15–17 for a different account of the

period.) From 745 BCE Tiglath-pileser III was beginning the establishment of an Assyrian empire that would dominate the Near East for over a century. He campaigned in the west from 734 and was opposed by a coalition headed by Rezin of Aram, whose capital was Damascus, and Pekah of Israel. Judah, under Ahaz, would not join and the allies threatened to invade, depose him and enthrone a king, the son of Tabeel, who would join the coalition. Ahaz sent tribute to Tiglath-pileser who responded by destroying Damascus and incorporating its territory and much of the territory of Israel into his empire (Isa. 17.1-3). Israel was spared total conquest when Hoshea (732–722) paid tribute. Judah became a loyal Assyrian vassal. Ten years later, in 722/21, Samaria was destroyed by Sargon (ch. 20) and Israel ceased to be an independent kingdom. Judah remained a loyal vassal. Hezekiah succeeded to the throne in 715. Events of his reign are narrated, with some differences, in Isaiah 36–39 and 2 Kings 18–20. Hoping for support from Egypt, Hezekiah in 705/704 joined a coalition against Assyria. Sennacherib invaded Judah in 701, devastated the country, besieged Jerusalem, but did not take the city.

Isaiah has taken these events of 735–700 BCE and compressed them into images of invasion, devastation and remnant. He depicts an overwhelming army sweeping through the land from the north. Damascus, Israel and other peoples, for example, Philistia and Moab, are destroyed by the Assyrians in these decades; Judah is ravaged and Jerusalem left alone. A raging flood sweeps through Judah 'reaching up to the neck' (8.5-8). This is the imagery and scene of much of chs. 1–39 which present this vision of the period. The vision's impact and meaning go far beyond a mere rehearsal of the events of 735–700 for it is augmented by dreams and nightmares which lend it a cosmic, mythic setting and significance.

The symbolic quality allows Isaiah to extend the invading army to include the Babylonians. Under Nebuchadnezzar, the Babylonians destroyed the last of the Assyrian army in 605. He soon invaded Judah, destroyed Jerusalem in 587 and took a large number of Judeans into exile near Babylon. This is the period of the Exile which can roughly be dated from 600–540 BCE when Cyrus entered Babylon and allowed exiled peoples to return. The book of Isaiah anticipates the exile in its poetic compression and equation of events and empires over a century apart, 735–700 and 600–587. In 40–66, the book envisions the end of exile, return and restoration. At no point does Isaiah speak explicitly of the events of 600–540; there is no narrative of Babylonian invasion to match those of Assyrian invasion in 36–37. Chapter 39 closes looking ahead to Exile; 40 opens announcing its imminent end.

Ahaz and Isaiah. Aram and Israel attack, unsuccessfully, 'in the days of Ahaz', but it is 'the house of David' that receives the report; the same shift occurs in 7.10-13. Ahaz is both an individual and a symbol for Davidic dynasty and the monarchic principle itself; what he does and does not do is what kings in general do and do not do. This is not a flattering portrayal of the king, the messiah. As the temple shook at the sound of a seraph, the heart of the house of David shakes at this report 'as the trees of the forest shake before the wind [*rûaḥ*]'. The simile employs the tree imagery that is central to the following chapters; it denotes human frailty: humans are blown away by the wind. Humans on their own are weak; humans trusting in the Lord are strong.

Personal names are significant. Isaiah is the 'salvation of the Lord' or 'the Lord saves'; the book of Isaiah concerns the Lord's victory over evil and destruction. Uzziah, 'strength of the Lord', and Ahaz, '[the Lord] seizes, holds', are anything but their names. Hezekiah is 'the Lord supports, holds' (at 8.11). Shear-yashub, 'a remnant returns', is a central symbol of judgment and hope for Isaiah since something survives the ordeal.

'To save' is a causative form of *yāšaʻ. The verb occurs frequently, usually with the translation 'to save'(25.9; 33.22; 46.7; 63.1, 9), occasionally, 'to bring victory' (59.16; 63.5). The participle is 'savior' (19.20; 43.3; 60.16; 63.8). There are three nominal forms translated 'salvation' (12.2-3; 25.9; 33.2; 45.8; 62.1) and 'victory' (26.1, 18). The root, at other points in the Hebrew Bible, means to deliver, help and defend in times of trouble (Exod. 2.17; Judg. 2.16-18; 3.9; 6.14-15), especially through military might. Thus military victory or deliverance and help during distress are metaphors for 'salvation' in a spiritual and religious sense. In Isaiah, 'save' and 'salvation' can usually be translated with 'victory, deliverance'.

Isaiah and his son are to meet Ahaz by 'the upper pool on the highway to the Fuller's Field'. Water imagery is combined with the image of the highway, the road. The latter refers to actual, physical roads, to the cosmic routes that armies and returning exiles take and to the spiritual ways of the Lord that all should follow. Ahaz should not fear the invading kings. He should firmly trust in the Lord and he and his royal power will be firmly established (7.9b). *āmēn, welds the ideas of firm trust and establishment (at 1.21).

Trust, or belief, refers both to an attitude, an orientation toward the world, and to the corresponding way of life, the way of acting, that are based on the words of another, here those of the Lord spoken by the prophet. If one is trusting, she is called faithful (1.21, 26). The kings attack and Ahaz responds by readying his defenses for war. This is one set of actions. Isaiah counsels another—do nothing for although the kings have planned an evil plan, 'it will not stand, it will not be'. The Lord's word, the imminent destruction of Aram and Israel, will soon be (14.24-27; 40.8). 'Plan' is 'counsel' and 'advice' (5.19; at 36.5). Standing implies stability and duration and it intones a pole of the high–low antithesis; only the Lord and his plan are on high and endure.

'Stand' is *qûm, one of several verbs for being high, elevated, raised, lofty; it occurs in 2.19-21, 'the Lord rises'. *rûm is a synonym that occurs in 1.2, 'bring up [children]' and in 2.12-14, 'lofty, high'. It exhibits the variable meaning of being high. Height can be 'pride' (rûm: 2.11, 17) or the Lord's 'high and lofty [rûm]' throne (6.1). I will pay close attention to varied occurrences of 'high' and of the high–low antithesis, but I will not generally indicate the Hebrew term—these are only two—since the concept is at issue and not the particular word.

Ahaz doesn't trust and continues his war preparations. To ask for a sign and receive it would mean giving this up and doing nothing. The Lord provides a sign for Ahaz and the house of David involving a woman conceiving, birthing and naming, but the passage is enigmatic and has been the subject of many interpretations. The woman can be any actual woman, the mother of Hezekiah, the mother of a son of Isaiah or daughter Zion giving birth to the remnant.[1] The sign itself is ambiguous as it may consist of one element, for example, the child or the name, or of the entire process. There are royal overtones, but this does not unequivocally refer to a prince, actual or ideal, and the entire scene of ch. 7 does not paint the house of David in a favorable light.

1.   O. Kaiser, *Isaiah 1–12* (trans. J. Bowden; OTL; Philadelphia: Westminster Press, 1983), pp. 153-59; G. Rice, 'A Neglected Interpretation of the Immanuel Prophecy', *ZAW* 90 (1978), pp. 220-27.

Although curds and honey can be royal delicacies, they can also be natural food, all that is left to eat (7.21-22).

A child, an important motif in chs. 7–11, connotes innocence and beginnings and immaturity and weakness (3.4-12). The name, Immanuel, 'God with us', is likewise double-edged: with us to save us or to punish us? The sign, as it is developed in vv. 15-17, is double and involves both good and evil for Judah; this is thematized in the child's knowing what to choose and what to refuse. The land of the two kings attacking Judah is soon to be abandoned. The time reference, 'before the child knows . . .', picks up the hint of a temporal limit from 6.11. However, the king of Assyria keeps coming into Judah and 'in that day' he covers the land like an insect infestation. The army, Assyrian or otherwise, is only God's implement, his razor with which he shaves the entire body (1.5-6), a humiliating sign of defeat. 'That day' is a time of havoc but something remains: a few animals, briers and thorns, hunters and flocks trampling and feeding. 7.23-25 are a 'fulfillment' of the Vineyard Song and the scene that follows it.

Similar to plant imagery (at ch. 4), Isaiah covers all the stages of a human life. Conception, birth and naming are in chs. 7–8; parallels occur in 51.2; 54.1; 66.7-9. The image of giving birth and the labor pains that accompany it are frequent in Isaiah and have quite different connotations. They can indicate great anguish (13.8; 21.3), heavy breathing (42.14) or futility and fruitlessness (23.4-5; 26.17-18; 33.11; 59.4). 11.6-8 and 66.10-13 speak of suckling babes and infants, the earliest stage of life. Other passages describe young children and youths: 1.2; 3.4; 10.19; 49.19-23. Young women, workers, farmers and warriors indicate various times in the prime of life. Marriage imagery belongs to this stage (49.18; 54.4-6; 62.4-5). Old age and elders are the final stage before death (3.2; 24.23; 65.20).

Chapter Eight

The prophet resumes his first person account and weaves in material from the preceding chapters, not just ch. 6. He is given a symbolic name to write on a tablet; this is the first suggestion that something is written, not just spoken. Reading and hearing are both involved in the reception of the word. Maher-shalal-hash-baz, 'the spoil speeds, the prey hastens', is double-edged like the sign of Immanuel. Positively, it is the Assyrian rush against Damascus and Israel. In its negative meaning, it alludes to the Judahites who want the Lord to speed and hasten his work and plan which are for their destruction (5.12, 18-19). Isaiah gets firm—see 7.9b—witnesses who have symbolic names. First is Uriah, 'the light/fire of the Lord'; light/fire is one of the most prevalent images in Isaiah. The other witness is Zechariah ('may the Lord remember'), son of Jeberekiah ('may the Lord bless'), which intone the importance of remembering (and forgetting) and blessing in Isaiah.

The prophetess is the second woman who conceives and bears a son. Isaiah gives the symbolic name to the child invoking its positive meaning. As with Immanuel, the child and his knowing signify the imminence of what his name implies. Damascus and Samaria will be spoil and prey before the child knows how to speak. And Assyria keeps coming. Immanuel was to refuse evil; this people refuse the gentle waters of Shiloah. Therefore, the waters of the river flood the land, reaching to the neck and, by implication, leaving the head, Zion-Jerusalem, intact. (See 7.8-9 where the capital is the head; head, $rō'š$, uses the same consonants as remnant, $šĕ'ār$.) But, Isaiah says ,'the Lord protects your land, O Immanuel, with his outstretched wings' (see 31.4-5 for the bird image).

The people take this assurance as an opportunity to recite an incantation—vv. 9-10 are marked by repetition and inner assonance—against the nations interpreting Immanuel in its positive sense. The Lord and Isaiah have none of it. The Lord holds him by the hand—*$ḥāzaq$, 'to hold, support', plays on Hezekiah ($yĕḥizqiyyāhû$: 'the Lord holds')—to prevent him 'from walking in the way of this people', that is, sharing this false assurance. The people, as in ch. 5, have things turned around; vv. 9-10 may be a proper statement of hope but not at this time. They should not fear the two kings and their conspiracy for they will soon be destroyed by Assyria; they should fear the Lord who will bring Assyria upon them also. (The theme of holiness continues with Isaiah's sanctification of the Lord.)

Sanctuary (60.13), stone (28.16) and rock (26.4; 30.29) usually connote stability and support; ironically, for both houses of Israel, the northern and southern kingdoms, the Lord will be these as immoveable objects to crash into and stumble over. For those in Jerusalem, he will be a trap and a snare. Isaiah looks beyond the events of 735–700 to those of 600–587 when even

Jerusalem falls, 'when many will stumble; they will fall; they will be smashed; they will be snared; they will be taken' (8.15; 28.13). Isaiah can recite his own incantations.

The testimony and the teaching (*tôrâ*) are bound and sealed 'in my disciples', that is, those taught (*limmēd*) by me. Teaching and learning are common motifs in Isaiah: 1.17; 2.4; 29.13, 24; 30.20; 50.4. The parable in 28.23-29 emphasizes wisdom as knowing proper times, places and amounts. The people 'back then' in the eighth century did not have this proper knowledge; they had everything backwards taking light for darkness and sweet for bitter. Isaiah 'back then' had this knowledge, this teaching and testimony, and handed it on through his 'children and disciples'. These are figures for all who listen to or read Isaiah whether those depicted later in the book who are no longer deaf and blind or postexilic readers of the book of Isaiah. The book is figured by the teaching and testimony. Reading implies writing which was introduced in 8.1 (29.11-12).

'To wait' and 'to hope' are close in meaning to 'to trust, believe and be firm' (7.9b; 8.1). Although a number of verbs are used for the concept, I do not distinguish them in my remarks since my focus is on the idea of waiting and hoping. The latter combine an orientation to the world and the way of life flowing from it; these are based on the words, heard and read, of another. At Sinai Moses recites the Lord's words, immediately writes them down and then reads them to the people (Exod. 24.3-8). The Lord came to Moses in a cloud 'so that the people may hear when I speak to you and trust you forever' (Exod. 19.9). The issue is trust and faith based on hearing and reading, not seeing; this is after the signs and wonders of the plagues and the event at the sea. Now the signs and wonders are Isaiah and his children, perhaps including Immanuel, who are 'from the Lord of hosts dwelling on Mount Zion' (Isa. 2.3; 4.5). Will people now hear and read and trust forever? The Lord is hiding his face, but this is not forever (6.11; 30.18-21; 54.6-8).

8.19–9.1 is reminiscent of 2.9-22 and 5.25-30 because of their repetitive and impressionistic style; they have an incantatory sound that is impossible to capture in translation. Isaiah imitates in sound the people as they consult ghosts. The imagery and contrasts of these verses are central to Isaiah—human and divine; the dead and the living; darkness and not light. There is oppression, hunger, cursing and not blessing, and thick, impenetrable darkness. The final verse, with obscure references, captures both space and time. It extends from Zebulun to the way of the sea, probably the west, and to the nations in the east; and it extends from the former to the latter times (1.26; 2.2).

Chapter Nine

Against this backdrop of gloom, 9.2-7 present the people's hope in a new king; however, this is a hope presented from the perspective of the postexilic book. The hopes for a king are interpreted both by their context, 8 and 9.8–10.4, and by their form. The people say one thing, but we read another. This type of ironic reading is indebted to Watts's commentary.

The people, the house of Jacob (8.17), called to walk in the light of the Lord (2.5), emerge from the darkness into a great light. They address their king in vv. 3-5 and describe his glorious rule in vv. 6-7; however, the 'you' in vv. 3-4 can be the Lord, the true king (6.5; 33.22), which undercuts the role of the human king. In his victories, the king has built up the nation and its joy. This is the first mention of the pervasive theme of joy and happiness. The darkness without dawn (8.20) is followed by the greeting of the rising sun. The jubilation is like that at the time of harvest and of dividing spoils. (1.8 has a similar combination of pastoral and military imagery.)

Yoke, staff and rod are broken (8.9-10) 'as on the day of Midian'; the Lord 'defeated Midian at the rock of Oreb' (10.26). The allusion is to Judg. 7.25; Gideon, the 'Hewer', defeated the Midianites and killed their leaders Oreb, 'Raven', and Zeeb, 'Wolf'. (This is the raven that dwells in the demonic land, Isa. 34.11, and the wolf that dwells with the lamb, 11.6; 65.25.) The allusions to the story of Gideon and his son Abimelech, 'My Father is King', darken the triumph of Isaiah 9 with the dismal view of monarchy in Judges. Gideon refuses to be king 'for the Lord rules over you' (Judg. 8.23), but he leads Israel into idolatry (8.24-27). Abimelech slaughters his brothers, becomes king in Shechem and is denounced by his surviving brother Jotham, the same name as the king of Judah. He tells a parable of the trees seeking a king. Three refuse; the bramble accepts and warns them that if the offer is not 'in good faith' then fire will break out and consume all (9.7-21). Burning can cleanse bloodiness (Isa. 1.15-16; 4.3-4) or it can consume bloody garments 'which are burned as fuel [food] for the fire' (9.5). This fire breaks out, burns the land and 'the people become like fuel for the fire' (9.18-19). The people speak of a royal victory like the day of Midian, but we read of violent kings who mislead and destroy their own people like Gideon and Abimelech (Isa. 5.12; 9.16).

A child, a son, is born. He is the new king who brings victory and glory, and he is one of the magic children of chs. 7–8 whose names combine judgment and remnant. The staff is gone from the shoulder and is replaced by the government. The word for government is based on the word for prince (1.23; 3.4) and avoids the word for king. His name is extraordinary, but in Isaiah these things are usually ascribed to the Lord. The Lord's counsel stands (7.3-9; 14.24-27); the Lord plans wonders (25.1; 28.29; 29.14). The Lord is Mighty God or Divine Warrior (10.21; 42.13). He is the people's father (63.16) and is forever (26.4; 45.17; 57.15). He brings peace (26.3, 12) and joy (55.12), peace like a flooding torrent (66.12).

'Peace', šālôm, is a significant notion in Isaiah; it connotes welfare (38.17), prosperity (48.18; 54.13; 66.12) and wholeness (53.5). *šālēm, in its various stems, implies completion, performance and fulfillment (19.21; 38.12-13; 44.26, 28; 60.20) and vindication and repayment (34.8; 57.18; 59.18; 66.6).

The messianic rule and peace are without end, geographic or temporal. It is upon the throne of David and his kingdom that it is established 'in justice and righteous, from now and forever'. (In 6.1 and 66.1, the throne belongs to the divine king.) In the Psalms, the terms for establish and uphold are used for the king (Pss. 2.6; 18.36; 20.2), the Lord as king (9.8; 29; 93) and for all of creation (8.4; 24.2; 93; 96.10). 'The zeal of the Lord of Hosts does this' (Isa. 9.7). (See 5.1-23 for the doing and work of the Lord.) The phrase is repeated in 37.32 in the context of the remnant of Mount Zion. The people speak of a Davidic king and monarchy being established; we read of the Lord's work of judgment that leaves a remnant.

The remainder of 9 and the beginning of 10 break into four sections each ending with the refrain, cited from 5.25, that the Lord's hand is still stretched out: 9.8-12; 9.13-17; 9.18-21; 10.1-4. The sections are concerned with Israel, the northern kingdom; Ephraim is its main tribe and Samaria, its capital. The people have despised the Lord's word (5.24), now the Lord sends it (6.8-9) and now they will know (1.3). They are proud, on high. They replace the good that has been destroyed with finer material. Sycamores have been hewed down ('Gideon'); they put cedars in their place. Yet the Lord is against tall cedars, symbols of pride (2.13). With poetic justice, the Lord 'raises up'—the verb is used of the Lord's exaltation in 2.11, 17; 12.4; 33.5-6—enemies who eat Israel (1.18-20) as Sheol swallowed the Judahites (5.13-17).

The Lord's anger has not turned back; neither have the people turned to the Lord, the one who struck them (1.5). As in 3.1-3, the Lord cuts off, removes, everything; the merisms—head and tail; palm and reed—and the combination of body and plant imagery signify totality. The leaders are swallowed or confused; the word has two meanings (3.12). The punishment is extreme. The Lord does not have pity on the least because the people are godless and foolish.

Their wickedness is like a fire that consumes all; it eats briers and thorns (5.6; 7.24-25). Ironically, the people's pride goes up in smoke and it is not the guiding smoke of 4.5-6. The Israelites seize and eat, but they are still hungry; Ephraim and Manasseh band together against Judah, and they are not satisfied. The series opened with Israel's enemies eating him (9.11-12); now they eat each other, mirroring the chaos of ch. 3.

Chapter Ten

10.1-4 is a Woe! Oracle and a transitional passage. The refrain at the end of v. 4 connects it with the preceding series in ch. 9, while the Woe! ties it to the oracle against Assyria that follows in 10.5-15. Other Woe! Oracles occur in 1.4, 24-26; 3.9-12 and 5.8-23 and are addressed to Jerusalem and Judah. With these parallels, 10.1-4 broadens its immediate audience to include the latter. The leaders of Judah (3.1-12) and Israel (9.14-16) mislead; they are all like the princes of Jerusalem denounced in 1.21-23; the Lord is against them because of their violence against the weak and the poor (3.13-15). Widows and orphans are their 'spoil and prey' (Maher-shalal-hash-baz).

In v. 3 the prophet questions the people directly using the themes of 'doing' (5.1-19) and of the storm 'from afar' (5.26). With a sarcastic twist, the prophet asks 'Where will you abandon your wealth?' Wealth or power is 'glory' (*kābôd*: 3.8; 4.2-5; 6.3; 8.7). They have abandoned (*'āzab*) their glory, the Lord; therefore they abandon their wealth, their land is abandoned (6.12; 7.16), and their glory burned (10.16-18). Prisoners and dead signify defeat (3.25; 22.1-3). Despite all this, the Lord does not relent.

The remainder of ch. 10 is a mixture of judgment and rescue. The Woe! is against Assyria, the Lord's implement, his staff and rod (9.4) whom he has sent against his godless people (9.17). (Assyria was mentioned by name in 7.17-20 and 8.1-8.) The announcement of the impending defeat of Assyria includes a description of the devastation they have wrought on others, especially Israel and Judah. Assyria is to perform the Lord's work by taking spoil and prey (v. 2) and by trampling the people like mud in the street (5.25). But Assyria has much more in mind and intends to destroy many nations, not just punish two.

Trampling or treading is an image that occurs at several significant points; it is conveyed by a number of verbs. The most frequent is *rāmas* which occurs here as the noun *mirmās*, trampled ground. The noun is in 5.5 and 7.25, the vineyard and the land are trampled; the other occurrence is in 28.18 when the Israelites become trampled ground. Because the people trample the Lord's courts (1.12), they are in turn trampled upon by beasts and by Assyria.

The Lord quotes Assyria in 10.8-11 and 13-14. Such quotations are frequent in Isaiah—see 3.6-8; 4.1; 5.18-19; 7.5-6; 9.10—they offer direct evidence of evil intent behind the speaker's actions. (See 2.3 for an opposite example.) Assyria exalts himself. His commanders, that is, his 'princes' (1.23), are kings; as he has done to all the other kingdoms, so will he do to Samaria and Jerusalem who are 'filled with idols' (2.8). He stresses his 'doing'. Verse 12, the Lord's work or 'doing', is bracketed by the two quotes. He will punish the pride (*rûm*) and haughtiness of the king of Assyria; for Israel, judgment and rescue are inextricably intertwined.

'By the strength of my hand I have done it.' In saying this, Assyria joins the drunkards who pay no attention to the work, the doing, of the Lord's hands (5.12). Hand is a symbol of power; it is the Lord's hand, not Assyria's, that is stretched out over his people (1.25; 5.25; 9.12-10.4). But Assyria claims wisdom and understanding. He has removed borders and brought down rulers 'like a bull' or 'like the Mighty One' (1.24). Assyria claims God's power and work as his own. He has gathered in peoples as one gathers in abandoned (*'āzab*) eggs, but the mother bird that has abandoned them may return (see 8.8b for a bird image applied to God). And not one chirped like a bird or the dead (8.19; 29.4). Assyria's pride is twofold. He is doing more than he was sent to do and he thinks that the doing is his own accomplishment.

Such thinking is ridiculous; an instrument is not greater than the one who uses it. Verse 15 employs words from vv. 5 and 12 to indict Assyria's pride, his being on high, and employs images of cutting and wielding to anticipate the coming punishment.

'Therefore' (5.24) introduces the announcement of punishment. The Lord is sending a debilitating disease into his corpulent nobles and a blaze under his glory, his army and wealth (8.7; 10.3). The Light of Israel becomes a fire and his Holy One a flame; briers and thorns (5.6; 7.24-25; 9.18) are consumed in a single day. Judgment on Assyria becomes judgment on Israel, and we move to the universal invasion and ruin seen in 2.9-22 and 5.26-30. All is burned; as in 9.14-15, plant and body imagery figure totality. The forest is burned and cut down (6.13). The trees are so few that even a child can write down their number.

'On that day', the day of the Lord (2.12-21; 4.2-6; 7.18-25), the remnant of Israel, the northern kingdom, will no longer lean on the one who struck them but will lean on the Holy One of Israel, but he is the one who struck them (1.5; 9.13) and removed the things they could lean on (3.1). Although as numerous as the sand of the sea (Gen. 22.17; 32.13), only a remnant will return; is Shear-yashub the child who can write down the number of trees or grains of sand? The cosmic background comes forward in the enigmatic 'annihilation decreed; flooding judgment' which the Lord is 'doing' in the midst of the earth. This mirrors the devastation 'in the midst of the land' (5.8; 6.12).

Because of this devastation, 'therefore' the Lord speaks to 'my people, inhabitants of Zion'. They are not to fear, but the assurance is muted since they will still be struck and beaten by the Lord's rod Assyria. (For the war oracle, Fear not!, see at 35.4; Ahaz is to fear not [7.4].) The Lord's wrath may not be forever, but it is in full effect now. As Isaiah and his disciples, the people must wait and hope (8.17). The references to Midian and Egypt combine the mixed messages of Exodus and Judges. 'In that day' the hopes of 9.2-7 are fulfilled and the oppression lifted; there is no mention of a king.

10.27b-32 envisions the advancing army of 5.26-30 which is both Assyria and the Lord. The poetry is impressionistic and difficult to convey in translation. 'This very day' he stands at Nob and 'waves his hand' at Zion-Jerusalem (10.13-15). A nightmarish scene—*hinnēh* with a participle (3.1)—follows. The divine forester is hewing ('Gideon') the tall, lofty trees; all the forest and the Lebanon fall to his iron axe.

Chapter Eleven

The forest is gone, but stumps and roots remain (6.13). Verses 1-9 are a vision, a dream of the age that succeeds this horrific judgment. Its pictures and images are messianic to the extent that they are royal imagery, but it moves beyond them to the paradisiacal world before Eden.

A shoot comes from the stump of Jesse, a branch blossoms from his roots. The destruction that has reached even to the roots (5.24) has not been total; the process of seed and growth begins anew. Jesse was David's father and 'the stump of Jesse' implies that the dynasty, the tree, of David is gone and that this shoot replaces it. The spirit of the Lord invigorates and energizes the shoot (at 4.4). It is a spirit of the wisdom and understanding which are not present in the people (1.3; 5.21; 6.9-10; 10.13!); the people, especially kings, follow their own counsel (7.1-9; 9.6), but the branch follows that of the Lord. 'Might' implies 'The Mighty God' (or Divine Warrior) of 9.6 and 10.21 (42.13). Although knowledge is lacking in the people (1.3; 5.13), the vision ends with the earth filled with the knowledge of the Lord. Fear of the Lord, and not of others, is proper (25.3; 29.13; 33.6). The shoot delights ($h^a r\hat{\imath} h\hat{o}$) in the spirit ($r\hat{u}ah$). Fear of the Lord is his very breath.

Verses 3b-5 are the actions of the shoot. He has a divine or superhuman capacity to judge by other than what he sees and hears. Judge, decide, see and hear are constant themes in Isaiah. Judging and deciding are what the Lord and his teaching do (2.4a); the shoot can be a manifestation of the divine teaching. As in chs. 1, 3 and 10, judging benefits the despoiled and the poor; the defense of their rights is sustained with force. Despite the fancifulness of the vision, the violence of judgment is not absent. He strikes with the rod of his mouth; Assyria is the Lord's rod. Like the burning spirit of 4.3-4, the branch kills with the breath of his lips. Righteousness and faithfulness (at 1.21-26), are worn as cloths wrapped around his waist; the closeness parallels the breath and delight of v. 3a.

The dream is a variation on the story of judgment, salvation for a remnant, and ultimate restoration. Verses 6-9 return us to the close of Genesis 1 when animals and humans ate grasses and not each other. Flocks feeding connote both desolation and peace (5.17; 7.21-22). Wild and domesticated animals feed and pasture together; Isaiah's encyclopedic style shows itself in the 13 terms for animals with two types of lions and snakes. A small child, not just a child, leads them; infants, still sucking or just weaned, play with serpents. The three terms emphasize the smallness, innocence and weakness and thereby the total peace that surrounds the animals and children. There is no violence. However, Isaiah uses animals and children because this is a dream, not a picture of an adult and real world.

The climax is fantastic. No one hurts or destroys—the verbs occur in 1.4b as 'do evil' and 'deal corruptly'—on 'my holy mountain'. Israel rejected the Holy One (1.4; 5.24). The earth is filled with both the glory and the knowledge of the Lord (6.3) 'as the waters cover the sea'. Flooding waters reach only to the neck (8.8).

'In that day', a day of salvation, the root of Jesse, like the mountain of the Lord, will be a standard for peoples and nations to come to, 'a glorious resting place', that is, the land or Zion (Deut. 12.9; Pss. 95.11; 132.8, 14). 'In that day' the Lord gathers, 'a second time', the remnant of his people 'who remain from Assyria, Egypt, Pathros, Cush, etc.'.These nations, including the coastlands, are part of the Table of Nations in Genesis 10 which occurs before the scattering 'over the face of the entire earth' which follows upon humanity's attempt to build the tower and the city of Babylon—the usual translation Babel obscures the name (Gen. 11.1-9). 'That day' is a time beyond the book of Isaiah when the Lord gathers all his dispersed and scattered people, not just those taken into exile to Babylon.

Verses 13-14 envision, at the same time, an end to the hostilities of the Syro-Ephraimite War and a return to 'the days of old', the time of Joshua or even before, when Israel was one people and successful against her enemies. In his dream, Isaiah moves back to times of unity and prosperity for Israel, for humanity and for all flesh before the divisions, expulsions and scattering of Genesis 2–11 and Judges. In 11.15 Isaiah visualizes the Exodus when the Lord 'waved his hand' (10.32) and dried the sea with 'his breath'. He sees a highway from Assyria for the remnant 'as there was for Israel when he came up from the land of Egypt'. References to Egypt and Exodus frame the reference to Assyria. (See 7.18 and 19.23-25 for the conjunction of Assyria, Egypt and Israel.)

Chapter Twelve

Chapter 12 is a hymn that concludes 1–12 and serves as a transition to 13–23 and to 24–27 and 40–66. As in ch. 1, the people are addressed in three groups. Verses 1-2 are masculine singular; 3-5 are masculine plural; 6 is feminine singular and addressed to Zion. The Lord's anger has turned away; the refrain of 5.25 has been canceled and the 'comfort' of 1.24 realized.

Verse 2 alludes to Moses's Song of the Sea (see Exod. 15.2); salvation, 'Isaiah', occurs three times in vv. 2-3. The poet, in accord with the Exodus allusion, intones joy and water. Although names have been frequent to this point in Isaiah, this is the first mention of the name of the Lord. The other themes are familiar: knowledge, doings and divine exaltation (2.11, 17). The Holy One of Israel, who has been despised (1.4; 5.24), is great in her midst.

Chapter Thirteen

The superscription indicates a new section, but not totally new since it is part of the Ahaz pericope of 7.1–14.32. The title is an 'Oracle on Babylon' or the 'Burden of Babylon'; the word for oracle also means weight or burden. In my reading, burden indicates that what follows weighs down on us; it is a nightmare.

Babylon. This is the first mention of Babylon. It was an ancient city and city-state that had imperial status under Hammurabi in the early second millennium BCE and under the Chaldeans, particularly Nebuchadrezzar (605–562), in the mid-first millennium (2 Kings 24–25). As part of the Assyrian Empire, it was frequently an instigator of rebellion, especially under its king Merodach-baladan (710–700; Isaiah 39). It was a powerful religious and cultural center even when it had no political power; both Assyrian and Persian kings participated in religious ceremonies there to gain greater legitimacy in the eyes of their subjects. In later times it became the legendary city of power, wealth and, at times, of evil (Revelation 17–18).

In Israel's history Babylon is the enemy that destroyed Jerusalem and Judah in 600–580 and took Judeans into exile near Babylon. Babylon has a symbolic status as a powerful and oppressive city and empire; its conquest by Cyrus symbolizes the end of exile. In the Hebrew Bible, Babylon is first mentioned in the Table of Nations in Genesis 10. Nimrod's kingdom began with Babylon in the land of Shinar (Isa. 11.11). Babylon is Babel, the site of the city and the tower, where humanity is 'scattered over the face of the whole earth' (Gen. 11.8).

In Isaiah Babylon is the city whose fortunes waxed and waned from the late eighth to the early sixth centuries and the symbol of imperial power and wealth, the symbol of oppression, exile and dispersion. Babylon is a proud and arrogant city, fortified and on high. Babylon is both similar to and in contrast with

Jerusalem-Zion. Assyria is haughty, but Assyria is a king and an army, not a city; Nineveh is its actual capital (Isa. 37.37) and not a personification. Finally, of all the peoples and nations in Isaiah, only Babylon has total destruction pronounced upon it.

The Burden of Babylon. The oracle continues the themes of the destructive day of the Lord (2.9-22) and the incessant advance of the army (5.26-30), and it intensifies the imagery through repetition and detail. The poet generally says things in threes and fours. Verses 2-3 describe the muster of the cosmic army on a bare mountain which contrasts with the vision of 'the mountain of the house of the Lord' (2.2-4). The verses are a good example of the poet's repetitive style. Lift a signal (5.26; 11.10); raise the voice; wave a hand (10.32). The soldiers are consecrated (holy), mighty, proudly exulting; they are both high and haughty. Previously the army was whistled for (5.26; 7.18-19). Whoever the army is—the hosts of heaven, Assyria, Egypt or Babylon—they are the Lord's instruments, 'the weapons of his fury' (13.5; 10.5, 25). In vv. 3-5 we both hear and see the scene: the tumult and clamor of a great multitude, kingdoms, nations and an army. They come from a distant land (5.26), the end of the heavens, 'to destroy the entire earth'. Verses 6-8 report the reaction to the invasion. This is the Day of the Lord of 2.9-22, not 4.2-6; it is near because the army comes from afar.

The poet achieves his impressionistic style by piling up terms and images; the effect in Hebrew is even more pronounced because of the sonorous quality of the repetitions. This is a high point in Isaiah's depiction of the monstrous invasion of the world, a hellish version of his story of sin and judgment; this time little, if anything, remains. The imagery is familiar even if intense and extreme. The poet, in v. 8, employs the image of childbirth to impart the pain and agony of the labor, not the birth of a child (chs. 7–8). This is another aspect of Isaiah's encyclopedic style; he uses images and themes for as many effects and meanings as possible.

Verse 9 is a scene—*hinnēh* with a participle—cruelty; wrath; anger; desolation; destruction. There is no light, only darkness; four heavenly entities are listed: stars, constellations, sun and moon. In 11-13, the Lord describes what he is doing in the effusive, impressionistic style: evil, wickedness, iniquity, pride, arrogance, haughtiness and ruthlessness. The high are brought low; humans are removed. In an ironic twist of an image, they are rarer than pure gold (5.8-10, 13-17; 6.11-13). The heavens and the earth shake (v. 5; 5.25) at the Lord's fierce anger (v. 9).

The result of this Day of the Lord is death, dispersal and devastation. 'A hunted gazelle; sheep with none to gather': 'hunted' is the same root as the 'dispersed' of Israel in 11.12 whom the Lord gathers. Isaiah employs the same words for opposite effect; judgment and salvation, dispersal and gathering are intertwined and cannot be resolved into a simple narrative. Violence and brutal death affect all, men, infants and women.

Verse 17 is a second scene (*hinnēh* with a participle). The Lord will stir up Cyrus when the time comes (41.2, 25; 45.13). The Medes are in the Table of Nations (Gen. 10.2) and, in Isa. 21.2, are called, with Elam (Gen. 10.22; Isa. 11.11; 22.6), to attack Babylon. Both the Medes and Elam are peoples to the east of Assyria and Babylon. The Medes were a particularly troublesome power for both of the latter from the eighth to the middle of the sixth centuries when they were conquered by Cyrus.

Isaiah is overlaying and compressing historical times, the eighth- and sixth-century struggles between the above peoples, and fitting them into his religious and poetic categories of sin and judgment, rebellion and invasion. The invasion is devastating and leaves few, if any, survivors. An army is called to punish the rebels. The latter are all humanity, the entire earth or a particular land and people; the army is cosmic or human. For Isaiah, Babylon is human and cosmic. It is a historical power that troubled the Assyrians, that destroyed Jerusalem and that was conquered in turn by Cyrus; however, we also need to take into account that Isaiah says little about the historical Babylon. Babylon is more-than-human; its designs and its fate are mythic and cosmic.

13.1-16 portray a cosmic invasion and slaughter. 17-19 give it a historical slant with the entrance of the Medes and Babylon, the Chaldeans. (The latter are the tribe that ruled the city Babylon from the middle of the eighth century; Abram came from Ur of the Chaldeans: Gen. 11.28-31.) The Medes, however, are more-than-human; they think nothing of silver and gold. They slaughter children without compassion and thereby accomplish the divine judgment (9.17; 13.14-16).

Babylon is 'jewel of the kingdoms; splendor and pride of the Chaldeans'. Jewel, splendor and pride all connote high, visible and brilliant; they are applied to Zion in 4.2. The root of splendor, *pā'ēr* (at 46.13), is used of finery (3.18), pride (10.12) and the axe vaunting itself (10.15). Zion, a woman, is desolate and will be splendid; Babylon, a woman (vv. 19-22 are feminine singular), is splendid and 'will be like Sodom and Gomorrah when God overthrew them' (1.7-9). The image of total devastation ushers in the demonic world of negation; in v. 20 the word 'no' is used four times with four different verbs and two phrases for 'forever'. This is followed by five verbs with six wild, demonic creatures as subject; this is the dark side of the peaceable kingdom (11.6-8). Chapter 13, marked with the immediacy of participles and imperatives, ends with the note that the time of Babylon's end is near as is the Day of the Lord in v. 6.

Chapter Fourteen
Chapter 14 follows directly upon 13 and at first counters the nightmare with a dream of restored Israel. There will again be divine compassion (9.17!; 13.18!) and choice. The Lord will give Israel rest in their own land; the verb 'to give rest' occurs in vv. 1, 3 and 7 and the noun 'resting place' is in 11.10. This is the land that is now desolate and empty (1.7; 6.11). Others, aliens, join them. Peoples bring them back and, turning the tables on them, the Israelites enslave the peoples and rule over those who oppressed them. There are hints of the Exodus here and in v. 3 in the mention of pain and hard service.

14.1-2 are comparable to the close of ch. 11 while 14.3-4 parallel 12.1, 'You will say on that day', with 'On the day the Lord gives you rest . . . you will raise up this taunt against the king of Babylon'. (In both instances 'you' is masculine singular.) 'Raise up' is the verb that underlies the 'oracle/burden' of 13.1 and 14.28. 'Taunt' is a word that also means 'likeness' and 'simile'; the taunt uses the comparison of parody. The song is against the king of Babylon; it describes the actions and fate of a man, not a woman. Lady Babylon returns in vv. 22-23.

Similar to the oracle against Zion in 1.21-26, the song is a lament 'How!' or 'Alas!' that contrasts past with present; Babylon, however, is not refined and restored. The oppressor has ceased; the verb occurs in 13.11 and underlies 'Sabbath' (1.13; 56.2-6). The taunt plays upon the rest and peace that are on the earth since the king of Babylon is gone; meanwhile the underworld is all astir at his arrival there. The Lord has broken the staff and rod of rulers; there is an underlying comparison with Assyria at work in the poem. 'Rulers' employs a homophone for 'taunt'; ruling and being taunted are connected in this parody.

The king struck peoples in unrelenting wrath; this interjects an unsettling comparison with the actions of the Lord. The violence is contrasted with an idyllic scene of the earth at rest and trees rejoicing; this differs from 7.1-4 where the king of Judah shakes like the trees and is told to be at rest. Trees introduce the antithesis of high and low, up and down, which is a mainstay of the taunt. 'Since you have lain down, there does not come up against us a cutter (down).'

Sheol beneath trembles (5.25; 13.13); it stirs up (13.17) shades, the leaders of the (under)world. The scenes of death and descent of 2.9-22 and 5.13-17 are expanded; 'ereṣ is land, earth and underworld. The sarcasm is heavy. The kings rise up from their thrones, but they are dead and in the underworld. They address the king of Babylon and emphasize that 'you are like us'. 'Ruling', 'being taunted' and 'being like' the dead are likened since all sound alike in Hebrew. Pride, 'the din of your harps', is brought down. The Judeans play harps (5.12). Hebrew homophones for 'harps' mean 'withered' (1.30), 'folly' (9.17), 'corpses' (5.25) and a near homophone means 'fall' (14.12; 21.9). The king has maggots and worms both beneath and over him. 'Beneath' opens and closes the scene in 14.9-11.

The lament is renewed in v. 12 with a second 'How!'; 12-20 continue the high–low contrast and expand upon vv. 4-11. Fallen from heaven, hewn down, is Helel Ben-Shachar, an early version of Lucifer, whose name means brightness. He storms heaven. 'You said in your heart.' As Assyria's so are the king's words turned against him (10.7). Verses 13-14 brim with words for high and above. He will be enthroned 'in *the uttermost parts of Zaphon*', the mountain of the divine assembly. 'I will be like Elyon [Most High]', a divine title. Assyria mistakes God's work for his own; the king of Babylon thinks himself God's equal. 'But you are brought down to Sheol, to *the uttermost parts* of the Pit.' Verses 16-20, the speech of the dead to the king, repeat words from 9-11, add to them and sharpen the contrast between the king's glorious past and humiliating present. Although dead, he doesn't have a tomb; he is cast out and covered with the slain 'like a trampled body'. (For 'trampling', see at 10.6; this is another verb, *bûs*.) All this 'because you destroyed your land, you killed your people'; again the troubling comparison with the Lord's actions.

Verses 20c-22a go back to the cosmic scene of ch. 13 with the Lord as speaker; this is not just a denunciation of Babylon.

Unlike 1.26 and 4.3, there is to be no name for 'the offspring who do evil'; this phrase is applied to Israel (1.4). The command to prepare 'a slaughter for his sons because of the sins of their fathers' is like a prophetic denunciation of Israel; rising and filling the world with cities alludes to the Table of Nations and Babel. The prophet is laying traditions one on the other to produce this multi-layered statement. 'I rise against them' recalls 2.9-22 and indicates the ultimate power behind all the devastation. 'Saying of the Lord of Hosts' marks a closure, and the Lord in v. 22b shifts from the general to the particular; he cuts off name and remnant from Babylon, makes 'her' a swamp and 'sweeps her with a destructive sweeper'.

'The Lord has sworn' (5.9) and the oath is familiar. 'I have planned and purposed.' 'To plan' is used by Assyria (10.7); to counsel, plan, is the verb used in 7.5-7; 8.9-10; 9.6; 11.2 (at 36.5). The Lord's plan is, it stands (*qûm*); but Babylon comes down. The plan is to break Assyria and his yoke (14.5; 9.3), to trample him (v. 19). The prophet goes from the particular to the general. This purpose is for all, not just Assyria, and this hand is stretched out over all, not just Israel (5.25; 9.11); no one can annul (8.10) it or turn it back.

Ahaz died in 715 and 'there was this oracle/burden'. Isaiah does not see this oracle as in 1.1; 2.1; 13.1. The oracle warns the Philistines not to rejoice 'because the rod smiting you is broken'; Israel does just this in 9.2-7, but falsely places its hopes in a human king, not the Lord. The oracle against Philistia, as all the Oracles Against The Nations in chs. 15–23, can turn against Israel; as I have said before, Isaiah cannot be resolved into a simple fable of good versus evil, in this instance with Israel good and the nations evil.

The pattern of the oracle is familiar; there is a temporary respite but the invader keeps coming, devastates the land and a remnant, here the weak and the poor, remains and feeds in peace. The oracle brims with words and images from the preceding chapters. There is a root, like the root of Jesse (11.1), but a serpent comes from it, 'a flying serpent'. The word is *śārāp*, but this seraph does not fly to cleanse and purge (6.2-6). There is feeding and lying down amongst the ruins (5.17; 13.20-21; 17.2), not in the peaceable kingdom (11.6-8). Root and remnant are killed (5.24; 14.22). Philistia must wail (13.6) 'because smoke comes from the north [Zaphon: 14.13] and there is no straggler in its ranks'. This is the cosmic army of 5.26-30 and 13.1-9.

Amidst all this death and devastation what can one say to 'messengers of a nation' who are perhaps those coming to Zion for the Lord's teaching and word; this rounds out chs. 2–14. 'The Lord has founded Zion.' This is messianic creation imagery, similar to the establishment spoken of in 9.7 in relation to David's throne, but here applied only to Zion; no king or kingdom is mentioned. (For parallels to the word 'to found', see 28.16; Pss. 24.2; 78.69; 89.12.) Zion is a refuge (Isa. 4.6) for 'the poor of his people', the oppressed (3.13-15) and the remnant.

Chapter Fifteen

Chapter 15 both starts and continues the Oracles Against The Nations (hereafter: Oracles); these are a separate group of speeches against nations other than Israel and occur as distinct collections in Jeremiah 46–51, Ezekiel 25–32 and Amos 1.3–2.5. With the exception of Amos, the collections all include statements of hope for Israel. Although all four prophets have a limited number of nations in common, mainly Philistia and Moab, there are larger numbers in common if we compare two or three of the prophets. However, the nations denounced are in different order in the prophets and the collections are placed in different parts of each book. On the whole, the Oracles address historical nations, accurately reflect their geography and probably represent historical events or series of events, but this is expressed in poetic and symbolic forms and structures and our attention is turned, therefore, to the role of the oracles in each prophetic book, that is, to the symbolic history and geography.

In Isaiah, the prophet's denunciation of other peoples begins in 2.9-22 with the judgment of humanity, continues with the specific condemnations of Damascus and Assyria—only Isaiah has an oracle against Assyria—and develops into the cosmic assault on the world and on Babylon. Chapter 14 closes with a renewed statement of the coming destruction of Assyria and a warning to Philistia not to place any hopes in Assyrian defeat.

The oracle to Philistia was in 715 BCE, the year of Ahaz's death; the next date is 711, Sargon's attack on Ashdod (20.1); the final date is 701–700, Sennacherib's unsuccessful siege of Jerusalem (chs. 36–37). To reiterate my perspective, Isaiah is compressing and poetically representing events, nations and characters from 735–700, overlaying them with others from 625–540 and later and fitting it all into the categories of his vision of God, world and humanity. The dates provide a framework in the book, not a chronological guide to ancient history. The geography in Isaiah is also symbolic and not a map of an actual invasion.

Philistia, Edom, Moab and Ammon are listed in 11.14. Philistia is on the Mediterranean coast immediately west of Judah; Edom, Moab and Ammon are in Transjordan east of the Dead Sea and in ascending order from south to north. All four are indicted in the Oracles in the other prophetic books. Isaiah omits Edom and Ammon in chs. 15–23 because Moab, in 15–16, stands for all of Transjordan. Damascus and Aram receive brief treatment, 17.1-3, because of the material in chs. 7–8. 17.4-11 returns to Israel and Jerusalem while most of 18–20 concern Egypt and its relations with Israel and Assyria. To this point in 13–20, Isaiah has covered much of the ancient near east from Assyria and Babylon, through Damascus and Aram, Palestine and Transjordan down into Egypt. Chapter 21 returns to the east and southeast including Elam, Media, Babylon and the Arabian Desert; 22 focuses again on Jerusalem and 23 goes northwest to Tyre and Sidon, back on the Mediterranean coast. The biblical world of ancient Israel is thereby traversed. I emphasize the biblical world and not the postexilic world since neither the Persians in the east nor the Greeks in the west are included.

The Burden of Moab includes both chs. 15 and 16. It is written in the impressionistic, lyrical style of 13 and should be read as much, if not more, for its impact and imagery as for its meaning. There is a great deal of wordplay and assonance in the Hebrew, for example, the words for night (15.1; 16.3) and wailing (15.2-3; 8; 16.7) are near homophones. Wailing and crying are carried over from 14.31 (15.2-8; 16.9); the oracle describes and imparts an emotional effect rather than a series of events. The large number of place names, at least 20, coupled with the intoned destruction and mourning, form a litany signifying total devastation. (Most of the names occur in Num. 21.10-35 and Jer. 48.1-47 which are rich intertexts that we cannot now explore.)

Much of the impassioned force of the poem is achieved by the familiar strategy of repetition and piling up words and images. Weeping and wailing; baldness, shaving and sackcloth; high places, streets, roofs and squares. 'My heart' in v. 5 can be the prophet, the Lord or even Zion who is introduced in ch. 16. The picture is defeat, panic and headlong flight. Waters are dried up and desolate; the grass is withered. They carry away what they have gained. They cross the Brook of Willows; willows is a homophone for desert, the Arabah. (At another time, brooks flow in the desert [35.6].) Waters are filled with blood and Dibon becomes Dimon in a play on blood (*dām*). A lion attacks the remnant (5.29-30); even the remnant cannot avoid the disaster. This could be the Lord speaking, 'I bring', or the prophet or Zion who voice this as a curse.

Chapter Sixteen

The opening apparently refers to Moab sending messengers to Hezekiah in Jerusalem appealing for aid; perhaps they go to the steward Shebna (22.15-25). However, specific royal terms are avoided; this is a ruler and they go to 'the mountain of the daughter of Zion' (10.32). The contrasting 'daughters of Moab' are like fluttering birds from a scattered nest; this recalls Assyria's bragging (10.14). Verses 3-4a are apparently addressed to Zion since the imperatives and pronouns are feminine singular. Since the poem is situated at Zion, we can read it from her perspective and with her reaction. The messengers request that she give counsel and make a decision; the latter word is rare but the concepts are familiar. As in 4.5-6, the dark of shade is protective; hiding is good. (But not when the Lord hides his face: 8.17.) Moab is like Israel; both have outcasts and sojourners or aliens (5.17; 14.1). 'The destroyer' employs the same verb as 'laid waste' in 15.1, marking an inclusion of 15.1–16.4b.

16.4c-5 is a short dream sequence of the people of Jerusalem, reminiscent of 9.6-7, of the time when the destroyer and his destruction are past, when the trampler (5.5; 7.25; 14.19, 25) has vanished and when a throne is established (2.2; 9.7; 14.32) in steadfast love. This is the first occurrence in Isaiah of the word and concept *ḥesed* which is important in most of the Hebrew Bible, but is not frequent in Isaiah. (55.3 combines the term with David and sureness or faithfulness.) This is the tent, not the palace or city, of David and it is a just and righteous judge, not necessarily a king, who sits there. As in 9.2-7 the people's hope for a new king is shifted away from an actual king.

The people speak in v. 6 and they alone charge Moab with arrogance. Neither prophet nor God make any such charge; they only react to the destruction. They wail; they do not accuse. A similar observation holds for Philistia. Their joy is ill-timed for the invading army is still coming, but they are not accused of pride or rebellion. I will say more on this as we progress in our reading of the Oracles.

The wailing resumes with v. 7. Moab is compared to a vine whose branches have spread out, even across the sea, but they have been chopped and cut. Isaiah implements and develops vine and tree imagery in a wide variety of ways and contexts. The lament picks up the plant imagery from 15.6-7 and turns it into a scene like that in 5.1-7. It is opposite that in 9.2-5 since the shout of battle and harvest are both silenced. 'The wine treader' is a variation of the trampling image (at 10.6; 63.1-6).

Verses 12-14 are closing comments. Moab approaches Zion for aid as though going to a sanctuary to pray; he does not succeed and only wearies himself (7.13). As in 1.21-26, past and present are contrasted; the future is not a time of restoration, but of glory brought into contempt. This juxtaposes the two words and concepts: contempt (lightness, littleness, triviality, humiliation) and glory (*kābôd*: weight, greatness, importance, exaltation); a similar contrast occurs in 3.5; 9.1; 22.18; 23.9. The once great multitude (13.4; 10.22) is a pathetic, miserable remnant, but still a remnant. Isaiah cannot be resolved into a simple fable of good Israel versus the evil nations.

Chapter Seventeen

The Burden of Damascus is brief because the fate of Aram and Damascus, along with that of Israel and Samaria, was sealed in 7.1–8.4. From that context we know that Judah and Jerusalem are to trust and to wait; they are not to respond to the crisis with either siege preparations or overtures to Assyria. Judah, in the person of Ahaz and the Davidic house, does both. The demand to trust and to wait holds throughout the period 735–700 as envisioned by Isaiah; Judah and Jerusalem are to trust in God and not become ensnared in coalitions against Assyria. In the latter part of the book, we will see that waiting and trusting should characterize human life at any time and place.

The oracle opens as a scene (*hinnēh* with a passive participle): Damascus is removed (*sûr*) as a city; it is a ruin ('a falling'), abandoned (*'āzab*) (7.16). Flocks lie down and nothing disturbs them; this pregnant scene alludes to both dreams and nightmares in 5.17; 11.6-8; 13.20-22; 14.30. The verb 'to disturb' refers to trembling in fear (10.29; 19.16; 41.5) or in awe (66.2, 5). Not being disturbed can be part of a curse (Deut. 28.26; Jer. 7.33) or of a blessing (Lev. 26.6; Jer. 30.10; 46.27; Ezek. 34.28). As frequently occurs in Isaiah, the pastoral changes to the military: the fortress (2.15) comes to an end (13.11; 14.4). The fortress, like the tower at Babel-Babylon, is a symbol of the evil, powerful city that is high, fortified, proud and violent. This city takes on many manifestations including Zion-Jerusalem at points in her story. However, the overall story of the evil city contrasts with that of Zion, the mountain of the Lord. While Zion is cleansed and restored, the evil city crashes into the dust, never to rise again (24.10-13).

Damascus is like Samaria, 'the glory of the Israelites'. Both splendid cities are brought down and reduced to a few berries left on an olive tree after both harvest and gleaning 'in the valley of Rephaim'. (The shift from body to land occurs in 1.5-7 and 10.16-19.) Rephaim is near Jerusalem and the term also means 'shades', the dead who stir at Babylon's approach (14.9). The tiny number is reminiscent of pitiful Moab. However, a day is coming when humanity, including Moab, Aram and Israel, will look to their Maker, their Doer (the participle of *'āśâ; at 5.1-7), and not to the idols they have made; this day follows upon the judgment of 2.9-21 (31.7). Verse 9, unclear in its specifics, speaks of strong cities that are abandoned and a desolation.

The prophet turns this into a denunciation of Zion—vv. 10-11 are feminine singular—a reversal of the hymn in ch. 12 which proclaims the Lord's saving deeds. ('Proclaim' is a causative form of 'to remember'.) Zion has forgotten her saving God; she has not remembered—Zechariah, 'the Lord remembers' (8.2)—her strong rock. Rock is a place of death (2.10, 19-21), a stumbling block (8.14) and the Lord (26.4; 30.29; 44.8). Zion has turned elsewhere. The horticultural image of sacred groves (1.29-30) refers to worship of a fertility god and, at the same time, symbolizes involvement in international intrigue and coalitions against Assyria. As the farmer with the vineyard, they plant and nurture, but harvest only disaster. ('Slips' is a homophone for 'prune' and 'pruning knife' [2.4; 5.6; 18.5], 'strength' [12.2] and 'sing' [12.5; 51.3].) There are alien gods in the people's midst (43.12); aliens consume their land (1.7) when they should be feeding their flocks (61.5). Harvest, which should be a time of abundance and joy (9.3), is a time of flight and sickness; Isaiah mixes pastoral, military and body images.

Zion, however, responds with a vision of her own drawn from the Lord's muster of his cosmic forces (13.2-16), his indefatigable army (5.26-30). Zion pronounces a Woe! upon the nations thundering and roaring against her for the Lord rebukes them and they flee afar, blown away like chaff (33.2-3; 40.24) by the whirlwind (5.28), gone by morning. Destruction is the spoil that is gathered by those 'who prey upon us'; they do not divide spoils with joy (9.2-4; 10.2). Zion's vision is accurate to the extent that, in Isaiah, this is the ultimate fate of the nations attacking Jerusalem; but it is inaccurate to the extent that this is not their immediate fate. Zion, like Ahaz, does not want to wait, does not want to delay her plans; she wants the dream realized now, this very morning!

Chapter Eighteen

The demand for immediate action and resolution continues with a second Woe!, apparently against Egypt which was ruled by a Cushite dynasty in the last part of the eighth century. (In Hebrew Ethiopia is Cush.) Although Cush and the Nile are mentioned in vv. 1-2, ch. 18 is not an oracle against Egypt. It has no title and is a continuation of 17.

It is unclear who is sending to whom; both Egypt and Mesopotamia are divided by rivers. The scene, however, continues the movement and activity of the close of ch. 17, employing familiar terms and concepts: swift, feared 'near and far', conquering or trampling (*bûs: at 10.6; at 14.19). Characteristic of Isaiah's predilection for diversity, 'near and far' (vv. 2, 7) employs a different Hebrew phrase than in other occurrences of the antithesis.

In response and in contrast to the sending of messengers, the prophet calls all, not just the people of Zion, to watch for the signal and to listen for the trumpet blast. The Lord's army is coming; it is seen and heard (5.26-30; 13.2-5). But the Lord speaks of quiet watching from his abode, not the immediate defeat of Zion's foes. This is the quiet of trust in a fearful time (7.4) and the quiet of desolation (14.7). Yet there is the activity of harvest before the fruit is mature; there is cutting, pruning and removing (*sûr), well-known actions in Isaiah. All is left (*'āzab) to birds of prey—this is Cyrus in 46.11—and wild animals. The poet does not specify the objects of the Lord's activity; the Lord cuts and hews all in his way (see 16.8 for Moab's 'shoots'), including Judah and Zion. It is after the harvesting, 'at that time', that the strange people, now involved in international intrigue, bring tribute 'to Mount Zion, the place of the name of the Lord of Hosts' (8.18). 'His name is exalted' (12.4). Peoples flow to Zion (2.2-4; 14.32) and not to Israel or the house of David (9.7; 16.5).

Summary of 15–18. Chapters 15–16 are the oracle on Moab which symbolizes other Transjordanian peoples involved in the coalitions; 17–18 are the oracle on Damascus and the

Syro-Ephraimite War which symbolize the onslaught that sweeps away Aram and Israel and threatens Jerusalem. The four chapters mix military and pastoral imagery. This composite of themes and images drawn from the Syro-Ephraimite crisis figures the twin themes of trust in the Lord and avoidance of entanglement in international intrigue and coalition. The Lord saves, but it is in his own time and in his own way; the people want victory now and want God to work it through their king.

Chapter Nineteen

Chapters 19–20 are the Burden of Egypt. Egypt was a symbol of wisdom and esoteric knowledge; in the first millennium BCE, Egypt was ancient since the Old Kingdom, the time of the great pyramids, lay 1500–2000 years in the past. It was the kingdom of the Nile, comprised of Upper and Lower Egypt. In the period envisioned in Isaiah 1–39, 735–580 BCE, Egypt's fortunes and power waxed and waned. However, a main strategy of her foreign policy was involvement in the politics of the states in Syro-Palestine to use them as a buffer against the empire, whether Assyrian or Babylonian, to the east. The buffer could be formed by rebellious states, whether on their own or in alliance, who opposed the great empire or by the same states fighting amongst themselves and thereby tying down the empire's forces. Egypt supported the states with grain and financial aid and promised, but seldom delivered, military aid in the form of the Egyptian army.

For Isaiah Egypt is an ancient and powerful people, noted first in the Table of Nations (Gen. 10.6), the people of oppression and of the Exodus, who symbolize an unreliable, untrustworthy ally and a strategy, a plan, that will not be, that will not stand. Egypt is a broken reed that pierces the hand of any who lean on it (36.6). Like Babylon, Egypt is, at the same time, a historical and a symbolic nation. The oracle against Egypt continues and develops many of the images and themes of the preceding chapters.

Chapter 19 opens with a scene, *hinnēh* with a participle, in vv. 1-4; the close is marked by 'says the Lord, the Lord of Hosts'. The Lord comes to Egypt. 'Swift cloud' recalls the swift messengers and army (18.2; 5.26) and the Lord's command of the clouds (5.6). The Lord stirs up civil war within Egypt. This reflects the division of Egypt into two parts and mirrors the division of Israel and Judah and the wars between them (7.1–8.4; 9.8-12, 18-21).

Egyptian spirit and counsel are confused. Like the Israelites, they consult mediums (8.19-20) and are ruled by a harsh king (3.1-15; 10.1-4). Verses 5-10 depict the effects on the land; Egypt, the land of the Nile, is arid. With a plethora of words and images, the poet pictures the desiccation; this contrasts with the brief statement about Moab's aridity (15.6). As an example of the terminological diversity, 19.5 uses three different words for water and for dry; v. 6 repeats two terms and adds one for water and three for dry. Both what is already there and what is newly sown dry up; the Nile can no longer support fish or flax and cotton plants. The economy is devastated. Workers are crushed—as are the Lord's people (3.15)—and grieved. 'Grieved' means something like 'of swampy spirit'; 'swamp, pool' refers to disaster (14.23) and restoration (35.7; 41.18).

Verses 11-15 develop the theme of rulers from v. 4. The leaders of Egypt, the land of wisdom and wonder, are foolish and deluded. If they are so smart, why can they not foretell what the Lord has planned for Egypt? (Similar questions about prediction punctuate chs. 40–48.) To plan and counsel, $y\bar{a}$'$a\d{s}$ (at 36.5), is a leitmotif in Isaiah, and the Judahite leaders are not any more discerning of the Lord's ways and plans than the Egyptians (5.11-23). The Egyptian leaders, as Israelite and Judahite leaders, have led their people astray (3.12; 9.13-17) by oppressing them and, even more, by provoking Assyrian invasion. The rulers stagger 'like a drunk in his vomit' (28.7-8). There's nothing to be done by anyone, 'head or tail, palm branch or reed' (9.14). On the other hand, the Egyptian leaders are denounced for confusion and foolishness, not for rebellion, sin or pride. Egypt, unlike Assyria and Babylon, is not personified; Egypt is not a man or woman who confuses God's work with his own; who thinks herself God's equal.

Chapter 19 closes with five comments on 'in that day': 16-17, 18, 19-22, 23 and 24-25. The prophet moves beyond the time of destruction into the future of his dream; Egypt, like Israel and unlike Moab and Damascus, has a glorious future. Egypt will respond with fear and terror to the Lord's hand and to his purpose, and this terror turns to awe. Verse 18 is enigmatic, but does recall the time before Babel when one language was spoken. In 19-22, however, the prophet portrays the Lord and the Egyptians in a relationship exactly like that of the Lord and Israel; the account, and its specific words, reads like a summary of the Exodus and Israel's history in the land. 'The sign and the witness' recall chs. 7–8. Like Israel, Egypt has a future beyond the time of striking and beating, a future of healing and return.

'In that day there will be a highway from Egypt to Assyria.' At the close of ch. 11, the highway led from Assyria to Israel as it had from Egypt to Israel; now Israel is left out since Egyptians and Assyrians come together to worship. This is similar to the nations flowing to the Lord's mountain without the people Israel as mediator and to humanity recognizing their maker (17.7-8). Egypt and Assyria symbolize the whole world. They stand for west and east, south and north, and a foreign nation, Egypt, that is not an invading enemy or enemy of the Lord and one, Assyria, that is both. This is a high point in Isaiah's dream of unity and peace, a time of blessing, not of destruction, 'in the midst of the earth'. A time when the Lord pronounces a blessing: 'Blessed my people Egypt; the work of my hands Assyria; my heritage Israel.' Yet this is a vision of a future, 'in that day'.

Chapter Twenty

The narrator abruptly shifts back to present reality with the prosaic 'In the year that the Tartan came to Ashdod'. (I leave the title Tartan untranslated; see the Rabshakeh in chs. 36–37.) This is 711 BCE. Sargon, king of Assyria, sent him and he captured Ashdod, a Philistine city, fulfilling the warning to Philistia (14.28-31); the brief story is about more than just Egypt. 'At that time' is a specific time, not the fanciful time of 'in that day'. The Lord spoke through Isaiah, son of Amoz; as in chs. 7 and 36–39, the short narrative sets the stage for speech.

Isaiah had stripped and gone about naked and barefoot; he is a witness. In 8.16-20 he is a witness against Israel who has not done what the Lord said and who has gone about naked and barefoot (3.16–4.1). To reiterate, the story is about more than just Egypt. 'My servant Isaiah': the noun 'ebed, servant or slave, occurs first in 14.2 when the enslaver become slaves; 'ābad, to serve or worship, occurs there and in 19.9, 21-23. I will follow the transformations of servant and servants as we progress through the book.

Isaiah is 'a sign and a portent' (8.18). As he goes about naked and barefoot, so will all of Egypt and Cush (Ethiopia) be led into captivity and exile by the king of Assyria, in a sense fulfilling the vision of 19.1-15. However, 'they are dismayed and confounded because of Cush their hope and Egypt their boast'. Both the hope and the boast are false; Egypt is a symbol for false trust. Egypt cannot help herself or anyone else (30.5; 31.1-3; 36.6); this contrasts her with the Lord, Israel's helper (41.10-14; 44.2). 'They' are 'the inhabitants of this coastland', the Syro-Palestinian coast including Philistia, Judah–Israel and Sidon and Tyre. This is a major Isaianic image: another nation falls and the army keeps coming towards us. 'In that day' signals a time both historical, the late eighth century, and symbolic, any time of disaster and fear. Each word of the inhabitants's lament is pregnant: hope, flight, help, deliverance, escape. They flee for help; there is none; then they flee in defeat (10.3; 13.14; 30.15-17). The only hope for escape is turning to the Lord, not to Egypt and international intrigue.

Chapter Twenty-One
Burden of the Wilderness of Sea. Whether the title is an obscure reference to southern Mesopotamia or a result of textual error, it is an interesting combination of wet and dry, two of Isaiah's main images. The poet writes in the same impressionistic, lyrical style as he used in 15–16, and he strives for affective impact with the repetition and imagery. The poem is words to be read and heard and a vision to be seen; with a slight adjustment in the Hebrew, 'wilderness of sea' becomes 'words' and the title, 'Burden of Words'. What is not stated is who sees, who speaks and where they are. I read the poem as an unfettered vision that shifts perspective and site, and in which the expression is more important than the speaker whether prophet or unnamed seer.

The poet sees and hears of the fall of Babylon; he reports this and his anguished reaction. The poet speaks of Babylon's fall, and fall implies Babylon's pride, her height; otherwise he does not mention Babylon's arrogance. The vision sweeps in on the poet as the whirlwind of an invading army (5.28; 17.13). The reaction is similar to the anguish caused by the muster of the cosmic army (13.1-8). The hard vision is both heard and seen. The Elamites and the Medes attack; this accords with both an eighth- and a sixth-century setting. Since the oppressor has ceased so does the mourning (14.4). As in 13.8, childbirth connotes agony, not delivery. The pain is so great that, paradoxically, the poet cannot hear or see (18.3). He heaps up words for anguish: pangs, dismay, appalling, horror and trembling (19.16-17).

Oblivious to the approaching storm, the Babylonians feast; in this they share much with the people of Jerusalem (5.11-12;

22.13-14). They polish the shield for show, not for battle. The poet sets up a watchman. The watchman is to tell what he sees, and when he sees the army, he is to listen carefully. (Listening, hearing, are important functions in Isaiah: at 1.18-20; 28.23; 34.1; 48.18.) 'He cried: A lion!' Even if this is a scribal error, it is understandable since the advancing army roars like a lion (5.29; 15.9). The watchman is diligent both day and night; he sees a rider coming (*hinnēh* with a participle). 'He answered': the message is crucial, not the speaker. 'Fallen, fallen is Babylon.' This is Lady Babylon: the eighth- and sixth-century city; the rebel and the oppressor; Babel, the site of unity and dispersion; the evil, fortified city.

The news is delivered to Israel. Verse 10 is rich in its form and in its allusions. 'My threshed one' (feminine singular): threshing is a form of trampling (at 10.6; 14.19; 16.10). 'Winnowed one' is literally 'son of my threshing floor' (masculine singular). What I hear from the Lord I tell to 'you' (masculine plural). As in chs. 1 and 12, the poet addresses Israel in all its manifestations: woman, man and men.

Burden of Dumah. Dumah is a town in Arabia, and in Hebrew the name means 'silence'. In Pss. 94.17 and 115.17, it is the silence of the grave. Although one calls and the watchman answers, both the question and answer are enigmatic, a type of silence.

Burden of Arabia. Dedan and Tema are sites in Arabia; they aid the fugitives from Babylon (16.1-4), ironically with food and drink (21.5). Sword, bow and battle allude to the advancing army (5.26-30; 13.1-18).

Chapter 21 ends as 16 did. The glory of Kedar, another place in Arabia, comes to ruin in a year, 'according to the years of a hireling' (16.14), and his remnant is pathetic. The similarities between chs. 15–16 and 21 set off 15–21 with a minor inclusion. Chapters 22 and 23 bring the Oracles to a close by returning to the close of ch. 14. Chapter 22 denounces Jerusalem while 23 is the Burden of Tyre; Tyre, like Philistia to the southwest, is on the Mediterranean coast to the northwest.

Chapter Twenty-Two
Burden of the Valley of Vision. The oracle is against a city. The title is ironic since it is the valley and not the mountain; in

Isaiah cities are usually raised up, on high, whether the height of glory or of arrogance. The chapter divides into two parts, vv. 1-14 and 15-25, with the first part split into two. In 1-7, the prophet addresses the city and its inhabitants ('you' is feminine singular); in 8-14, he makes it clear that he is denouncing Jerusalem. In the second half of the chapter, the Lord sends the prophet to announce the fall of Shebna and of his successor Eliakim. With the exception of vv. 24-25, the chapter, in the Hebrew text, is in verse form (see REB and NIV).

The opening scene is similar to that in Babylon (21.5); there is rejoicing in the midst of disaster. Shouting, tumult and exulting are characteristic of the Lord's army (13.2-5; 17.12), not of the ones being attacked. Many have died in the city from oppression and civil war, not from battle (3.25!); the rulers have fled, a typical action in these times (16.2-3; 20.6; 21.14-15). Although they tried to flee far away, they were captured; the play on far and near continues. 'I' lament 'the destruction of the daughter of my people' (16.1-2), with weeping and refusal to be comforted (12.1; 40.1). The 'I' is the poet and the ruler of the city.

'For the Lord of Hosts has a day.' This is a time when the Lord is against the high and haughty (2.12-19; 13.6), when he tramples (*bûs: 14.19; at 10.6) them in the valley and when their exultant tumult turns to the tumult of defeat. This is the nightmare of the Lord's Day, not just the time of an attack on Jerusalem. Walls come down and shouts go up. Kir bares the shield for battle, not for show (21.5). The city's valleys are filled with chariots (2.7); the cavalry is at the gates (21.7-9). The city is Jerusalem, Babylon and any arrogant citadel.

In v. 8, the poet shifts from a cosmic to a specific vision. The Lord has taken away the shelter of Judah. 'To take away' means 'to exile' (5.13), 'to betray' (16.3) and 'to reveal' (22.14). 'Shelter' is related to 'booth' and 'protection' (1.8; 4.6) and figures Zion. Like Isaiah, Judah goes about naked. The people act as they did in chs. 5 and 7. The city is under siege and for the people it is 'the city of David', not Zion or the city of the Lord. They look to the royal armory (1 Kgs 7.2-5); they store water supplies (Isa. 7.3; 8.5-8); they destroy part of the city to fortify the walls, ignoring that the Lord is against fortified walls (2.15). But the preparations are in vain because 'you do not look to him who is doing it; him who fashioned it long ago you do not see'. This continues the themes of seeing and doing (5.1-19) and introduces the term 'to fashion, plan' (yāṣar: 27.11; 37.26; 43.1, 7, 10, 21) in the sense of

making or forming like a potter (*yôṣēr* 29.16; 30.14). 'Long ago' is
the same phrase as 'from far away' (v. 3; 5.26); being near or far
is both physical (33.13; 34.1) and temporal (13.6, 22). Distance
and time figure each other.

Verses 12-13 are the epitome of Isaiah's notion of rebellion
and sin: the harsh contrast between what the Lord calls for, what
he wants, and what he gets (1.2-3; 5.11-23). He calls for weeping
and gets feasting. The irony is heavy. In chs. 3 and 5, because of
revelry and feasting, the Lord sends baldness and mourning
(3.18-26; 5.11-23). At this point the people's iniquity is removed,
atoned for, only through death. At other points, Isaiah's guilt
(6.7) and that of the people and of Jerusalem (33.24; 40.2) are
atoned for without death.

Shebna and Eliakim. This is a tale of the arrogance of the
nobility and an allegory of the fate of Jerusalem. The two parts
of ch. 22 open with the question 'What do you mean by . . . ?'
Shebna is hewing and carving—two participles—a dwelling on
the height, in the rock; these are terms of strength and stability
but it is a tomb that he is making. The fate of the king of Babylon echoes in the background (14.19-20); height is an image of
pride and rock, of death (2.10). But the Lord is hurling him—
hinnēh with a participle—into a wide land, not the confines of a
tomb. Glorious chariots, a sign of military pomp, are a shame 'to
your master's house'; Hezekiah is not named. Shebna is acting
like a king with his own military forces. This is the juxtaposition
of glory (*kābôd*) and contempt, shame, first noted at 16.14; the
story plays upon the different denotations of *kābôd*. Shebna, set
on high, is thrown down.

The Lord promises to 'call my servant Eliakim'—the name
means 'the Lord raises up, makes stand [*qûm*]'—and, in an elaborate coronation ceremony, to make him Shebna's successor. 'To
bind' (the girdle on), *ḥāzaq*, plays upon the name Hezekiah (at
8.11). His absence is understandable since Eliakim is a virtual
king with authority over Jerusalem, Judah and the house of
David. He has its key 'on his shoulder'. A key is not 'the government on his shoulder' (9.6), and a peg, even in a firm (*'āmēn*)
place, is not an image of stability. 'Throne of honor [*kābôd*]' is a
stronger image, but in v. 18 'glory' is juxtaposed with 'shame'.
Too much is hung on him; 'all the weight [*kābôd*] of his father's
house' from greatest to least, even jars. 'Jars' is a homophone for
the silenced 'harps' of the king of Babylon (14.11) and the 'corpses'

in the streets (5.25). 'In that day', the time of defeat, the peg will give way, be hewn down ('Gideon': 10.33; 14.12) and the burden on it cut off. (Note the verbs of destruction.)

This tale of two royal officials is symbolic of the fate of others since the plot of the story is a recurrent pattern in Isaiah (see ch. 20). A time of glory and power for one person or nation is followed by their defeat and demise; this ushers in a time of rejoicing and power for another, but this is not permanent since disaster and defeat also overtake them. In Isaiah those who think themselves in a firm place are hewn down.

Chapter Twenty-Three

The Oracles close with the Burden of Tyre. Tyre and Sidon were two important Phoenician city-states on the Mediterranean coast north of Israel who maintained an elaborate system of trade routes and colonies around the entire Mediterranean basin from Egypt to Tarshish, probably southern Spain. Tyre, whose name in Hebrew is a homophone for 'rock', was a city built on a rocky island several hundred yards offshore; it resisted sieges by Assyrians and Babylonians and was not conquered until Alexander. It is a dual symbol of trade and travel—note the terms in vv. 2-3—and of the impregnable fortress, 'the stronghold of the sea'; the oracle plays upon both of these aspects and weaves in images and themes from the preceding chapters. Tyre's travel is for trade, not for international intrigue.

As with the oracle on Moab, the prophet opens with wailing and waste. Most of the poem, even parts of vv. 13-18, is written in the impressionistic style and as a series of addresses directed to Tyre and Sidon. They are to mourn their own destruction, their disgrace. They have not given birth or raised children (1.2); this is a third meaning of the childbirth motif. The other two are actual birth (7.10-16; 8.1-4) and the agony of labor (13.8; 21.3). All on the coast, from Egypt to Tarshish, lament the ruin of Tyre; the entire western expanse of the Mediterranean is symbolized by sea (v. 4). Like Jerusalem and Babylon, Tyre is an ancient, exultant city; she has travelled afar.

Her fall is not a historical issue but an image of the fall of the mighty and a question of who planned this? The answer is in 14.24-27 and 23.9: the Lord of Hosts. The plan and purpose are already known. The Lord brings down, defiles and humiliates, the proud and honored of the earth. This plays upon the contrast of glory and contempt (22.18). Glory is figured with images of crowns and jewels. The Lord has stretched out his hand, a recurrent image of divine power and judgment (5.25; 9.12; 11.15; 14.26-27); he makes kingdoms tremble, another symbol of power (5.25; 13.13; 14.9). Sea, kingdoms and Canaan figure totality. Strongholds are destroyed and daughter Sidon exults no more; there is no rest for them in their far flung trading empire (see 7.19; 11.2; 14.1-7 for different notions of rest).

Ironically, it was the Chaldeans (13.19), not the Assyrians, who destined Tyre for the wild creatures that inhabit the demonic land that Babylon becomes (13.21). We are back in the violent Day of the Lord of ch. 13 and in mythic, not historical, time. Tyre is a desolation, a ruin. The poet rounds off w. 1-14 by repeating his opening lament and, with v. 15, moves forward to 'that day'. Tyre will be forgotten for 70 years 'like the reign of one king', a much longer period than the few years of a hireling (16.14; 21.16), but at the end of that period the harlot city will sing of remembrance and restoration. Tyre is like Zion, a harlot city who is restored (1.21-26), and the chapter closes with a vision similar to that at the close of 19. Tyre returns to her wide-spread trade; 'harlot' stands here for serving and dealing with others, not for sexual misconduct. Her goods are dedicated, 'holy', to the Lord; this recalls the consecrated, 'holy', warriors (13.3) and rounds out 13–23. The goods are not hoarded but are spread abroad for 'abundant food and fine clothing'—the word clothing means covering, shelter (4.6; 22.8)—'for those who dwell before the Lord'. Given the parallel with 19.23-25, this includes many more than just the people of Israel.

Summary. The Oracles come to a definite conclusion even though their beginning is spread across chs. 10 and 13–16. Against the backdrop of the divine army called from the ends of the heavens to destroy the entire earth, the Oracles speak of violent times, of the violence of human history. They speak of universal judgment and of universal peace when Egypt, Assyria and Israel worship the Lord and when Tyre supplies them food and clothing. The nations and the individuals are both historical and symbolic, particular and general. They are the nations of the Table of Nations in Genesis 10. Isaiah envisions a return to this state of unity before the scattering and dispersion at Babel-Babylon (Genesis 11), but this unity requires a unity of judgment. All of the nations, including Israel and Judah, must suffer through the catastrophic invasion of the divine army; the particular invasions of Assyria, Babylon and Persia become symbols or allegories for both the violence and the victories of human history.

Chapter Twenty-Four

Chapters 24–27 are markedly different in style and content from their context and, unsurprisingly, assessments of them have varied greatly. The chapters include chants and songs whose repetition and assonance are observable even in English; there are a considerable number of Hebrew words used for the first time, and occasionally for the only time, in Isaiah; the poet(s) speaks in general categories with few of the particulars of 17–23 and 28–33; although the poet describes a great deal of devastation, the call is for praise more than for wailing. These differences have caused many to isolate 24–27 in the book of Isaiah and to treat them as an eschatological or apocalyptic collection, hence the frequent title *The Isaianic Apocalypse*, and to consider them amongst the latest material in the book. This is by no means a majority opinion and almost every aspect of the chapters, for example, inner structure and unity, relation to their Isaianic context and date and identity of the speakers, is open to debate.[1]

Although the chapters do stand apart, they are closely connected with the rest of Isaiah in style, vocabulary, imagery and themes. The chanting style is an intensification of the style found, for example, in 13 and 15–16; the repetition and piling up of words and images may be more striking in these chapters, but they are not unique to them. The poet writes in a cosmic, symbolic mode. Attempts to separate material about 'righteous' Israel from that about 'wicked' nations are even more futile than in earlier parts of Isaiah. Speakers are generally unidentified. I call the main speaker the poet to reflect the anonymity and I employ multiple identifications for those who utter imperatives and for those who say 'I' and 'we'. Chapters 24–27 are both summary and transition and they mark a stage in the transformations taking place in the book of Isaiah; while reading these

1.   See D.G. Johnson, *From Chaos to Restoration: An Integrative Reading of Isaiah 24–27* (JSOTSup, 61; Sheffield: JSOT Press, 1988), pp. 11-17 for a brief review of the major questions and opinions.

chapters, we move beyond or away from particular nations and individuals.

Chapter 24 is similar to 13 in its vivid presentation of world-wide destruction. Both 13 and 24 are intense in their depiction and imagery and they form an apt frame for the Oracles in 14–23. In places, chs. 24–27 mirror the proclamations of salvation and hope that are interspersed within the Oracles. However, with a few exceptions, the particular peoples and nations of the Oracles, Israelite and foreign, are absent from 24–27 whether it is judgment or salvation that is pronounced on them.

Although I discuss ch. 24 in four sections—1-9; 10-13; 14-20; 21-23—the divisions are for purposes of clarity and do not reflect different poems. Verse 1 opens the scene—*hinnēh* with a participle—of the Lord laying waste to the earth, the land; the word *'ereṣ*, in both meanings of whole earth and particular land, occurs 15 times in the chapter. The devastation is total. 24.1-13 describe the utter ruin without any reaction of wailing or mourning (contrast chs. 15–16). Verse 2, akin to the scene in 3.1-3, lists six pairs. Much of the chapter works with sets of three, as does ch. 13, and not the more usual two. The earth is despoiled 'for the Lord speaks'; the Lord's speech sets the entire book in motion (1.2). The world withers as flowers wither (1.30; 28.1, 4). (For world, *tēbel*, see 13.11; 14.17, 21; 18.3.) Homophones for 'wither' are 'corpse' (5.25; 26.19), 'harp' (5.12; 14.11) and 'foolishness' (9.16; 32.5-6); for this word play, see at 14.11. 'Heaven' is the 'height' (*mārôm*) on which Shebna builds (22.16) and it is based on **rûm*, to rise, raise (at 7.7). The verb connotes arrogance (10.15; 26.5), child raising (1.2) and divine exaltation and heaven (6.1; 32.15; 33.5).

The inhabitants of the earth have transgressed teachings and violated statutes; the latter may mean that they have lost all sense of measure since the word 'statute' occurs with this meaning in 5.14. The eternal covenant is broken, annulled (8.10; 14.27; 33.8). This is the first appearance of the term covenant, *bᵉrît*, in Isaiah; the term does not appear often in the book and occurs in different contexts when it does (42.6; 49.8; 54.10). Teachings, statutes, covenant, curse and guilt belong to Isaianic cultic imagery (at 1.10-16).

In the midst of v. 6, the poet shifts to other typical Isaianic imagery: eating, fire, tiny remnant (13.12; 16.14), mourning and ceasing, coming to an end (13.11; 14.4). Verses 7-9 reverse the celebration of 9.2-5 and the feasting of 5.11-23. There are strong allusions to the Vineyard Song, to the descent into Sheol and its images of eating (5.13-17) and to the dryness and aridity that befall Moab (16.10) and Egypt (19.5-10). The instruments and the drink are those listed in 5.11-12, 22.

Verses 10-13 depict the ruin of 'the city of chaos'. Chaos is *tōhû* and alludes to 'the formless void' (*tōhû wābōhû*) of Gen. 1.2. (Both words occur in Isa. 34.11; see 29.21; 40.17, 23 for *tōhû*.) The peaceable kingdom of 11.1-9 pictures conditions at the close of Genesis 1; chaos is the darkness and waste at the start of Genesis 1 before creation. This is the mythic city of evil, pride and strength; in Isaiah, it is embodied in Zion, Samaria, Damascus, Tyre and Babylon. It is broken like Jerusalem (8.15; 28.13) and Assyria (14.5, 25, 29). It is closed in on itself. In contrast and at other times, Zion's gates are open to the influx of nations (2.2-4; 60.11). Verse 11 repeats and condenses 7-9. The remnant, what is left, is desolation (6d). There is harvesting and gleaning (17.6) 'in the midst of the earth' (5.8; 6.12; 10.23; 19.24), among the nations. This time no city is left standing like a booth in a vineyard.

Verses 14-18 present difficulties for the reading because of the indeterminate speakers. 'They lift their voices; they sing for joy'. The response in 14-16a is unexpected given chs. 13–23 where wailing and horror are the normal reaction to the announcement of disaster. The response accords more with the hymn in ch. 12 which shares terminology with 24.14-16a. Chapter 12 is a hymn to be said 'in that day' which follows upon the ingathering of the dispersed; it is a prayer of the returned remnant of Israel. Therefore, I read this section in ch. 24 as a prayer of the remnant, but the remnant of both Israel and of the nations, that is, all who are left after the destruction of the city of chaos. What Israel and Zion do, all can do.

They sing and shout (12.6) because of the majesty of the Lord (12.5). Majesty is the Lord on high; if humans raise themselves on high, majesty turns to pride. In 11.11-16 the Lord gathered the dispersed from the entire earth; in 24.14-16a, it is people across the entire earth who praise the Lord: west (the sea), east ('regions of light'), the coastlands (11.11) and the ends of the earth (11.12). (There is a similar boundless praise of the Lord in 42.10-13.) Because the city is gone, someone—the poet? Zion? an unidentified member of the nations?—requests the glorification 'of the name of the Lord, the God of Israel'; this reflects the all-encompassing view of passages such as 2.2-4 and 19.19-25. More than just Israelites can glorify the God of Israel. Those left speak in their own voice: 'We hear songs from the corners of the earth', not just in Zion. They praise the glory, the splendor, of the Lord, the Righteous One (5.16); splendor is like a jewel, a diadem (4.2; 13.19; 23.9).

An unspecified inhabitant of the earth—an individual? a nation? the city of chaos?—objects to all the joy and chants his misery. He pines and wastes away (10.16; 17.4) because 'the treacherous deal treacherously'; they attack Babylon (21.2) and are themselves done in (33.1). Israel acts treacherously (48.8). There is no escape because terror, pit or snare will take them. The days of the Flood return (Gen. 7.11), and the earth (feminine singular) trembles from its heights (*mārôm*) to its depths, its foundations (Isa. 40.21): broken, torn, shaken. Its rebellion weighs upon it; it staggers like a drunk (19.14), a hut (1.8); it falls and cannot rise (*qûm*). Earth, as feminine singular, symbolizes the lofty city that crashes down. 'Lies heavy on' is *kābēd* (at 43.4), the verb related to *kābôd*, and the crash parallels that of Shebna and Eliakim (22.15-25).

After the downfall of earth and city, 'in that day' the Lord punishes, or decides the fate of, heaven and earth.[1] God decides the fate of all whether for weal or for woe. In that day, even the cosmic hosts (13.4-5) are consigned to the pit with the earthly kings (14.15-20). The highest go to the lowest.

The sun and the moon are disgraced. At the advance of the heavenly army, they lost their light (13.10). In 24.23 the poet uses two different and unusual words for sun, 'the hot one', and moon, 'the white one', which he employs again in 30.26 for the opposite image of brilliant light. They are disgraced 'because the Lord is king in Mount Zion and in Jerusalem'. This alludes to the prophet's vision of 'the king, the Lord of hosts' (6.5), the only other time to this point in the book that God is called king (33.22; 41.21). The final phrase of the chapter is difficult and ambiguous. 'Before his old ones' is usually translated 'his elders' in a positive sense; however, the elders are condemned in 3.13-15. (The word is translated 'aged or old men' in 47.6 and 65.20.) Divine glory balances the shame of the sun and the moon.

1.   For the latter meaning of *pāqad*, see Watts, *Isaiah 1–33*, pp. 325-26; the verb, significant in chs. 24–27 occurs in 10.12; 13.4, 11; 23.17; 26.14, 16, 21 and 27.1, 3.

Chapter Twenty-Five

Verses 1-5, a hymn similar to ch. 12, are an immediate response to the preceding. The speaker, 'I', is unidentified and can be a member of Israel or of the nations; if the latter, this is a recognition similar to that in 2.3. The terminology and imagery, as in much of 24–27, are characteristic. 'To exalt' is 'to raise' (*rûm*; 1.2); high and low, combined with strong and weak, are a central contrast in the hymn. The hymnist praises the name of the Lord in response to the request in 24.15 (12.3). The praise gathers significant terms: do; wonderful and wonders (9.6; 28.29); of old or from afar (5.26; 22.11; 37.26); faithful and sure. (The latter are both **'āmēn*: at 1.21; 7.9; 16.5.) The themes are characteristic of Isaiah. The high is brought low; the strong glorify the God who protects the weak and lowly; God is a shelter from the storm.

The fortified city, *'îr b^eṣûrâ*, puns on Zion, the besieged or guarded city, *'îr n^eṣûrâ* (1.8; 27.3). Assyria reduces 'fortified' cities to heaps (36.1; 37.26); the Lord is against all 'fortified' cities (2.15; 27.10) including Babylon (13.19-22), Damascus (17.1-3), Jerusalem (22.10) and Tyre (23.1-14). Ruined palaces are demonic haunts (13.22; 34.13) that are never rebuilt, although Jerusalem is an exception (44.28). 'Strength' and the related noun 'stronghold' are common in Isaiah: 12.2; 17.9-10; 23.4, 11, 14; 25.4; 45.24; 49.5; 56.11; 62.8. 'The ruthless' are 'the tyrants' laid low by the Lord (13.11); the same root is used of the Lord who rises 'to terrify' the earth (2.19-21). The poor are the oppressed (3.13-15; 10.2) and those protected by the Lord (14.30-32). The Lord's canopy over Zion (4.6) is expanded into protection for all the needy, all seeking refuge (14.32). Although vv. 4c-5 are not clear, they do utilize imagery of storm, heat and shade (32.1-2).

'On this mountain' is analogous to 'in that day', except that it emphasizes place, not time. It introduces the first of three comments: vv. 6-8, 9 and 10-12. The first counters the judgment scene in 24.21-23. 'This mountain' is, at once, Mount Zion, the mountain no longer occupied by the city of chaos and the mountain where the divine army is mustered (13.2). The bounteous feast prepared by the Lord undoes the dearth of wine and joy described in 24.7-13 and counters the deluded feasting in Jerusalem (5.11-23; 22.13) and Babylon (21.5).

'On this mountain' he swallows the veil covering peoples and nations. 'To destroy, swallow' and 'to confuse' is the polysemic verb we encountered with leaders who swallow those led (3.12; 9.16) and with the Lord confounding the plans of Egypt (19.3).

'Covering' is similar to 'hut' and 'shelter' (1.8; 4.6) and 'cover' (22.8). The act in v. 7 is ambiguous. To remove a cover exposes those beneath to the blazing sun and allows judgment to fall upon them; to remove a shroud removes a sign of death and allows the once dead to feast. 'The Lord swallows death forever' counters Sheol's swallowing the Jerusalemites (5.13-14) and is the reverse of Death's swallowing Baal in the Canaanite myth. He wipes away tears as, at another time, he wipes away sin (43.25; 44.22). He removes (*sûr*) disgrace as a husband removes disgrace from a wife (4.1; 54.4). 'From all the earth' marks the dispersion announced in 11.11-12.

'In that day it will be said' indicates time. The anonymous speaker continues. 'Our God' recalls 'my God' (25.1) who is the God of all (19.24-25; 2.2-4). 'We wait' (26.8); the farmer and the Lord waited but were frustrated (5.1-7); Isaiah waits (8.17). As noted at 8.17, waiting is close in meaning to trusting; to trust and wait is to not turn to violence and imperial dreams. 'Save' and 'salvation' are ubiquitous in the book of Isaiah, 'The Lord saves'; joy and salvation are linked in ch. 12. 'This mountain' returns the emphasis to place.

Moab—see chs. 15–16—stands for itself, for Transjordanian peoples and for the nations in general. 'Trodden' is 'threshed' in 21.10 (for 'trampling', see at 10.6). The image of swimming in a dung-pit is disgusting and humiliating. Spreading hands recalls Israel's similar futile act (1.15). The chapter closes with the high and proud, the fortified walls, being brought low, 'cast to the ground, even to the dust'; ground and dust are death, the underworld (2.9-21). The image contrasts with the Lord's hand resting on the mountain (v. 10) and returns to the opening of the chapter.

Chapters 24 and 25 present a cosmic overview of the Lord's judgment on the high and mighty and his protection of the lowly and weak. Judgment is famine, destruction and lowering; protection is a banquet, a refuge and a song of joy. The chapters allude to and thereby bring together all the preceding material except that they broaden it into an all-embracing nightmare and contrasting dream.

Chapter Twenty-Six
'In that day' and 'in the land of Judah' combine both time and place. The chapter begins with a song in vv. 1-6; vv. 7-18 are a complicated song or prayer to the Lord; vv. 19-21 are a concluding

call to the people who utter the prayer. The chapter advances beyond 25 for the saved, the righteous, now have a city of their own.

In the style of these chapters, the song 'is sung'; no singer, Judahite or alien, is named. The song alludes to the Vineyard Song (5.1-7; 27.2-5) and the song of Tyre (23.15-16) and extends the imagery and themes of strength and trust and the high brought low. The saved sing as a group. 'We' have a strong, open city in contrast to the closed city of chaos (24.10, 22; 25.2); 'our city' is fortified with salvation (victory: at 7.1-3), not with stone (22.8-11; 25.12). Any can enter if they are righteous and faithful (*'āmēn); this maintains the world vision of 2.2-4 and anticipates that of 56.1-8. In verses 1-4, the song stresses peace, trust and stability. The everlasting rock is the rock that Zion forgot (17.10). Verses 5-6 return the stress to the violence that marked 25.1-5; salvation and peace cannot come without judgment. The Lord brings the lofty city down to the earth and into the underworld (25.12); 'height' is mārôm which can mean 'heaven' (at 24.4, 18, 21). The contrast of heaven and the netherworld recalls the king of Babylon's fate in 14.12-15. The needy trample the debased city (rāmas: at 10.6; 25.10).

Verses 7-21 are a loosely structured section uttered by the saved, the protected, who speak as a group 'we' and once as an individual 'I' (v. 9). They address the Lord, 'you', and speak about 'them'. The image of the level road connects with the foot image in v. 6. It alludes to similar 'ways' in 2.2-4; 11.15-16; 19.23-25; 40.3-5 and contrasts with leaders who twist the way (3.12; 8.11; 9.16; 10.2). Name and remembrance are combined in 12.4 and again in 26.13 where 'to proclaim, acknowledge' are a form of *zākar, to remember. Yearning and desire add an emotional charge to waiting. The hope is for the Lord and for his judgments in the earth. 'Judgment', mišpāt, is court procedure, including the sentence, the punishment and its execution (at 1.21; at 3.13-15; 4.4; 28.17). When his judgments are present, the entire world (24.4) learns righteousness (ṣedeq: at 1.21) which is frequently paired with justice (mišpāt). People should learn goodness and justice (1.17) and the ways of peace (2.4).

Verses 10-14 narrow the view and contrast 'we' and 'you' with 'them', the wicked. They neither learn righteousness nor see the majesty and uplifted hand of the Lord. In Isaiah, the lack is predicated of both the nations and Israel. Verse 11b reads, 'may they see and be ashamed of a zeal of [for] a people'; there is no possessive pronoun, 'your'. Zeal is the Lord's martial fury (9.7; 37.32; 42.13), but human zeal or jealousy leads to civil war (11.13). However the phrase is understood, it does not equate 'we' with Israel and 'they' with the nations. Israel and nations alike do not see the Lord and his work; Israel and nations alike can learn and be saved. Fire, adversaries, enemies, and eating intone the scene of 1.7 and the smelting of 1.24-25. 26.12 contrasts 'our' peace with their destruction. 'O Lord! You do all our works.' Neither Israel-Judah (5.12, 19; 22.11) nor Assyria realize this (10.13). 'To acknowledge the Lord's name' alludes to v. 8 and 12.4.

Verse 14 pronounces 'they are dead, they do not live' implying that 'we' are alive. Their fate is destruction without remembrance (at 26.8, 13). Verse 15 recalls 9.3. There is no 'but' in Hebrew, only 'you have increased'. The Lord has increased 'the nation' and 'the land', not 'us' or 'your nation'. Verses 14-15 contrast the dead and the living and proclaim the Lord's care for the latter. He has enlarged, or 'pushed afar', the ends of the land or of the earth (5.26; 11.12; 13.5). Verse 16 is obscure, but it does contrast the narrowness of distress with the earth's enlargement (at 28.20).

The poet employs the image of childbearing to impart the notion of futile work, 'we bring forth wind', as he did in the oracle on Tyre (23.4). The people can do things (v. 12), but can 'do no saving [or victorious] acts'. In RSV 18d is 'the inhabitants of the world have not fallen' (v. 9d). RSV and NRSV reflect the ambiguity of the Hebrew phrase since 'fall' or 'let fall' (v. 19) can mean destruction (death) or birth (life).

In 19, the poet counters both 14 and 18. 'Your dead live; your corpses rise [qûm].' 'Dwellers in the dust' can be mourners or the dead, Israelite and foreigner (2.9, 19; 26.5). They awake and sing for joy as does Zion (12.6) and the whole earth (14.7). 'Dew of lights' is an image of morning, beginning and life. 'The earth gives birth to, lets fall, the shades' coupled with the disclosure of blood and slain (v. 21b) counters the death scene of 14.9-19 and the preceding image of futile labor. The destruction and death that the Lord has visited upon the earth in chs. 24–26 and in 1–23 can be overcome by resurrection. Resurrection is an appropriate image for Isaiah since the low, the fallen, are raised, given birth to ('be fallen').

The Lord, or the prophet, comes on scene to tell 'My people'—Israel? Egypt? Any who survive the cataclysm?—to lock themselves in. For awhile at least they and their strong city are like the city of chaos. The short time of the Lord's fury was first noted in 10.25; see 6.11-12 for the idea of a time limit to the punishment. Chapter 26 closes with a scene—*hinnēh* with a participle—which balances v. 21; the people go in while the Lord comes out. The scene recalls 24.1 (and 13.9-11) and rounds off 24–26. Throughout the chapters wrath, judgment, death and grief stand in tension with peace, salvation, life and joy; the righteous contrast with the wicked, 'we' with 'they', but the various distinctions do not line up into a separation of dead wicked and live righteous or dead nations and live Israel.

Chapter Twenty-Seven

'In that day' moves into a future beyond 26.21 and continues the theme of deciding the fate of and punishing. Leviathan is a powerful creature from Canaanite myth (see Pss. 74.12-14; 104.25; Job 41.1) usually connected in the Hebrew Bible with creation as the story of God's victory over chaotic forces; these forces can be personified as Rahab (see Ps. 89.9-11; Isa. 30.7; 51.9-11) and as a sea dragon. The victory over chaos is relevant since ch. 24 described a return to the chaos before creation. Chaos is overcome and the cosmic destruction reversed; therefore, ch. 27 can once again mention Jacob-Israel.

Verse 1, which stands on its own, brings together distant past and future. Punishment 'in that day' corresponds with creation 'in the former days'; both connote establishment of peace and order. Leviathan is myth and mythic time transformed into poetic time and poetic imagery; Isaiah presents a vision of the world, not a myth of the distant past. His world is, at once, past, present and future.

Verses 2-5 are a transformation of the Vineyard Song (5.1-7) and of the oaks and gardens in which the people delighted (1.29). We are still 'in that day' and there is no specified singer, only an imperative (masculine plural) 'Sing of it!' However, the Lord, not a group, responds with an affirmation of his constant care of the vineyard. He is its 'keeper' and 'guard'; these are from the same verb used in 1.8 and translated as a 'besieged city' (at 25.2). The besieged city transforms into the guarded vineyard. The vineyard, masculine in 5.1-7, is thought of as the city, feminine, and spoken of as feminine, 'her', in 27.2-4. This is the last occurrence for the term for 'thorns' used in the phrase 'briers and thorns' (5.6; 7.23-25; 9.18; 10.17; see 32.13). The Lord may have no anger, but he will burn up the briers and thorns, that is, the vineyard. Verse 5 shifts from city, 'her', to people, 'him'. To avoid his fate, he can take hold of—Hezekiah: 'The Lord takes hold of' (at 8.11)—the Lord's 'protection' which is the term for strength and stronghold (12.2; 25.4; 26.1). Instead of rebellion and violence, the people should make peace with the Lord (26.3, 12).

The chapter, and 24–27, closes in vv. 6-13 with a series of statements combining salvation and judgment, sin and its removal, which summarize the preceding and anticipate the following. Verse 6 counters the destruction of root and blossom (5.24) and the negative pictures of plants (1.29-30; 5.1-7; 17.10-11) with the image of Israel as a flowering and productive plant (11.1, 10) 'who fills the world with fruit' (14.21c). The earth is filled with the glory and knowledge of the Lord (6.3; 11.9). Plant images as signs of restoration increase in frequency and detail from 32.16-20 and reach their apex in 60–62.

Verse 7 is a chant of striking and killing which recalls the beaten body of 1.5-6 (9.13; 10.20-26; 14.29). The Lord contends with his people (*rîb*: at 3.13-15) and with their enemies (49.25; 50.8; 51.22); his breath blows them away (10.3; 17.13; 40.24). Atonement for and removal of guilt and sin recall the prophet's vision in ch. 6 (*sûr*, to remove, is in 6.7 and 27.9; at 1.16). Altar stones are 'crushed to pieces', that is, 'scattered'. Asherim, sacred poles, do not stand (17.7-8); the poet continues his play upon high and low. 'The fortified city' is a ruin in 25.2; there is word play on 'the besieged city' of 1.8 which is 'the guarded vineyard' in 27.3. The two cities, the city of chaos and the strong city (24.10; 26.1), are different yet similar; they are both alone and abandoned (6.12; 17.2, 9), pasture land for flocks (5.17; 7.21-25; 17.2). Zion, at different times, is both cities. As previously, Isaiah mixes pastoral and military imagery (1.8; 17.1-6; 27.4). Calves strip branches; the branches dry out, are broken like the city of chaos, and women use them to light a fire. Dryness is punishment since the dry burns: 1.29-30; 5.24; 29.5-6; 40.6-8.

This people, unnamed and unidentified, do not understand; they are like Israel (1.3). They make a fire which can consume them (9.18-21). God has no compassion or mercy on them; this counters the liturgical name of the Lord in Exodus 34 (see Isa. 9.17; 13.18). At other points the Lord does have compassion on Israel (14.1; 30.18-19; 33.2). He is the people's maker (17.7) and fashioner or former in the manner of a potter (at 22.11; 29.16; 44.2; 45.9).

The closing comments move beyond the harsh judgment to 'that day', a time of ingathering; they expand the vision of 11.10-12, 15-16. Threshing is an agricultural image akin to refining in which some are destroyed and some saved (1.25; 21.10; 28.23-29). 'Gathering' alludes to the harvesting and gleaning, the small remnant, in 17.4-6. The promise is addressed to Israel, but the extent 'from the Euphrates to the river of Egypt' recalls the sweeping vision of a united Egypt, Israel and Assyria at the end of ch. 19. 27.13 shifts to the third person. 'The trumpet' alludes to the global call of 18.3; Egypt, Israel and Assyria are connected in a context of worship of the Lord 'on the holy mountain at Jerusalem'. This is where peoples and nations come to learn the Lord's ways and the ways of peace.

Chapters 24–27 which stand apart from their context, are nevertheless tied to Isaiah in terms of style, terminology, imagery and themes. They form a retrospective on 1–23, especially the Oracles in 13–23, and an anticipation of what follows. They bring major themes to the forefront—rebellion and sin followed by destruction and devastation; the evil, fortified city against the strong, righteous city; the contrast of high and low, life and death, and righteous and wicked. However, even less than in the first 23 chapters can we resolve these themes into simple narratives that distinguish past, present and future, the fates of the wicked from the fates of the righteous and, more narrowly, wicked nations from righteous Israel. These plots and distinctions are there, but their edges blend and blur. The nations and Israel share similar fates whether weal or woe. Judgment and salvation occur at the same time; they are intertwined—smelting is an impressive image of the combination—and cannot be separated into actions that chronologically follow one another.

Chapter Twenty-Eight

After the general depictions of chs. 24–27, chs. 28–33 refer again to particular peoples, especially Judah, Assyria and Egypt; they are more like 1–23 than are 24–27. We will see that they also look ahead to 40–55 and 56–66. Chapters 28–33 contain most of the themes and imagery of the preceding chapters and expand upon many of them; the section is an excellent example of the need to read Isaiah as much for how it is said as for what is said. The six chapters, although loosely and variably structured, do have a certain movement that builds to a conclusion and climax of promise in 33 before the worldwide devastation of 34.

28.1-4 is a Woe! Oracle. (Woe!, *hôy*, is a division marker: 28.1; 29.1, 15; 30.1; 31.1; 33.1; see 5.8-23; 10.1-5; unfortunately, NRSV obscures the repetitions.) The leaders of Ephraim, a major northern tribe and a title for Israel, the northern kingdom, are the objects of the denunciation. The remainder of 28–33 are against Judah and Zion-Jerusalem; 28.5-6, 7-13, which have an unidentified object, are transitional.

Verses 1-4 combine typical Isaianic terminology and imagery. Pride is on high. 'Proud' (*gē'ût*) and 'valley' (*gê'*) are a pun. High (head) contrasts with low (valley; cast down). The beautiful flower withers and is trodden on (*rāmas*, at 10.6; 1.29-30; 25.10–26.6). The leaders of Samaria, like those of Jerusalem, are drunks (5.11-12, 22; 22.12-14). Verse 2 is a scene—*hinnēh*—which describes Assyria with storm imagery (5.26-30; 17.13; 25.4-5; 27.8; 30.27-33); he is like overflowing, flooding waters (8.7-8; 10.22). 'To hurl down' is the same verb as 'to rest' in 25.10; the Lord's hand is powerful for weal and for woe (40.10-11). To be a ripe, succulent fig is to be eaten, swallowed (at 25.6-8), as soon as seen; Samaria, like Jerusalem, goes down Sheol's gullet (5.13-14).

Verses 5-6 interrupt the denunciation and glance ahead to 'that day', a day of the Lord's beauty, justice and strength. The picture alludes to the splendid remnant and the spirit of justice described in 4.2-6; 11.1-5; 16.4-5 (the oracle on Moab). The closing phrase, 'at the gate', refers both to the site of judging and holding court and to the place where an attack would have to be stopped.

'These also', in v. 7, refer to the leaders of vv. 1-4 and 6; they can be in both Samaria and Jerusalem and serve as a transition to the particular denunciation of Jerusalem's rulers starting in v. 14. The theme of drunkenness continues from vv. 1-4; vomit and filth intensify the disgust. No longer is there the dearth of wine of 24.7-11; nor is this the feasting on the mountain (25.6-7). 'Confused' is the same root as 'to swallow' which occurs in v. 4 as 'to eat' (at 25.6-8); the justice is poetic: what they swallow (eat) swallows (confuses) them.

Vision and seeing were introduced in v. 4. Priest and prophet are those who should best know the teaching of the Lord; knowledge, understanding and seeing are central themes in 28–33 and are introduced in the opening verses of the book. The comprehensibility and accessibility of the divine word and revelation are core issues in this section. 28.9-13, a difficult passage, juxtaposes teaching, knowledge, explaining or understanding (27.11) and message ('hearing'), all key terms involving the reception of the Lord's word. But there are none to receive it except infants who are too young (3.4, 12; 11.6-8!). For them the word is a meaningless chant:

ṣav lāṣāv ṣav lāṣāv qav lāqāv qav lāqāv zᵉ'êr šām zᵉ'êr šām (vv. 10 and 13).

'They' are infants and the leaders who are like infants in their intellectual capacity.

The Lord speaks to 'this' people, not 'his' people, in a foreign tongue; this parallels Isaiah and his preaching, that is, the book of Isaiah. God speaks to them of rest and repose (14.1-3), but they are not willing to listen or hear (1.19-20; 30.9). They stumble; they are broken, snared, captured (24.17-18); this alludes to 8.15 which is in a context of confusion and ignorance. 'Therefore', vv. 14 and 16, looks to what has just been said and calls attention to what is about to be said (at 5.24). 'Hear the word of the Lord' doubles the emphasis. 14-16 revolve around who has said what. 'Scoffers' is a pun on Zion, and 'who rule' can also mean 'who sing or quote proverbs' (Num. 21.27); in either sense the prophet uses it sarcastically.

The leaders have a Covenant with Death, an Agreement with Sheol. 'Agreement' puns on 'vision', yet this agreement has no vision. (For covenant, see at 24.5.) At one level this covenant is a treaty with Egypt to offset the threatening power of Assyria, 'the overwhelming waters' of v. 2; however, it signifies far more than that in Isaiah since life and death are a central antithesis in the book. Chapter 1, especially vv. 19-20 and 27-28, presents the choice, and these rulers have chosen death (22.12-14). Finally, Death and Sheol are allusions to the Canaanite god Death (at 5.13-14); a treaty with him should offset the Lord's attack, 'the overwhelming scourge' (8.7-8; 10.26). Lies (9.15) are their refuge, not the Lord who is in Zion (4.6; 14.32; 25.4; 32.2).

The Lord's countering speech is a scene—*hinᵉnî*: Look at me!—which is just as much a chant as a statement; meaning and impact go together. The stress is on stability and trust (*'āmēn). This is not the false security of siege preparations (22.8-11); Isaiah turns actual fortifications into a symbol of trust in the Lord. In sharp contrast to lies and rubble, trust has a foundation built with justice and righteousness (26.1; 60.17-18). Storm and flood sweep away lies and rubble, and the covenant is annulled (24.5; 33.8), it does not stand (7.7; 14.24-27). 'Beaten down' is the 'trampled ground' (*mirmās*; v. 3) of the vineyard (5.5; 7.25; at 10.6).

The terror of understanding the message (v. 9) is captured in the couplet about the short bed and narrow cover. The image associates the people with Babylon (14.11) and reverses the protective cover over Zion (4.5-6; 22.8). 'Narrow' is from the same root as 'distress, to be in straits' (8.22; 25.4; 26.16; 30.20; 49.20; 63.9). This message, however, expands. The Lord rages high, Mount Perazim, and low, the valley of Gibeon; both are sites of decisive Israelite victories (2 Sam. 5.17-25; Jos. 10.1-15) which now symbolize divine victory over Israel. The reversal makes the Lord's deed (ma'ªśeh; at 5.1-5, 12) truly strange and alien (1.7; 2.6; 17.10; 25.2, 5; 43.12). Both the Lord's speech and work are foreign to this people (v. 11).

The repetition of 'scoff' closes vv. 14-22, the oracle against the rulers. 'Bonds' are like the narrow blanket and 'decree of destruction' alludes to 10.22-23; 'the whole land' is 'the whole earth'. The specificity of 28.1-22, with the latter phrase, shifts to the generality of the teaching of vv. 23-29. This is a parable of a farmer who, unlike the preceding people (v. 9), is instructed by God. The call to hear is general so that all, not just Judahites, can learn from this. The agricultural terms and imagery are characteristic and inclusive—plow, plant, harvest and thresh; dill, cummin, wheat, barley and spelt. However, plowing, scattering, crushing, beating, and staff and rod (the terms of 10.5 in reverse order) refer to more than just proper farming techniques. One does not beat forever (10.24-26; 26.20) or crush totally. This is a focal point for Isaiah's imagery of trampling and threshing (at 10.6; 14.19; 25.10; 27.12; 41.14-16).

'This', which comes from the Lord, has an ambiguous antecedent in vv. 1-22 and 23-28. It is a strange work of judgment and salvation; it concerns Judah, Israel and the nations; there is destruction over the entire earth but it does not last forever and some do remain. The Lord does wonderfully with his plans (9.6; 25.1); he magnifies wisdom. This moves into the realm of the miraculous, beyond human comprehension. This is a strange teaching since trust in the Lord is not the obverse of a covenant with death. The latter leads to destruction; the former to refining, threshing and gleaning.

Chapter Twenty-Nine

The chapter continues the strange mix of judgment and salvation, of ignorance and blindness, and of understanding and seeing. Verses 1-8 are addressed to Zion ('you' is feminine singular)

called Ariel. The meaning of the name is disputed and there are
several possibilities: 'hearth of God', 'lion of God', and 'underworld' (especially in v. 2b). David camped there and there were
celebrations there, but now death and lamentation. The image of
the besieged city from 1.8 is developed. Siegeworks are raised
up, and deep from the earth, the dust, the underworld 'you speak;
like a ghost, you whisper and chirp'. Allusions are multiple: the
devastation of 2.9-22, the descent into Sheol of 5.13-14, the
ghosts who chirp of 8.19, the dwellers in the dust in 26.19, and
those who have a covenant with death in 28.14-18. Even in death,
there is a faint remnant.

Verse 5 shifts from judgment to salvation, from Zion to the
aliens attacking her (1.7; 28.21). The dust of death is now fine
dust and chaff, the product of the previous threshing, that is
blown away. (See 17.12-14 and 25.1-5 for the fate of aliens and
tyrants.) Unexpectedly Zion is visited, her fate decided, by the
Lord in a violent storm—vv. 6b-7 are a chant—in 'a flame of
devouring fire'. 'Eating' and 'fire' are common images in Isaiah;
to this point in the book, they are combined indirectly in 1.7 and
directly in 5.24 (with dust); 9.5, 18-19; 10.17; 26.11. Zion's fate is
salvation since the attacking nations disappear like a dream.
The poet expands the simile in v. 8 with hunger and eating, thirst
and drinking (5.11-14). Zion awakes and the multitudes are
gone.

Verses 9-10, addressed to 'you' (masculine singular), shift yet
again. The leaders, especially the prophets, are drunk, not with
wine as in 28.7-8, but in a deep sleep akin to the dreamer and to
the Adam (Gen. 2.21), and with a blindness akin to that of the
people (Isa. 5.12; 6.9-10; 22.11). Eyes are closed; heads are covered. The image of closure turns into that of a sealed and unread-
able book in vv. 11-12. The image hearkens back to Isaiah's
teaching and testimony that are bound and sealed while he waits
for the Lord (8.16-20); book and teaching are figures for the book
of Isaiah which has an impossible time finding an understanding and receptive readership. Isaiah's possible audience is comprised of those who find the book impenetrable and of those who
cannot read.

Verse 13 contrasts near and far, outer (mouth and lips) and
inner (heart), to depict the false worship of 'this people' (1.10-15)
and their feigned fear of God (11.2-3; 25.3; 48.1-2; 58.1-5). Their
learning is merely human. In v. 14, 'so' is the stronger 'therefore'
(RSV; at 5.24; 28.14) which looks back to the preceding verses and

not just v. 13. This is a scene like 28.16: Look at me! (*hinᵉnî* with
a participle). 'Amazing' and 'shocking' are the same root and con-
nect the scene with 28.29 where the root is translated 'wonderful'. The wonderful counsel again involves judgment since
wisdom perishes. As in vv. 10-11, wisdom is hidden and hiding is
a punishment.

This is a Woe! for those who hide their plans so that God will
not know them. Deep and dark contrast with high and light
which are associated with sight and knowledge; these themes
and contrasts are central to chs. 28–33 and to the entire book of
Isaiah. The people pervert, overthrow, things (1.7; 5.20-21; 13.19).
They are like Assyria (10.15) since the made confuses itself with
the maker. The terms in v. 16 are characteristic of Isaiah: potter
and former are the same word (at 22.11; 27.11); 'deeds', 'thing
made', 'maker' and 'make' are all forms of *ʿāśâ* 'No understanding' is the root for 'discernment' in v. 14c. Verses 13-14 and 15-16
are paired through their description of the topsy-turvy world of
this people.

Verse 17 introduces a dramatic shift. It turns 'the little while'
before the Lord's wrath passes (10.25; 26.20) into 'a little while'
until the glorious restoration, 'in that day'. The close of the chapter, vv. 17-21 and 22-24, is a gathering point for Isaianic themes
and images for salvation and for the evil times that precede it.
Lebanon, a symbol of pride and height (2.13; 10.34; 14.8), turns
into a fruitful field, a Carmel, and Carmel is regarded as a forest. (Note the contrasting use of 'regard' in v. 16.) The poet
employs the double meaning of *karmel*: an orchard or fruitful
field and a mountain on the Mediterranean coast (33.9; 35.2; 1
Kings 18). Karmel and forest were both burned in the destruction that precedes the restoration (10.18). All deaf and blind are
healed, not just the people of Israel (6.9-10). The sealed book is
heard and the darkness penetrated (5.30; 8.22–9.3; 24.22). Sight
causes joy for the poor who find refuge in the Lord (14.30-32;
25.4; 26.6). Tyrants, the ruthless, and scoffers are cut off (13.11;
25.3-5; 28.14, 21-22); they are those who corrupt the legal process (1.17, 23; 10.1-2) and turn the plea of the righteous 'into chaos
[*tōhû*]'.

'Therefore' takes the vision of peace for all and applies it to
Israel. The Lord redeems or ransoms (*pādâ*: 1.27; 35.10; 51.10);
shame is gone (1.29; 24.23; 26.11). Jacob sees properly (5.12;
17.7-8; 22.11); his children are the Lord's work as is Assyria
(19.25). Holiness alludes to Isaiah's vision in the temple (6.3). 'To

stand in awe' is the same root as 'the tyrant' who is no more (v. 5); one type of fear or awe is replaced by another (see at 25.3 for comment on the root). Finally, humans who have erred and wandered in spirit, as in the preceding chapters and particularly in vv. 13-16, 'know understanding and learn instruction'.

Chapter Thirty

However this promise is for 'that day'; now is a time of Woe! for the rebellious children (1.2, 23) because of their involvement in intrigue with Egypt, the symbol of false security and unreliable help (ch. 20). Judah is a sinful people (6.7!; 27.9!); they should seek refuge only in the Lord and Zion (4.6; 14.32; 16.3-4; 25.4). Doing a plan that is not the Lord's leads to failure (7.5-7; 14.24-27). 'Alliance' is a multiple pun since the word means 'shelter' (25.7; 28.20) and 'idol' (30.22; 42.17) and it alludes to the covenant with Death; people go down to Egypt and Sheol (5.14). 'Protection' is the root for strength and stronghold (at 27.5). As in ch. 20.5-6, hope turns to shame (29.22!) and humiliation. Verse 5 generalizes the point: all are disgraced by a people who cannot help others.

Verses 6-7, Burden of the Beasts of the Negeb, intensify the theme by contrasting the immense effort of carrying tribute on pack animals through a country filled with savage animals with the useless people who are their goal. (Distress and animals allude to scenes in 5.29-30; 8.21-22; 14.19-31; 49.8-12!) Egypt's help is worthless, vain (see Qoh. 1.2, 4). The Lord renames Egypt Rahab, the dragon destroyed at creation (27.1; 51.9-10). Naming and renaming are central motifs in Isaiah (1.26; 4.1-3; 7.14; 8.1-4; 62.4).

'Now' (v. 8) keeps us in the present of this past time and 'write' alludes to writing in ch. 8 and 29.11-12. The book is a witness, a testimony (8.16-20), for the 'latter day' (1.26; 2.2), the time of the readers of the book of Isaiah. Isaiah moves from the present of the past to the present of his readers. 'For they are . . .' (v. 9) holds us in the indefinite time of vision. People, of the past, present and future, who do not listen to the Lord's teaching are rebels (1.20,23; 28.12). They want visionaries—the terms are from 'to envision' (1.1; 2.1; 22.5)—who tell them comforting lies, not a stern vision (21.2). 'Way' and 'path' are central images for God's will (2.3), for the Exodus and the return from exile (11.15-16) and for the unity of all people (19.23-25), but this people want none of these possible meanings. Holy One of Israel is a

motif marking the depth of sin (1.4; 5.19, 24) and the height of
trust and power (6.1-3; 10.20; 12.6; 17.7; 29.19, 23).

'Therefore' (at 28.14) occurs five times in the chapter—vv. 7,
12, 13, 18 [twice]). The second occurrence introduces a denunciation, in vv. 12-14, that is a simile within a simile. They reject
'this word', an impersonal reference to the Lord's word. Reject or
despise is one of a group of terms for rejecting the Lord (5.24;
8.6), evil and idols (7.15-16; 31.7; 33.15). They should rely upon
the Lord (10.20; 12.2; 50.10), not perversity or Egypt. A third
'therefore' marks the announcement of destruction; 'this iniquity' refers to the context and to all sin (1.4; 5.18; 13.11; 26.21).
With poetic justice, sin becomes its own punishment (9.18; 28.4)
when the high wall suddenly breaks and crashes. The military
simile turns to a domestic simile of a broken pot—'crash' and
'break' are the same verb—and the latter image is related to the
images of dust (17.12-14; 27.9). The poet juxtaposes fire and
water, symbols of weal and woe.

Verses 15-17 are the second speech of the Holy One, and it
continues the contrast of reliance on the Lord with trust in military power and alliances. Salvation or victory ('Isaiah') and
strength lie in quiet and trust (7.4; 17.4; 18.4), not in swift cavalry (2.7). Ironically, the horses's swiftness is needed for the people's retreat before a swifter army, the indefatigable force of
5.26-30. The people are left alone like daughter Zion. 'Flagstaff'
and 'signal on a mountain' allude both to the call of the cosmic
army (5.26; 13.2) and to the return of dispersed Israel (11.10-12).
Verse 18 follows from the latter allusion. The Lord can be gracious (14.1; 26.10) or not (27.11). He waits so that those who wait
on him may be happy (8.17; 25.9).

The remainder of the chapter goes from the harsh vision of
reality to dreams and nightmares; it is difficult to read because
it is a concentration of so many terms and images that carry the
themes of weal and woe. Impact and impression are just as
important as message. I comment on a few of the terms and note
parallels as examples, but I am not trying to be exhaustive on
either score.

The people will call and the Lord will hear and answer; previously the process has been blocked (1.15). Calling and answering
are a frequent theme in 40–66 (41.17; 49.8; 65.25; 66.4). Harsh
food and drink, hunger and thirst, are for a set time (5.13; 26.20).
Teaching, hiding and seeing accord with chs. 28–30, while hearing and walking in the way allude to passages throughout 1–30.

Scattering golden and silver idols is a work to be done on the Day of the Lord (2.7-21). Planting seed, rain and harvest counter the dearth of famine (1.30; 5.6-10; 10.17-19; 17.10-11; 24.1-13) with the abundance of tilling, feeding, cattle, winnowing and brooks on mountains. The image of plenty expands the image of restoration in 29.17 (27.6; 28.23-29). The profusion of terms mirrors the richness of the dream. But the dream is unsettled by a moment of death, 'when towers fall'; the poet cannot speak of something high without contrasting it with the low. Verse 26 counters the darkness of 24.23 with the incredible brilliance of the moon ('the white one') and the sun ('the hot one') when the Lord binds and heals the wounds that he has inflicted (1.5-6; 9.13; 19.22).

A nightmare scene—*hinnēh* with a participle—replaces the dream; it recalls the horrific vision of 5.26-30 and 13.1-16 and the frequent imagery of fire and rage. The metaphors are oral: lips, tongue, jaws, breath and eating. The fiery flood invokes the watery flood; both reach to the neck (8.8). Sifting as an action is kin to smelting and winnowing (1.25; 27.12). The leaders of both Israel and Egypt have led their people astray (3.12; 9.16; 19.3-14).

The poet closes the chapter with allusions to a variety of passages. Verse 29 intones song, joy (9.2-3; 12.1-6; 24.14-16) and the stability of the mountain and the rock (17.10!; 26.4). Verses 30-33 employ imagery of hearing and seeing, fire and storm to proclaim the fall of Assyria, the Lord's rod and staff (10.5). This concentration of allusions serves to bind and unify the book of Isaiah; at the same time, the prophet employs many words for the first, and sometimes the only, time here. The section, 30.19-33, is an example of both Isaianic diversity amidst unity and the encyclopedic style.

I offer a few examples of the variety. 'Hide' (v. 20) is a third verb added to the two in 8.17 and 26.20. The verbs 'to turn to the right' and 'to the left', are used only here; right and left occur in 9.20 and 54.3. 'Covered' and 'plated', v. 22, occur only here as do 'cattle' and 'oxen'; 'donkeys' is in v. 6. Other examples are 'silage', 'bridle' and 'jaw' (see 50.6). 'Brooks' is translated as 'streams' in 32.2, and 'sifts' puns on 'wave' (10.15; 11.15).

Chapter Thirty-One
Chapter 29 ends with a dream, 30 with a nightmare (at least for the nations); both are followed by a Woe! against Israel for false reliance on Egypt and human power and for not looking to the

Lord. 31.1-3 are a mix of the specific, Egypt and Israel, and the general, humanity. The verses allude to 30.1-4, 16 and 5.12. The Lord is wise, not humans whether Israelite or Egyptian. He both brings evil and rises against it (45.7); evildoers and workers of iniquity are Israel (1.4; 10.1), Babylon (14.20) and humanity (29.20; 32.6). The contrast of human and divine, flesh and spirit, applies to Egypt, Israel and all peoples (2.22; 40.6-8). The Lord stretches his hand over Israel (5.25; 9.12) and over all nations (14.26-27). Helper and helped stumble and fall (3.8; 8.11-15; 28.13); all perish as one (1.27-31).

In vv. 4-5, the prophet, referring to the Lord's personal revelation to him, takes the image of a terrifying lion (5.29-30; 30.6) and twists it so that the lion with its prey is not terrified, like Assyria (30.31), by the shepherds who attack him. In vv. 4-5, 6-7 and 8-9, the prophet pronounces hope and promise for Israel and destruction for Assyria, but read more closely the message is ambivalent. 'The Lord of hosts comes down to fight upon Mount Zion' (29.7-8), but is this for it or against it (10.12)? Birds fluttering overhead are like the canopy over Zion in ch. 4. To protect or defend, *gānan*, is the root for shield (22.6; 37.33) and puns on garden, *gan* and *gannâ* (1.29-30; 51.3; see at 37.35).

Since Zion is both literal city and symbol of the place of the Lord, a haven and refuge (14.32), the poet calls the people to return (1.27; 30.15) to the Lord and his ways even though their rebellion is deep (29.15). Zion is secure; come back to her. 'In that day', they throw away, reject, their idols (30.12, 22) which their hands made (2.8; 17.7-8). Egypt is human; Assyria falls to a sword not human and is eaten by it (1.20). He flees (*nās*) and his soldiers are put to forced labor (*mas*); they desert the standard (*nēs*), the symbol of muster and return (5.26; 11.10-12; 13.2). The poet closes the chapter on an ambivalent note: 'Says the Lord whose fire is in Zion and whose furnace is in Jerusalem.' Who is burned in the fire and refined in the furnace?

Chapter Thirty-Two

32.1-8 is a vision: See! (*hēn* is similar to *hinnēh*). It is a messianic dream that emphasizes the peace, security and justice of the king's reign (11.1-5), but the king, who is mentioned only in v. 1, is not at the center of the vision. This is less royal and Davidic than the related vision in 16.4b-5. It is a king and he rules with princes, not alone. 'Each', in v. 2, downplays individual achievement and may include others besides king and princes. The imagery of shelter in a storm recalls Zion (4.5-6; 14.32) and the Lord (25.4-5). 'Dry place', ṣāyôn (25.5), puns on Zion, ṣiyyôn, where the Lord's fire is; the pun continues the association of fire and water in Isaiah (30.14). 'Streams of water' occurs in 30.25 where it is immediately followed by beneficial brilliance. In 32.2, on the contrary, the brilliant light is overwhelming and shade is necessary to escape it; the shade of a great rock, not the rock of Assyria (31.9).

As in 29.18, blind and deaf are healed and the curse of 6.9-10 reversed. In 4-8, the poet develops his picture of justice from 29.20-21; he composes the passage around a catalogue of terms contrasting good and evil. The rash hasten things out of time (5.19). 'Good judgment' combines the words for 'knowing' and 'understanding' which occur in 1.3. 'Stammerers' recall the drunks and scoffers of ch. 28; now, however, they speak 'readily' which employs the root for 'rash' but to opposite effect. 'Fool' and 'folly' (9.17) are near homophones for 'withering' (1.30; 24.4), 'corpse' (5.25) and 'harp' (at 14.11). Verse 5 shifts the attention to fools and villains. (For calling and naming, see at 30.7.) They work iniquity (31.2); they 'err' which is the root for 'wandering' and 'misleading' (3.12; 9.16; 28.7; 29.24). Verses 6-7 speak of hunger and thirst, evil plans and ruining the poor and needy of humanity, not just Israel (3.13-15; 29.19). The noble plan noble things and stand (qûm) by them (7.5-7!).

While vv. 1-8 are a description, 9-13 are a denunciation of wealthy ladies (3.16-26). Verse 9 plays on qûm from v. 8, to stand, and on trust which here is false ease and complacency. The short time till disaster contrasts with the 'little while' until restoration in 29.17. Trembling and shuddering befall humans (10.29; 19.16; 23.11), flocks (17.2), Sheol (14.9) and the entire earth (5.25; 13.13; 14.16). The pastoral desolation copies the scene at the beginning of ch. 24; the shift from body to land in vv. 11-12 is similar to that in 1.5-7; 10.16-19; 17.4-6. 'Thorns and briers', qôṣ šāmîr, continues the motif of 'briers and thorns', šāmîr wāšāyit (5.6; 7.24-25; 10.17), but marks a transformation by dropping one term and using a new one. Isaiah continues diversity amidst unity. 'Joy' and 'jubilant' recall the happiness of 9.2-5, but are used here in a context of arrogant joy, matching the false trust of v. 9. 'Jubilant' is arrogance in 5.14; 22.2; 23.7; 24.8.

Verse 14 is transitional and moves from judgment to promise, from grim vision to glorious dream. It alludes to scenes of the

crash and abandonment of the city of chaos (24.10-13; 27.10), of
Damascus (17.1-3, 9) and of Babylon (13.17-22). The high comes
low. A den is a place of death (2.19), but v. 14 closes with a scene
of pasturing and a note of joy, not with a demonic abode (5.17;
13.20-22; 14.30; 17.2). Complacency leads to trembling and
lamenting, and the peace amidst ruins turns into the peace following the fall of the wicked. The transformation into dream
occurs when 'there is poured upon us a spirit from on high
[*mārôm*]'. *Mārôm* is heaven, God's abode (at 24.4, 18, 21; 33.5;
57.15), and the heights (22.16; 26.5; 33.16). The poet closes the
chapter with an elaborate development of his dream of plenty
from 29.17 and 30.19-26. He presents a catalogue of positive
terms: peace, justice, righteousness, quiet and trust (7.4; 14.7;
18.4; 30.15). 'Forever' of destruction (v. 14) becomes 'forever' of
peace (v. 17). 'Dwell', 'abide' and 'rest' emphasize endurance. Are
'my people' Israel, Egypt or any who wait for him (19.25; 30.18)?
'Complacency and ease' (v. 9) modulate into 'security and quiet'
(v. 18); the same words occur in both verses. 'Forest' does double
duty as symbol of plenty in v. 15 and of oppression in v. 19. It,
and its counterpart the lofty city, are cut down (10.33-34; 24.10;
26.5-6). Happiness, which comes to those who wait for the Lord
(30.18), comes to those who plant by water, a symbol of life, and
who let cattle roam, a symbol of freedom and expanse. 'To let
range freely' is a form of the verb 'to send' which occurs in the
negative image of cattle being let loose in a 'deserted habitation'
(7.25; 27.10). The latter contrasts with the 'peaceful habitation'
of 32.18.

Chapter Thirty-Three

Chapters 28–32 develop contrasts of proper and improper trust
and reliance and instruction and knowledge. They mix judgment
and promise; vision, nightmare and dream; and Israel, the
nations and all humanity. With 33, the prophet brings this section to a close by repeating many of the themes, terms and images
of the preceding five chapters. Formally, he rounds off the section by using the style of short, juxtaposed passages that he used
in 28–29. At the same time, 33 summarizes and concludes 27-33,
13-33 and 1-33. Temporally, the chapter is set in a timeless
present embodied in the thrice repeated 'now' of v. 10.

Verse 1 is a Woe! and a chant that applies to all destroyers at
all times (16.4; 21.2; 24.16). 2-6 are ambiguous. The 'we' who ask
the Lord to be gracious and who wait for him (8.17; 25.9; 30.18-19)

are Israel and, at the same time, all in Israel and among the nations who have been threatened with destruction and treachery. In their distress, they proclaim God's strength, his arm (40.10-11), and victory; this is reminiscent of the hymns in chs. 12, 25 and 26. The image is familiar: the Lord rises up—'majesty' is *rûm (at 7.7)—and peoples scatter (2.9-21). The image of caterpillars and locusts is degrading and recalls the insects of 7.18. The exalted Lord is an image that punctuates the book: 3.13; 6.1; 30.18; 57.15; 63.15. 'Dwelling on high' is to abide in Mount Zion (8.18; 32.15). The Lord's glory and knowledge fill the world (6.1-3; 11.9). Justice, righteousness, stability (*'āmēn), salvation, wisdom and fear of the Lord are all positive qualities (11.1-3; 32.16-18).

The scene in vv. 7-9 refers to preceding passages, especially in chs. 15–16 and 24. Envoys or messengers are figures for the international intrigue that Israel and others are relying on (18.1-2; 30.1-7). But the intrigue has been blocked; the international routes are deserted; agreements are broken and annulled (14.27; 24.5). 'There is no regard for humans' is a preferred translation of the last phrase in v. 8 since it makes the parallel with 2.22 explicit and marks Isaiah's move from history to the Day of the Lord, a day of mourning when the luxuriant turns desolate. This is the reverse of the dreams in 29.17; 30.19-26; 32.15-20 and a glimpse of the terrible nightmare of ch. 34.

In vv. 13-16 all are called to know the Lord's doing and strength. Near and far are an antithesis used in a variety of contexts: 5.25-26; 6.12; 13.5-6; 46.13; 57.19. Sinners and godless fill Zion (1.28; 9.17); they tremble as the ladies did (32.10-11). They recite an entrance liturgy that is similar to Psalm 15 except that these people speak of living with fire and flame (31.9) whereas the psalmist speaks of dwelling in the Lord's holy mountain. Verse 15 contrasts righteous with wicked behavior (1.23; 10.1-4; 29.20-21; 32.1-8). With a twist of the motif, the righteous are blind and deaf to evil. The distinction of righteous and wicked is a central contrast in Isaiah and directly related to images such as smelting and winnowing which remove the evil and leave the good.

Verse 16 is a crescendo with imagery of height and stability. The righteous dwell with the Lord. The terms for 'live', 'heights' and 'refuge' are the same in v. 5 for 'dwell', 'high' and 'exalted'. The Lord and his name are exalted (2.11, 17; 12.4). Fortress is a symbol of security (26.1-3), not a high place to be brought down.

Assured (*'*āmēn*) food and water counter hunger and thirst (5.13; 30.20; 32.6). In 17-19, the prophet addresses the righteous as a group ('you' is masculine singular). He hearkens back to the sight of a king in 32.1 and scans the immense land, now empty of the invading army. The terror is past and the people remember the invaders who once tallied their resources to assess tribute. 'To count' recalls the tiny remnant that a child can count (10.19). They no longer see or hear the foreigners speaking an alien language (29.9-13).

The prophet interrupts the reverie. Look on Zion! She, not a king or army, is the focus of their vision, a vision of peace, expanse and freedom that contrasts with distress, narrowness and constraint (28.20; 33.2). She is a city, a quiet habitation (32.18), an immovable tent with fixed stakes and ropes. (The image is expanded in 54.2.) The image recalls the throne in the tent of David in 16.4-5; now both king and David are displaced. Zion is not a fortress (26.1-2), but a safe place with rivers that no warship can navigate; Egypt and Tyre cannot come there with their intrigue and trade (19.1-15; ch. 23). 'Majesty' and 'stately' are the same word and allude to the majestic trees that the Lord fells (10.34).

In v. 22, the people declare the royal visions of 16.4-5; 32.1-8; and 33.17 fulfilled, but not with a human or Davidic king. The Lord is judge (16.5), ruler ('one who makes decrees': 10.1-2), king and savior (12.2-3; 33.2). Verse 23 is problematic because the antecedent of 'your' (feminine singular) is not clear; I read it as addressed to a foreign ship whose 'rigging' is loose unlike the taut 'ropes' of Zion (v. 20; these are the same word). 'Mast' is 'flagstaff' and 'sail', the 'signal' of 30.17, a scene of defeat and flight. Booty is divided as in 9.3.

Chapter 33 closes with promise. No one who dwells there ('in her') is sick (1.5; ch. 38) and their iniquity is forgiven or lifted up (2.9!; 6.7; 22.14!; 27.9). In this chapter, the poet has intensified themes of failed intrigue and alliances and defeated and withdrawn armies to present his dream of a place and time of peace, justice and freedom. The dream is elaborated in ch. 35, but not before the horrific nightmare of 34.

Chapter Thirty-Four

Chapters 34–35 bring the contrast of judgment and salvation to a crescendo. Chapter 34 depicts the depths of the nightmare, the eternal demonic land; ch. 35 adds new glory to the dream of the restored, paradisiacal land. Its brilliant picture is exceeded in the last half of Isaiah, particularly in 60–62. The sharp contrast of evil and good, however, does not mean a final end to evil or a total separation between evil and good for they continue to be mixed in the rest of Isaiah.

Chapter 34 breaks into clear sections that develop the scene of horrific destruction, an intensification of ch. 13 and related passages. The divisions that I work with are vv. 1-4; 5; 6-7; 8-12; 13-15; and 16-17. In the first section, peoples come near to hear, not to attack. (See 41.1; 43.9; 49.1; 51.4 for analogous calls.) All are summoned: nations, peoples, earth and world. The Lord is enraged and furious; the latter term connotes heat (42.25). The Lord's wrath, signified by a group of terms, is common in Isaiah (10.4, 25; 13.3, 9, 13; 27.4; 30.30; 48.9; 54.8-9).

The Lord is against the nations and their armies. This is not a call to arms as in 13.2-5, but a call to witness God's destruction of the nations. God acts alone, not as the leader of an army (59.15-19; 63.1-6). 'To doom' is the word for the ban and 'utter destruction' of holy war in which everything, animate and inanimate is destroyed as an offering to God (11.15; 37.11; 43.28; see Joshua 6–7 for the ban on Jericho). The sight of corpses recalls the gruesome scene of Sheol in 14.19. The army was mustered on the mountains in 13.4; now the mountains flow with blood. (In 13.7 and 19.1, 'flow' refers to melting in fear.) The army rots (5.24); the heavens roll up like a scroll, like 'garments rolled in blood' (9.5). (For 'withering', see my comments at 14.11 and 28.1-4.) Dryness and languishing parallel passages such as the dry garden in 1.29-30, Moab in 16.8-11, Egypt in 19.5-10 and the earth in 24.1-13 and 33.9. In 36.16, the Rabshakeh uses vine and fig tree to portray a false peace.

In v. 5, the Lord speaks within the horrific scene. 'My sword' is the symbol of violence and war (1.20; 2.4; 14.19; 22.2; 31.8; 51.19; 65.12; 66.16). 'To drink its fill' is translated 'to drench with tears' (16.9) and, for opposite effect, 'to water' (55.10; 58.11). The sword comes down—Look! *hinnēh*—on Edom. Edom is listed with Moab and Philistia in 11.14. Philistia is condemned in 14.28-31 and Moab in chs. 15–16; in 25.10 Moab is a symbol of the haughty who fall. Edom is denounced in itself and as a symbol of a violent power (63.1-6). 'A people doomed', under the ban, can be Edom or Jacob 'whom I gave to utter destruction' (43.28).

In vv. 6-7, the poet expands the Lord's statement and the scene of 2-4. He repeats words 'sword', 'blood' and 'slaughter' and adds new ones. 'Sated' is 'filled' and it, along with the list of animals, alludes to sacrifices and 'hands filled with blood' (1.11-16). The satiety is signified in v. 7 by 'soaked with', the same word as 'drunk its fill' in v. 5, and 'made rich with fat', as 'gorged with fat' in v. 6. The animals stand for rulers and their nations; 'goats' (1.11) are the 'leaders' in Sheol who rise to greet the king of Babylon (14.9). 'Sacrifice', *zebah* and 'slaughter', *tebah*, pun on each other. Verse 7 depicts the fall. 'Land and soil' are 'earth and dust' which connote the underworld (2.9-21; 5.13-17; 14.9).

'For', which introduces vv. 8-12, refers back to vv. 1-7. This is the Day of the Lord, a day of retribution (2.9-21; 13.6). 'Vengeance' alludes to the Lord avenging himself on Zion (1.24); in 61.2 and 63.4, the 'day of vengeance' is a time of favor and redemption for Israel. 'Vindication' is repaying (at 9.6-7). 'Cause' (*rîb*) connotes legal arguments and struggles (27.8; 45.9); is this struggling on behalf of Zion, as in 51.22, or against her, as in 3.13? 34.9 has only 'her' streams and soil, and the antecedent can be Bozrah or Zion. Destruction befalls all; in the next chapter, restoration is available to all.

The fiery stream is an image introduced in 30.27-28, 33; fire and burning are familiar images. In 35.6 restoration is streams of water flowing in the desert (66.12). The Lord's breath is like a 'stream of sulfur' (30.33). Water, soil (dust) and earth are a merism for totality. The unquenchable fire looks to the beginning and close of the book (1.31; 66.24). (For rising smoke, see 9.18-19.) The different phrases in v. 10 accentuate the everlasting waste. 'To lie waste' is *ḥārēb*, 'to be hot and dry' (5.17; 19.5-6; 25.4-5); it puns on sword, *ḥereb*. Being impassable is not the protection it was for Zion in 33.21.

This picture of a demonic land filled with fiendish creatures develops the scene that follows the fall of Babylon (13.20-22). Through mention of possessing, dwelling, measuring and allotting, it is also a parody of the story of Israel's division of the land as told in Joshua 12–21 and a counterpart to the dwelling on heights and in Zion (33.5, 16, 24). 'Confusion' and 'chaos' are *tōhû* and *bōhû* (Gen. 1.2; at Isa. 24.10). At another time, the Lord measures with justice and righteousness (28.17). As the Lord renamed Egypt Rahab (30.7), this diabolical region is named 'No Kingdom There' (1.26; 32.5; 62.4). 'Nothing' implies annihilation.

Verses 13-15 elaborate the description by including noxious plants and more desert animals. 'Strongholds' and 'fortresses' are familiar words in Isaiah, but the words for 'thorns', 'nettles' and 'thistles' occur only here, although the image is familiar. 'Haunt' is the word for 'habitation' or 'pasture' (27.10; 32.18; 33.20); in 35.7 'the haunt of jackals' becomes a resting site. It is characteristic of Isaiah that words, images, etc., have double and even opposed meanings; the demonic kingdom is the shadow side of the peaceable kingdom. Some of the creatures appeared in 13.20-22. Lilith is either a 'night hag' because her name is similar to the word for night or a 'storm-demon' in parallel to a Mesopotamian demonness.[1] 'Place to rest' is a perversion of Israel's rest (14.1-3) and 'shadow', of the protective shade in 25.4-5 and 32.2.

To intensify the parody even more, the prophet directs us to read in 'the book of the Lord' that not one is missing or is without its mate; this is an allusion to the pairs on Noah's ark (54.9-10). 'Book' is the 'scroll' of v. 4. Will reading be any more successful than in 29.11-12? God's mouth commands and his spirit gathers, here demons, at another time, the dispersed of Israel (56.8). The casting of lots, the apportioning and taking possessing, re-emphasize the parody of the book of Joshua. However, by parodying other positive parts of Isaiah, of Joshua and of other biblical books, the chapter binds itself to them and thereby underlines the fact that for Isaiah the processes and states of judgment and salvation are inextricably intertwined.

Chapter Thirty-Five
After the nightmare comes the dream and the dream counters the nightmare on many points. I already noted the transformation of streams and haunt in 35.6-7. However, 34–35 are a pair which present juxtaposed and contrasting views of judgment and promise. They counter each other, but one does not cancel or replace the other. The two chapters, in the approximate center of the book, present in an explicit manner the inextricable blend of judgment and promise, evil and good, in Isaiah. There is always the hope that someday the Lord will make a definitive separation and bring final destruction for the wicked and salvation for the righteous (66.24). This is a hope, a dream, and not the world we live in; even this hope is qualified since it is the Lord who creates good and evil, weal and woe (45.7). Isaiah does not describe a dualistic world.

1. Watts, *Isaiah 34–66*, pp. 13-14.

Verses 1-2 are a joyous song proclaiming the transformation and blossoming of the desert. The poet speaks as one of the restored, 'our God', and not as a member of the demonic family. In 34, the creatures gathered but did not sing or rejoice; in 34.5 they saw only the descending sword of the Lord, not the Lord in glory. Glory and majesty both are part of the imagery of light since they are seen and manifested (for glory, see at 10.3). The crocus replaces the thorn and thistle. Lebanon, Carmel and Sharon are double-edged symbols of pride (2.12-17) and of glory whether the glory is granted to another or withered (33.9). Sprouting and flourishing were introduced in 4.2 and are developed in 27.6; 29.17; 30.23-26; 32.14-20; 66.14; for the contrast of dry blossoms, see 5.24; 17.11; 18.5.

He encourages others in the community to strengthen hands and knees (external vigor) and hearts (inner vitality). The restoration is for all, not a privileged few. ('Strengthen' and 'be strong' are *ḥāzaq and pun on Hezekiah; see at 8.11; 41.6-7!) 'Do not fear!' is a command addressed to Ahaz (7.4), the people (10.24) and Hezekiah (37.6). Conrad notes that the phrase was originally a war oracle addressed to a king before battle; in Isaiah it undergoes a democratizing transformation and is addressed to the royal people.[1] Examples occur in 40.9; 41.10, 13, 14. 'Vengeance' recalls the Lord's Day and 'recompense' is analogous to 'vindication' in 34.8 (3.9-11; 59.18; 66.6).

Verses 5-7, marked by 'then' and 'for', describe the results of the transformation (see 11.1-5, 6-9 for a similar structure). Eyes and ears are 'opened' and 'unstopped' (these are the same verb); the conditions of 6.9-10 are reversed (29.18; 32.3; 33.15!). The lame walk (33.23) and the mute speak; the latter counters the stammering in 28.7-13. Waters flow in what was hot and dry; mere grass turns to reeds. The desolation of Egypt (19.5-10) is overcome.

Highway is a recurrent image with multiple connotations: a physical road; the moral and religious way, the way of the Lord; the route for Exodus and return (11.15-16; 27.12-13); and the way of peace for all (19.23-25). The image is developed here and is important in the last half of the book. 34 describes a place; 35, a way to a place, Zion, but Zion herself is not described. Verses 1-7 depict the transformed desert which can be crossed. It is

1.   Conrad, *Reading Isaiah*, pp. 36-49.

called The Holy Way and distinguished from No Kingdom There; it is the road for the remnant in Zion who are called Holy (4.3). (Note the motif of name and naming.) Isaiah was in the midst of people with unclean lips (6.5), but there are none who are unclean on this road or in Zion (52.1, 11). There are no fools here, as there were in Egypt (19.11). The road is straight; there are none who wander, stray, or mislead. (*tā'â, is frequent in Isaiah: 3.12; 9.16; 16.8; 19.13-14; 28.7; 63.17.) Lions are fierce (5.29; 15.9; 31.4); their taming is a sign of peace (11.7; 65.25).

This is the first occurrence in Isaiah of 'to redeem', *gā'al*, which occurs numerous times in 40–66. (The parallel term, *pādâ*, is not as frequent, occurring only in 1.27; 29.22; 35.10; 50.2; 51.11.) Although they refer to practices of buying back a human, especially a family member, or an animal, in the Hebrew Bible they generally have a set religious meaning and are often applied to God's redemption or ransom of Israel from bondage in Egypt.[1] Characteristic of Isaiah, redemption and exodus from Egypt are a figure for return from Assyria, Babylon and dispersion on the highway built for that purpose (11.10-16).

In v. 10 the poet rounds off the poem by repeating the joyous song of 1-2. (51.11 is a repetition of 35.10.) Zion is the goal, not yet the actual site where the ransomed dwell. (36–39 take us to Zion-Jerusalem to present scenes from the past and not from the time of salvation.) The people's 'everlasting joy' contrasts sharply with the 'everlasting waste' of 34.10. Nevertheless, the fact that sorrow and sighing must flee is a brief reminder that they are still present.

Chapter Thirty-Six

Chapters 36–37 are one story, with distinct scenes and stages, about Sennacherib's attack on Judah and siege of Jerusalem in 701 BCE. They narrate the image of daughter Zion from 1.8 and represent the later temporal pole of the events of 735–700 which Isaiah compresses into his image of the overwhelming army that keeps coming and yet leaves a remnant. After chs. 7–8, 36–37 with 38–39 are a second concentration of individuals with proper names, but this does not make 36–39 into a straight narrative of the past any more than it did with the story of Ahaz and the Syro-Ephraimite crisis. The narrative elements of time and setting set

---

1.   Watts, *Isaiah 34-66*, pp. 16-17.

the stage for lengthy discourses by the characters. The speeches of generals, kings and prophet comment on each other and on the entire book; they can be read in both a straightforward and an ironic manner. My comments deal partly with the chapters in themselves and partly with how they interact with the rest of Isaiah; I pay little attention to historical issues concerning the individuals and events or to the relationship between 36–39 and the nearly identical story in 2 Kings 18–20. There are involved, multiple relationships between chs. 36–37 and the rest of Isaiah. I comment on chs. 7.1–8.8; 10.5-15 and those parts of Isaiah that deal with true and false trust and reliance.

The first episode and round of speeches occupy 36.1–37.7. Hezekiah, first mentioned in 1.1, reigned from c. 715–686 BCE. Although his name is punned on at times (at 8.11; 27.5; 35.3-4), this is his first appearance as a speaking character. This is the last fixed date in Isaiah (1.1; 6.1; 14.28; 20.1). The reference to the pool in v. 2 connects the story with Isaiah's confrontation of Ahaz at the same place in 7.3. Ahaz and Hezekiah are compared and contrasted. Ahaz reacted with fear and self-defense; Hezekiah turns to the Lord for help.[1] The onrushing army stops at Jerusalem and the city is saved. However, Eliakim and Shebna are part of the delegation that meets the Rabshakeh, the Assyrian general (see at 20.1 for the title); they are doomed men (22.15-25) and cast a shadow over the narrative.

The majority of 36–39 is comprised of an intricate pattern of speeches within speeches and of quotes within these speeches; some of the speeches are written letters. Fewell, 'Sennacherib's Defeat', aptly subtitles her study of the 2 Kings account, 'Words at War'. There are spokesmen and messengers and, with the exception of ch. 39, no direct dialogue between any two characters. The Rabshakeh speaks for the king to the leaders and people of Jerusalem. This is analogous to the structure of God, prophet-messenger and people, but it is not an exact analogy.

In 36.2-4, the Rabshakeh is sent by the king of Assyria to Jerusalem to say to the delegation, 'Say to Hezekiah: Thus says the great king, the king of Assyria'. In 36.22, Hezekiah finally receives the message third hand. Verses 4-10 revolve around the issue of reliance and trust; *bātaḥ* to trust (32.9-11), occurs five times. Hezekiah should trust neither in Egypt nor in the Lord

---

1.   Conrad, *Isaiah*, pp. 34-51.

because Assyria's power is irresistible and, moreover, the Lord himself has sent him on this mission of destruction. In one sense, the proclamation is correct. Egypt is a broken reed, a fully unreliable ally (ch. 20; 30.1-4, 12; 31.1-3). To this point in Isaiah, most in Jerusalem and Judah, from Ahaz on, have relied on Egypt and on themselves and have not relied on or looked to the Lord. Finally, the Lord has sent Assyria (10.5-6), but it was to punish and plunder, not, as Assyria intended, 'to destroy' (10.7; 36.10). From 10.12 and 14.24-25, we already know the outcome of the exchange in chs. 36–37: the fall of Assyria.

Verse 5 is central to my reading of Isaiah. 'Indeed, is a word of the lips counsel and strength for war?' Word is a figure for book, and war for life. 'Indeed, can the book of Isaiah provide counsel and strength for life?' Counsel, *'ēṣâ*, connotes plan, purpose, knowledge, wisdom and skill (5.19; 8.10; 11.2; 19.3; 25.1; 28.29; 30.1). 'To plan, counsel', is *yā'aṣ (7.5; 14.24-27; 23.8-9; 32.7-8); the participle is 'counselor' (1.26; 9.6; 41.28). Strength is the courage and power to carry out what is learned from counsel even if the accomplishment only requires waiting for the Lord (30.15), doing nothing but turning to the Lord as Hezekiah eventually does.

The exchange on language in vv. 11-12 is ironic since the Judean leaders now want an incomprehensible foreign language to be spoken (28.11!; 33.19!). Verse 12 could be spoken by Isaiah just as well as by the Rabshakeh; both have been sent by their master to speak to all the people, not just their leaders. The people are doomed to eat and drink their own urine and excrement, a disgusting turn on the motif.

Verses 13-20 replay vv. 4-10 and their intertext, 10.7-14. The Rabshakeh speaks in the name of the king of Assyria and in the speech he quotes Hezekiah (vv. 15, 18). Deliverance is a major theme; 'to deliver', *nāṣal*, occurs seven times in the speech. Again, the Assyrian is partly correct. On the one hand, Hezekiah cannot deliver them; on the other hand, it is not a deception on Hezekiah's part to declare that the Lord will deliver them and that Jerusalem will not fall to Assyria. Verses 16-17 are a parody of Israel's 'peace' ('blessing') with the Lord and their possession of Canaan, a land flowing with milk and honey. They are a direct counter to the harsh reality of what the people are now eating and drinking. (For 'vine and fig tree', see 34.4.) Assyrian arrogance and ignorance are displayed here in vv. 18-20 and in 10.7-11 as the king equates the Lord with other gods and claims to have bested them all. The Lord cannot deliver Jerusalem from 'my hand', the symbol of Assyrian pride in 10.13-14.

The delegation is silent and says nothing; they are deaf and dumb (6.9-10; 35.5; 42.18-19). In this exchange of lengthy speeches, Hezekiah's command is notable for its brevity: 'Don't answer him'. Verse 22 closes out the first set of Assyrian speeches by repeating the names of the delegates from v. 2; the cloud over Shebna and Eliakim is still present and is noted again in 37.2.

Chapter Thirty-Seven

Hezekiah responds to the message by tearing his clothes and putting on sackcloth; this is what the Lord called for in Jerusalem (22.12; compare 22.8-14). Hezekiah goes to the house of the Lord and sends the delegation to the prophet Isaiah with a message; apparently prophet and temple are separate (6.1-4!). In contrast, the Lord sent Isaiah to Ahaz. Hezekiah, similar to the king of Assyria, does not speak directly to God or prophet. The message stresses humiliation and impotence; the childbirth image is employed (26.18; 33.11). The request reflects weakness: 'It may be . . .' If God has heard the Assyrian mockery, then he may rebuke him. Isaiah is asked to pray for 'the remnant'. No other action is asked for from God or prophet.

Isaiah's response, a message from the Lord, is brief; he may be answering before he is even spoken to. Hezekiah, like Ahaz, is told not to fear mere words because the Lord promises, in words, to cause the Assyrian to 'hear a hearing' and to return and fall by the sword (31.8-9). (For the war oracle 'Fear not!', see at 35.4.) There is no direct reference to deliverance of the city. This ends the first round in the war of words; the second round comprises 37.8-35. 37.36-38 is the summation of the entire story.

The king of Assyria, at this juncture, appears weak because he reacts when he 'hears' that Tirhakah is attacking. He sends messengers, not his general, and they go with a letter, which we learn of subsequently in v. 14, not with 'a great army' (36.2). The message, in vv. 10-13, repeats 36.4-7, 13-20, but speaks of the 'kings of Assyria', not of 'I' and 'my hand'. This is an empty threat no longer backed by the presence of the Assyrian army.

Hezekiah reacts forthrightly this time. He reads the letter, spreads it before the Lord and prays directly to him. (See 1.15 for futile acts of spreading and praying.) The prayer, vv. 16-20, emphasizes power and destruction, not humiliation and degradation. He

appeals, with exalted rhetoric, to the creator God of all, not just
of Israel; he calls upon God to hear Sennacherib's words and to
see the desolation brought by this nation (63.7–64.12). Ironically
the Assyrians have caused other nations to do what they should
do, that is, cast their idols into fire (2.18-21; 17.7-8; 31.7). Hezekiah closes with a direct request for salvation ('Isaiah') so that
all may know, and not just hear of, the Lord.

The Lord's response is sent through the prophet Isaiah and,
fitting with the intricate speech patterns, is addressed to the
king of Assyria; at no point do either the Lord or the king of
Assyria, the central antagonists, speak directly. Assyria has
scorned Zion; now Zion scorns him. To scorn is to shake one's fist
at (10.32). The king of Assyria filled his messages with questions; the Lord matches them with his own. Mockery, pride and
haughtiness are familiar accusations. Assyria rises against the
Holy One of Israel, not Hezekiah. As in 10.5-14, the Lord quotes
the king in vv. 24-25 to convict him with his own words. 'I' intones
pride and self-aggrandizement. The imagery of height associates
the king of Assyria with the king of Babylon who stormed the
'heights' of heaven and was thrown down to the 'depths' of the
Pit (14.13-15). Assyria goes to the 'far recesses' of Lebanon. (The
three terms are the same word.) He claims to produce water and
to dry up the rivers of Egypt, yet both are the Lord's work (11.15;
19.5-10; 41.17-20).

With a question that anticipates the disputes of chs. 40–48,
the Lord invokes his deed ('āśâ) and his fashioning (yāṣar) 'from
long ago'. (See at 22.11 for the play on long ago and far away.)
The first stage is for Assyria to destroy and bring down fortified
cities (23.7-11; 26.5-6). With characteristic imagery of weakness
and withering (34.4; 40.6-8), the Lord describes the defeated
inhabitants who include Israelites and Judahites. The Lord
knows and does not just hear. Assyria is only an instrument, an
animal or insect, who can be turned and sent back home (5.26;
7.18-20; 10.5, 15). Assyria is like Babylon in its pride, in its
assault on the heights, but Assyria returns home while Babylon
is destroyed, consigned to Sheol, and her land is turned into a
demonic land.

The Lord addresses Hezekiah in vv. 30-32 and gives a sign of
hope. The sign alludes to Ahaz (7.11, 14), Isaiah (8.18), hope
and judgment for Egypt (19.20; 20.3), Hezekiah's recovery (38.7,
22) and Israel (55.13; 66.19). This sign refers to time, three
years, and to plants and eating; it offsets the Assyrian proposal

to surrender and the reality faced by the besieged. Remnant and bearing fruit are connected in 4.2 and 27.6 (17.10-11!). Verse 32 quotes the Lord's doing from 9.7 which closes a messianic vision; in 37.30-32, however, there is no reference to the king even though he is addressed.

The king, 'my servant David', is named in vv. 33-35. Verse 33 rejects all military threats; 34 repeats 29; and 35 explicitates the Lord's promise to save Jerusalem. 'To defend' is the verb *gānan* which puns on garden, *gan* and *gannâ*, and on shield, *maggēn*, in v. 33 (at 31.5). Shield recalls the canopy over Zion in 4.2-6 and the play on garden looks to chs. 60–62 when the Lord's defense of Zion turns her into a garden like the garden of Eden (51.3).

The story ends abruptly and brutally. A final messenger, 'angel', comes who acts and does not speak. 'Bodies' refer to the death scenes in 14.19 and 34.3. The list of proper names serves to summarize the story of Assyria. (Assyria is mentioned again only in 52.3-6.) Assyria may continue to exist, but the Assyrian army has finally stopped coming and Zion and Hezekiah have been saved.

Chapter Thirty-Eight

The relief is short-lived for Hezekiah who becomes sick and is 'at the point of death'. The prophet Isaiah comes again, this time with a message of death: 'You are dying; you will not live'. The issue of life and death, which hovered over the previous two chapters, dominates this chapter. As he prayed before for Jerusalem and its people, Hezekiah prays for himself but he makes no explicit request for healing. The Lord should remember his faithfulness (*'amēn*) which contrasts with Ahaz's lack of same (7.9). Isaiah returns a divine message of healing. It is the Lord, 'the God of your father David', who speaks. Hezekiah will live for another fifteen years; this indicates that the time is still 701. The date is affirmed by the Lord's added promise to deliver Hezekiah and the city (37.35). The king's recovery and the safety of the city are connected. As in 37.30, there is a sign, a scene—*hinnēh* and a participle in v. 8—which involves a shadow going back and the sun going down ten steps ('steps' is based on 'to go up'). Hezekiah is granted fifteen more years; Jerusalem, about one hundred more years. The king's eventual death and Jerusalem's eventual fall are connected. As in Psalm 89.36-38, the promises to David are not eternal. Jerusalem is saved from Assyria this time and the onrushing Assyrian army stopped, but the army transmutes into the Babylonians and keeps coming.

Hezekiah offers a psalm, a writing, in thanksgiving for his recovery, his life. (See Psalms 22; 30; 32 for parallels.) The psalm employs characteristic Isaianic terms and images, particularly the contrast of life and death. Verses 10-15 describe the king's misery which mirrors that of Jerusalem and her people. Sheol is death (5.14; 28.14-18). 'Rest of my years' intones remnant (1.8-9; 4.3; 7.22). He is no longer in 'the land of the living' which is a symbol for both life and Zion (4.3). Tent and weaving are images of fragility and transience (4.5-6!; 33.20!); the lion, of strength and violence. The psalmist clamors, chirps (29.4), like a bird; he looks to heaven (*mārôm*) since God has done this to him.

Verses 16–18 are Hezekiah's request for life at a time of death. 16 is emphatic: life, spirit, health. 'Welfare' is peace (*šālôm*). He does not go down to the pit, the grave (14.15-19; 24.22; 51.14). As an inhabitant of Zion, he is saved and forgiven (33.24). 18 contrasts Sheol, Death and the Pit with thanks, praise, hope and faithfulness. 19 stresses life now and in the future, fathers and children, as all praise God's faithfulness. The Lord saves Hezekiah and the entire community; 'we' sing to him—'to sing', *niggēn*, puns on 'to defend', *gānan* (37.35)—'at the house of the Lord'. The house is the mountain of 2.2-4 and 11.9, a scene of light, knowledge, peace and life.

Verse 21 returns to the mundane reality of the present, to a specific cure for Hezekiah's ailment. The chapter closes with Hezekiah's open-ended question which can be asked by him and by any, Israelite and alien, who are concerned with life and the ways of the Lord. It is a question that the book of Isaiah strives to answer. 'What is the sign that I will go up to the house of the Lord?'

Chapter Thirty-Nine

As in ch. 37, a foreign king, Merodach-baladan, king of Babylon, sends letters to Hezekiah. He congratulates him on his recovery. ('To recover', *ḥāzaq*, puns on 'Hezekiah'; at 8.11.) The transformation of the oncoming army from Assyrian to Babylonian is underway. (See ch. 13 for more on Merodach-baladan.) Hezekiah welcomes the envoys and shows them everything, there is nothing he does not show them. Isaiah appears for a brief exchange with the king. In response to the first question, Hezekiah asserts that they have come 'from a far country' which alludes to the onrushing army (5.26; 13.5), 'from Babylon' which marks the transition from Assyria to Babylon. For the second question, Hezekiah repeats, in shorter form, the totality of v. 2:they saw every thing; there was nothing I did not show them. ('To show' is a causative form of 'to see'.)

The conversation ends with a message from the Lord. 'Look! Days are coming'—*hinnēh* with a participle—gazes a century into the future. Verse 6 emphasizes the totality that is to be carried to Babylon: everything will be taken and nothing, no remnant, will be left. The totality includes time: 'all that your fathers have stored up until this day'. This is an ironic comment on the limited relief granted to Hezekiah by the Lord, 'the God of your father David' (38.5). In 38.19, fathers and sons symbolized the continuation of life; here, its end. The sons are eunuchs 'in the palace of the king of Babylon'. The fate of Jerusalem and the house of David is grim in the face of the Babylonian army. But, beyond this, the fate of Babylon is likewise grim since jackals will live in its palaces (13.22). And, at a time even beyond this, eunuchs will come to the Lord's house, his holy mountain (56.1-8).

Chapter 39 closes with Hezekiah's ambiguous statement.[1] Is this self-serving? The word is good because it is for the future and Hezekiah will escape the disaster. Is it a calm acceptance of the fact that, despite life now, death will come for Hezekiah and for Jerusalem? Is it a prayer, as in 38.3, that this disaster, this death, not come too soon? There is irony in Hezekiah's reference to Isaiah's message of doom with the words 'good', 'peace' (38.17) and 'security' (*ʾāmēn: 38.3, 18-19).

This narrative of historical characters from the period of 735–700 closes Isaiah 1–39. Assyria has stopped and withdrawn only to be replaced, in a century, by Babylon represented by Merodach-baladan in 39. Jerusalem, saved and standing alone at the close of the eighth century, is, at that later time, destroyed. The monarchy and the Davidic line, represented by Hezekiah, are swept away. However, in the book of Isaiah, there is no narrative of the Babylonian destruction of Jerusalem to match the narrative of Assyria's attack in 36–37. Indeed, with the exception of Cyrus, no historical character after 700 is named. None of the major characters, Israelite or Babylonian, of the last days of

1.   See Ackroyd, *Religious Tradition*, pp. 157-64.

Judah and Jerusalem are mentioned. There is no Jehoiachin, Zedekiah or Nebuchadrezzar in Isaiah. On the other hand, from chs. 13–14 and 21, we know the outcome for Babylon. 'Fallen, fallen is Babylon; all the images of her gods lie shattered on the ground' (21.9).

As I have pointed out several times in the Introduction and in the Commentary, 1–39 contains all of the vision of Isaiah. Thematically, all the elements and various turns of the story of sin-judgment-salvation are here; the characters and their diverse manifestations are here: God, Israel, the Nations and humanity. We know that the hoped for outcome is salvation for the righteous and destruction for the wicked, in Israel and in the world, but that the reality is the inextricable melding of good and evil, salvation and judgment. A final resolution is hoped for, trusted in, but not yet experienced. Even though good and evil, righteousness and wickedness, are distinguished in Isaiah, such distinctions cannot be simply applied to religious, social or national groups in either Isaiah or the world.

The potpourri of Israel and the nations, of good and evil, of salvation and judgment and of merciful God and punishing God are expressed in a literary form that is a potpourri of styles that include the particular stories of 36–39 and the impressionistic dreams and nightmares of 24–27 and 34–35. Isaiah places form, how it is said, on an equal footing with content, what is said. The encyclopedic style, the diversity amidst unity, manifests itself in terminology, phraseology, imagery, wordplay, punning, etc.

Interlude

Chapters Forty–Sixty Six

Chapters 1–39 are anchored in the distant past and point to the ways of the Lord, the ways that the postexilic community should walk in. By 'ways' I intend religious, moral and political behavior and issues of reading and writing, interpretation and expression. In 40–66, the poet takes his materials from the past, uses them to interpret the more immediate past of exile and return and expresses this in different fashion from 1–39. As I noted in the Introduction, I am reading Isaiah as one book that was composed in the fifth century BCE. Although most of 1–39 depict times in the last half of the eighth century BCE and although their style is different from that of 40–66, I read them as an integral part of the book composed at the same time and by the same people as 40–66. I do not enter into arguments about historical authorship or about what other already existing materials, written or oral, contemporary or ancient, may have been included in the book of Isaiah.

Also as I noted in the Introduction, since I am reading Isaiah as a work composed perhaps a century after the return from exile, I am reading 40–66 as set back in the time of return and as portraying the hopes and fears of that community as they returned and began rebuilding. Isaiah sees a community fearful of the might of Babylon and despairing of any hope that their situation of oppression and imprisonment can be changed. The prophet, and here I distinguish the prophet-poet who speaks in these chapters from Isaiah the 'author' of the entire book, proclaims God savior. However, Israel's salvation comes through Cyrus. Many, because of despair or because of resentment that the savior is a foreign king, reject the message; the rejection is countered by repeated proclamations of salvation and repeated denunciations of the people for their sin, their hard-heartedness, their refusal to trust in the message of hope. Isaiah, the fifth-century prophet-poet-author, draws analogies between those times and debates and his times and the people arguing against his interpretation.

As I just said at the close of my comments on ch. 39, all of the vision of Isaiah, both in its form and its content, are in 1–39. If that is so, what does 40–66 add to the book and the vision? If anything, there is even more significance attached to style, to how it is said. This is reflected in the frequent observation, by many studying these chapters, particularly 40–55, of the power and the beauty of the poetry. Clifford's title, *Fair Spoken and Persuading*, is a fine example. 40–66 stand out, in large part, for their clear and memorable expression. To use a musical analogy, the last half of Isaiah are variations on the themes, terms and images, of the first half. As I have said several times, one major mode of variation is transformation; a previous element is repeated and with significant change and development.

The specific names, times and events of 1–39 give way to the traditional and indefinite references of 40–66. The Lord, Israel, the nations and idols, and all humanity are the main characters; there is no Nebuchadrezzar, Zerubbabel, Ezra or Nehemiah. Formally, the chapters follow the grandiose and all-embracing style of chs. 13; 24–27; 34–35. They mirror Israel's life in exile, in dispersion and as a small province and as small and widely scattered communities in the Persian empire, but they present a vision of this life and not a narrative of its characters and events.

Repetition is more frequent and intense; longer sections are repeated and repeated more times. The poet-prophet constantly and consistently turns back on himself as he moves ahead. The impressionistic style, the piling up of words and images, dominates the section. Isaiah's encyclopedic style continues in the combination of new words with previously used vocabulary; I will note a few examples but do not treat this aspect thoroughly because it is beyond the scope of the commentary.

There is a more dramatic cast to the presentation than in 1–39 because of the frequent use of debate and disputation and the need for persuasion, not just the announcement of judgment and the call for change. (From a form-critical perspective, both Westermann and Schoors treat the many genres present in these chapters; I am indebted to their work, but employ it in ways very distinct from their goals.) Others, 'they', are being asked not just to change their ways, but to accept Isaiah's interpretation of their situation and of their future and to live their life in accord with the vision. Although this debate may be implicit in 1–39, it is brought to the forefront in 40–66. This also brings Isaiah's vision to the forefront. In the commentary, we will pay more attention to the message and vision of the book than we did with 1–39.

The Lord is frequently the speaker and at times without an introductory formula such as 'Thus says the Lord'; even when there are such formulas, they serve more to identify the Lord than to subordinate his speech to the prophet's. Isaiah's vision and interpretation are the Lord's proclamation. Declarations of hope and salvation dominate over those of sin and judgment, although in decreasing proportion as we move beyond ch. 54.

Although the chapters are set in the sixth century and later, the poet looks back to the creation of the world and forward to the creation of a new heavens and earth. There are no date formulas employed as in 1.1 and 6.1. The setting is, at different times, in Babylon, in Zion–Jerusalem and Judah, at places in-between and in the entire universe. The all-inclusive cosmic time and space of parts of 1–39 play a larger role in 40–66 and are associated with salvation, not judgment. Especially in the promises of return and renewal, 40–66 move in a dream and mythic time and space. However, the dream is upset, not so much by nightmares of universal destruction as in chs. 2 and 13, but by reality; actual life, in Judah and in the world at large, does not reflect the divine promises of the dream. The remnant, which is an important image and theme in 1–39, is now on the scene, but the scene is not so new; the remnant struggles with the same problems and predicaments as eighth-century Israel did. This is the tension between belief and reality, hope and actual life, interpretation and the world (or text) interpreted.

Isaiah 40–66

Chapter Forty

The divine commission to comfort is quoted by an unidentified speaker and addressed to an anonymous group (the imperatives and 'your' are masculine plural). In vv. 3 and 6 an anonymous voice speaks and, in the latter verse, is answered 'and he said'. (I do not emend the Hebrew with the Greek to read 'And I said' as in NRSV and most translations.) The anonymity is deliberate since prophecy is being transformed; this is not the commissioning of an individual prophet as in ch. 6. The focus shifts to the role and function of prophet as one sent to speak a divine message; it is no longer a question of the identification of a specific prophet. The generalization was already at work in 1–39 since they devote little space to the identification and description of the eighth-century prophet.

The punishment announced so frequently in 1–39, including 39.5-7, is over for the people and for Jerusalem. (40–66 continue to characterize 'Israel' in the three modes of masculine singular, masculine plural and female singular.) Threatened exile and destruction give way to proclamations of return and rebuilding. Dry, impassable places have a highway through them for the Lord to approach and for the people to return. (See 2.2-3; 11.16; 19.23; 35.8-10 for parallels.) The highway is formed by levelling; high and low, usually in opposition, are on the same plane in this image. The way is both an actual road and proper religious and moral behavior. In these chapters, literal roads through actual places modulate quickly into symbolic paths traversed by metaphorical travellers returning to Zion, the Lord's holy mountain. I already hinted at this literal and metaphorical reading in my comments on 1.27-28 and 7.1-3. The tension of chosen people, 'our God', and a universal God continues since all see the Lord's revealed glory. (In v. 5, 'all people' is 'all flesh' which may include animals; the phrase is in 40.6; 49.26; 66.16, 23-24.)

To cry, *qārā'*, means to read in 29.11-12; v. 6, therefore, alludes to reading. In the book someone cries out and we read of this shout and its message; we also read the book of Isaiah.[1] Human transience, figured in the image of a plant blooming and then drying, applies both to foreign powers that have oppressed Israel and to Israel. Humans, including prophets, come and go 'but the word of our God stands forever'. An individual prophet such as Isaiah passes from the scene but his words, his book, remain to be read and proclaimed by others (at 36.5). Prophecy is transformed from words spoken at a particular time to specific people to a book, a grand poem and vision, available to all at all times.

Zion–Jerusalem is a herald or recipient of good news which she announces to the cities of Judah; this is the prophetic role. Height is positive. God appears on the scene although not yet speaking. *Hinnēh*, see!, occurs three times in 9–10. The Lord comes with both might and gentleness. Arm is a symbol of strength and compassion (28.2; 33.2); he is ruler and shepherd. 'Gathering' alludes to the return of the dispersed (11.12; 43.5; 66.18).

Verses 12-17 focus on the Lord's might as evidenced in his grand creation; his compassion is dealt with in 27-31. Verses 12-14 are a series of rhetorical questions asked in general and whose answer is the Lord or No one! The Lord as creator of the world was not a significant theme in 1–39, although it was alluded to in 4.5 and 37.16, but is important now, especially in 40–48. This expansion of the theme and imagery is a major contribution to the book. In 40 creation is emphasized by the variety of the descriptions of the creator in vv. 12-17, 21-23 and 26-28; many of the terms are used here for the first time or even for the only time in Isaiah. For example, in v. 12, 'hollow of his hand', 'span', 'measure' and 'balance' occur only once in Isaiah. On the other hand and in Isaianic style, the new occur amidst familiar terms and images. Heavens and earth, mountains and hills are frequent pairs; vv. 13-14 concentrate words for spirit, counsel, knowledge, teaching, way and justice. The Lord, unlike humans, needs no one to teach or counsel him (28.26).

Verses 15-17 intensify the chasm between the divine and the human by viewing the world from the divine perspective. Nations and islands look like a drop of water or dust; all of them are nothing and emptiness (*tōhû*: 24.10; 29.21; 34.11). In the middle of the comparison, v. 16 denies human ability to cross the chasm

1.   Conrad, *Isaiah*, pp. 130-43.

with any form of sacrifice.[1] In 18-20 the poet, opening with rhetorical questions, mocks those who would bridge the gap by making an idol that is like God. (This recalls the king of Babylon who
would be like the Most High: 14.14.) The details of the construction of an idol contrast sharply with the divine creation of the
universe; human making and divine creation are often contrasted
in 40–48 and we will cite this passage on several occasions.

The poet, with rhetorical questions in v. 21, expects knowledge
and understanding of his audience and employs creation—the
beginning—to mark time and space. His answer, in vv. 22-24,
crosses the chasm between heaven and earth. God lives in the
heavens and those who live on earth look like insects to him. The
rulers on earth are nothing (tōhû) because he makes them that
way. Divine might overwhelms human might. The rulers, not
humanity in general (40.6-8), are quickly dried and blown away
(5.24; 17.13; 29.5-6). Verse 25 is similar to 18 except that the
question focuses on whom, not what. Verses 19-20 mock idols; 26
marvels at the size and order of the heavens. The Lord has created and named each star. The Holy One speaks; holy is other-
ness which emphasizes the gap separating divine from human.

Against this backdrop, vv. 12-26, of divine power and cosmic
time and space, the poet returns to the people, named Jacob and
Israel, and takes up the theme of comfort and support from vv.
10-11. Israel thinks that his misery is hidden from God. (See
29.15 for another use of the image.) Questions from v. 21 are
repeated and answered with the assertion that the Lord is a God
of time and space who never tires or lacks understanding. He
who brings down the mighty supports the weak and weary. On
their own, even vigorous youths stumble (3.8; 8.14-15), but if
they wait on the Lord, they can fly and run without tiring. Waiting is in the same semantic range as hoping, trusting and believ-
ing; all refer to life lived in the world as though the dreams and
visions are reality (at 8.17; 25.9; 26.8; 30.18; 33.2).

Isaiah, here and throughout the book, places Israel's hopes,
regardless of time or place, in the might and compassion of the
Lord, the God of all times, places and peoples. The story of this
particular people is a part of the larger story of all peoples in
the entire world; from another perspective, the tale of Israel's
judgment and salvation is an example, a *mise-en-abîme*, of the

1.   Lack, *Symbolique*, pp. 20-24.

judgment and salvation of all humanity. In reading Isaiah we frequently encounter this double aspect. Proclamations and descriptions of Israel's fortunes are meant for this particular people and, at the same time, are symbols and allegories of the fortunes of others. In accord with this, I pay special attention to those places where a character is not identified or named; the servant in 42 and 52.13–53.12 and the woman in 54 are two excellent examples.

Chapter Forty-One

The questions and answers of 40 are a rhetoric to persuade people, both those within the text of Isaiah and Isaiah's readers, to recognize the Lord's power and might that can be used for weal and woe. This was variously exhibited in 1–39. 41 and following continue this rhetoric and, at many points, sharpen it into a debate, a trial of the nations and their idols. The Lord, who speaks in 41.1-13 without introduction, is prosecutor, judge, jury and executioner.

The Lord calls the nations to judgment, to the judicial proceedings.[1] Who roused a victor? 'Victor' is from *ṣādaq—at 1.21— which denotes righteousness and innocence to this point; in 40–66, the root in its forms, also denotes victory, triumph and deliverance. In 1–39, God raised Israel's conquerors from afar whether Assyria, Babylon or the cosmic army. This victor, however, conquers other nations and turns them to dust and stubble (40.6-8, 24). He approaches rapidly, scarcely touching the road; the indefatigable, onrushing army that was cosmic, Assyrian and Babylonian is now Cyrus coming to destroy oppressors and save the oppressed (5.25-30). His approach is one result of the highway and the divine support described in 40.3-4, 28-31. Both 'āśâ and pā'al are used for the Lord's doing (at 5.1-7, 12). Beginning, first and last, connote time, space and authority; the Lord envelops all in all ways.

The nations respond with fear. They encourage, ḥāzaq (at 8.11; 35.3-4; 39.1), each other to make an idol which may be like God (40.18-20). The making is a parody of divine creation; 'it is good', a mockery of God's creation (Gen. 1.12, 18, 31). The idol cannot be moved or toppled (Isa. 24.10; 54.10); neither can it move or do anything. 'But you' (masculine singular) introduces a major

---

1.   Muilenburg, 'Isaiah', p. 449.

contrast with the nations and their idols who are given up to the victor from the east. 'You' are treated differently. Israel–Jacob is the Lord's servant, chosen and friend (*'āhab* means to love, acknowledge, be attached to: 1.23; 43.4; 48.14). Abraham is called from the east and, analogously, the dispersed of Israel are gathered 'from the four corners of the earth' (11.12). God's call of Cyrus, the victor, is paralleled by his earlier and later calls of Abraham and Israel. 'Do not fear' (40.9) is a leitmotif in 40–66; it is the war oracle addressed to the royal people (at 35.4; 43.1, 5; 44.2, 8; 51.7; 59.19).

The free-standing pronoun is not necessary in Hebrew syntax since person, number and gender are indicated in verbal and nominal forms themselves. The use of such pronouns in Hebrew accentuates the speaker 'I', the one spoken to 'you' or about, 'he' or 'they'. It is usually difficult, if not impossible, to indicate the emphasis in English without a cumbersome translation. Although Isaiah uses pleonastic pronouns throughout his book, there is a noticeable increase in their frequency, especially that of 'I' and 'you', in chs. 41–49. The increase is associated with divine self-affirmation (vv. 10, 13) and with focus on God's distinctive care for his chosen, 'you'.

The lengthy assurance to Israel in vv. 8-10 is in the elaborate style characteristic of these chapters. The use of three parallel elements is frequent. For example, note the avowal of help in vv. 10 and 13. 'Holding the hand', *ḥāzaq*, contrasts with the idolaters' mutual encouragement in v. 6 and the action of taking one's hand is paralleled in 8.11 (Isaiah); 42.6 (the servant); 45.1 (Cyrus); 51.18 (Zion) and 64.7. All who fight against them are nothing. In verses 11-13, 'you' is Israel and the one from the east who is named Cyrus in 44.28–45.1 and before whom none can stand (41.25; 45.1-3).

Verse 14 is the third declaration of divine help and 'Fear not!'. Verses 14-16 are unambiguously addressed to 'worm Jacob' whose Redeemer is God (at 35.9). Jacob becomes a sledge to thresh mountains and hills (at 10.6; 28.27-28), to turn them to chaff that the wind carries away (17.3; 28.23-29; 40.24; 41.2). Israel plays a role in its own liberation by defeating enemies and by helping build the highway for the redeemed (35.8-10). They rejoice in the Lord (24.7-16; 35.1-2; 38.18-20; 45.25); they do not fear as do the nations (v. 5).

Verses 17-20 summarize the effect of chs. 40–41. The poor and needy (3.13-15; 14.30-32) are all those, whether in Israel or in the nations, who require divine sustenance. Thirst figures need (5.13; 21.14; 32.6; 48.21) and the Lord's answer is the provision of water and the transformation of the desert, a symbol of suffering and desolation, into a garden land (30.19-25; 33.16; 35.6-7; 44.3). The result is universal recognition and knowledge that the Lord did and created all this (40.5, 21; 41.4); this result was a significant theme in chs. 25–27. As noted at the close of ch. 40, Israel's salvation is placed in the context of worldwide judgment and salvation.

Verses 21-29 parallel 1-7 with the debate with idols. The argument revolves around prediction and understanding, not just performance. Not only has God, the King of Jacob (6.5; 24.23; 33.22; 44.6), done this but he already had predicted and explained what he was going to do. The idols do nothing, whether weal or woe, and no one fears them. They are nothing. An idolmaker chooses wood (40.20); the Lord chooses Israel (41.8-9); to choose an idol is an abomination (1.13). The play upon proper and improper choice continues in the following chapters and is analogous to earlier issues of proper and improper trust and reliance. The Lord repeats his call of one from the north who treats rulers 'as the potter tramples clay'; this is what Assyria did (10.6). Verses 26-28 emphasize speech; only the Lord can foretell and announce good news (40.9). An idol cannot give counsel (yāʻaṣ at 36.5); they are wind and emptiness (rûaḥ wātōhû).

Chapter Forty-Two

In vv. 1-4 the contrast between the idols and the divinely supported servant is introduced by hēn, Look!, a form of hinnēh. The affirmation of the servant is shorter than that in 41.8-10, and the Lord speaks about, not to, the servant. Granting the spirit recalls the shoot from the stump of Jesse who is amply endowed with divine spirit (11.1-2). The shoot judges, šāpaṭ, and the servant brings forth justice or judgment, mišpāṭ. (The noun occurs three times in these verses and refers both to a judicial process and to the final outcome and state of a just society; at 1.21; at 3.13-15.) With both the shoot and the servant we are dealing with royal or messianic terms and images, but not with a king. 11.1-9 and 42.1-4 involve all the earth and the nations; world rule is a messianic claim (at 2.2-4).

Unlike the shoot who kills with his breath, the servant does not even shout or quench a smoldering wick. The latter image is reversed when it is God's power, when armies 'are quenched like a wick' (43.17; 34.10!). The servant works faithfully, trustworthily (*'āmēn: at 1.21-26; 43.9; 61.8). He neither crushes nor is crushed in his drive to establish the teaching (tôrâ: at 2.3) that the world awaits (51.5).

Verses 1-4 are divine speech without introduction; v. 5 is an elaborate formula announcing the divine statement in vv. 6-9 (see 43.1, 15-17; 44.1 for similar formulas). The formula, reminiscent of 40.12-16, depicts God the creator of heaven and earth and of all humans upon the earth. He gives his vivifying spirit to his servant and to all people. God now speaks directly to the servant; the speech is framed by the repeated 'I am the Lord' employing the pleonastic pronoun (at 41.8-10). 'Holding the hand' was noted at 41.10, 13. The servant is a covenant and a light for the nations (49.6-8) so that those in darkness can see (29.18; 35.5), and what they see is the Lord's glory. This is all an integral part of the consistent imagery of light in Isaiah (2.2-5: Let us walk in the light of the Lord!). They realize that, in accord with the argument presented in 41.21-29, the Lord's past word has come to be and now he predicts new events for the future. He is Lord of past, present and future; he speaks and it is.

In 1892 Bernhard Duhm isolated four sections in Isaiah 40–55 (so-called Deutero-Isaiah) that he argued were distinct poems by a separate poet presenting an individual servant of the Lord and not personified Israel as in 41.8-10. His four Servant Songs are 42.1-4; 49.1-6; 50.4-9 and 52.13–53.12. (Duhm and others argue that the name Israel in 49.3 is a later addition and should be deleted.) Since Duhm, debate has revolved around the separation of the songs from their context, their extent and the identity and mission of the servant. Today few commentators regard the poems as the work of another writer or as radically distinct poems within 40–55; they regard the songs as intense personifications that are an integral part of the work. Many argue that the first two poems can be extended to 42.1-7 and 49.1-7 (12), but this does not materially affect the interpretation of the song's content.

The larger debates concern the identity and mission of the servant. This overlaps with the interpretation of 40–55. The proposed identities can be divided into collective (Israel or part of Israel), individual (for example, a ruler or prophet) or a combination. For example, Wilcox and Paton-Williams, 'The Servant Songs', see 42.1-4 and 49.1-3 as personified Israel and 49.4-6 and the last two songs as the prophet. Many scholars, noting the

frequent positive references to the nations, claim that Israel
and the servant have a mission to bring all the nations to worship the Lord; others just as strongly deny this claim.

My reading of the poems keeps them in their context which is
all of Isaiah, not just 40–55, and discusses how they fit this context and yet stand out from it. Accordingly I do not make a major
issue of the extent of the material; for example, I read 42.1-9 as
a single section. Isaiah, Eliakim and David, prophet and royalty,
are called 'servant of the Lord' ('ebed yhwh: 20.3; 22.20; 37.15)
since they, in different ways, do the Lord's work. The verb 'ābad
means to do and work (19.9; 28.21), to serve (60.12), to worship
(19.21-23) and to slave (14.3). It and the noun 'ᵃbōdâ, with the
roots 'āśâ and pā'al which are more frequent (41.4; at 5.1-12),
refer to the concept of the Lord's work and doing, whether weal
or woe (28.21; 32.17), and all that it entails. It is a work of judgment and salvation, war and peace, enslavement and liberation
whose ultimate outcome, however, is justice and righteousness,
peace and freedom (32.16-20; 42.6-7).

Therefore a servant of the Lord can be warrior or peacemaker,
conqueror or liberator, judge, prophet or faithful worshipper.
Any group or individual who do the work of the Lord can be a
servant. As I said in my discussion of 40.1-9, the focus should be
on what a servant (or prophet) does, on what their role and function are, not on who that servant is. The Lord's work can be done
by other than an Israelite prophet or king, and a faithful worshipper can be other than an Israelite. That the scope of God's
work extends to all people has been clear since ch. 2. However,
this is the scope of God's work and not the mission of any particular person or group. In 2.2-4, the nations come to the Lord; no
one goes out to bring them to the holy mountain. What does go
forth is the Lord's word (2.3) and, as noted before, the book of
Isaiah is one manifestation of the divine word. The servant is a
figure for the book and, in the book, we read of other servants:
Israel and Israelites, Cyrus, faithful worshippers and those who
wait on the Lord.

Verses 10-12 are the first of several hymnic interludes that
mark major transitions in the chapters (see 44.23; 45.8; 49.13 for
other interludes). Newness, glory and praise continue from vv. 8-
9; the theme of joy permeates Isaiah (at ch. 61; 9.3; ch. 12; 24.14-
16; ch. 35); the listing of places emphasizes the worldwide scope.
(Kedar is a descendant of Ishmael, son of Abraham [41.8; Gen.
25.13].) Verse 13 reintroduces the militaristic theme that typified

ch. 41; the Lord stirs up both Cyrus and his fury or zeal (9.7; 37.32). 'Soldier' is the 'mighty' God of 9.6 and 10.21.

Verses 14-20 are the Lord's speech without an introductory formula. His time of restraint is over. Breathing heavily like a woman in travail (37.3), he desiccates the wet so that it is passable; this is the highway image (40.4-5; 41.14-16; 33.21!). In other contexts the dry is made wet to provide sustenance for the poor and the thirsty (30.23-25; 35.5-7; 41.17-20). The Lord does not forsake them (41.17). 'Forsake' is *'āzab which I first discussed at the close of my comments on ch. 6 and noted the varied contexts it occurs in. People forsake the Lord when they should not (1.4, 28); they should forsake or abandon idols and evil (31.7; 55.7); because of sin, they are forsaken, their land abandoned (6.12; 7.16; 49.14; 60.15). I will continue to note this concern with what is and is not forsaken.

The ones not forsaken are the blind, the thirsty and the poor in Israel and among the nations. They serve the Lord and trust in him (12.2; 26.4; 50.10; 62.4, 12) in sharp contrast to those who trust in idols or other false hopes (30.12; 31.1; 36.4-9). The latter are put to shame, a major image for punishment (1.29; 19.9; 23.4; 24.23; 41.11; 66.5). There is hope for all deaf and blind (6.9-10; 29.18; 35.5; 42.6-7) since they cannot be more closed than the Lord's own servant and messenger and yet the Lord is still with the latter. The unrestricted scope of the hope lies in the indefiniteness of the nouns. Ironically, those who serve the Lord and are sent by him can be as blind as those who trust in idols.

Verses 1-4 pair justice and teaching; v. 21, righteousness and teaching. Despite the teaching's visibility (2.3), 'this people'— their identity indefinite—are locked in darkness (42.7) and are prey (8.1-4; 10.1-14; 17.14). 'Who?' echoes the questions in 40.12–41.4; 'you' (masculine plural) is Israel, humanity or the idols. Hearing contrasts with deafness. Verses 24-25 focus the general message on Israel; what the Lord does for all, he does for or to his people. The Lord put him in prison and made him prey. 'We' sinned; 'they' did not walk in his way and listen to his teaching. This can indicate a division within the Israelite community[1] and between Israel (we) and the nations (they). But it is Jacob who is punished with war and fire which are ubiquitous images for

---

1. Conrad, *Isaiah*, pp. 95-96.

punishment (1.7; 66.15-24). As so often the case, Jacob does not understand (1.3; 29.13-16).

Chapter Forty-Three

'But now' marks a sharp contrast with 42.21-25; judgment is off-set by salvation. The affirmation, in Isaianic style, repeats words and phrases from 40–42 and adds new ones. The Lord is Jacob's creator (40.28; 42.5) and fashioner. To fashion or form is *yāṣar* (at 22.11; 37.26); it is the action of a potter (29.16) and other arti-san (44.9-10). Fear not! is repeated in v. 5. Verses 1-7 form a compact unit because of reiterated words and phrases; v. 7 closes with called, created and formed from v. 1 and adds 'made'. The redeemed return to Zion on the Holy Way (35.8-10); the Holy One is Israel's Redeemer (41.14; 43.14). 'You are mine' and 'I am with you' (v. 5) are central expressions of the intimate relationship between God and people that flows from his creation and contin-ued support of them. To call by name connotes both authority and intimacy (40.26; 45.3-4). Because the Lord is with him, Israel will not be harmed by flood or flame. 'Overwhelm' refers to 'destructive' flooding (8.5-8; 28.2, 15-18; 30.28) and to 'overflow-ing' peace (66.12).

The Lord is Savior (43.11; 45.15, 21; 60.16; 63.8). 'Savior' is the participle of *yāša'* (see at 7.1-3). Salvation and savior are major themes in the book entitled Isaiah, 'the Lord saves'. The term for 'ransom' also means to blot out (6.7), forgive (22.14), expiate (27.9) and annul (28.18). Egypt, Cush (Ethiopia) and Seba are all part of the Table of Nations (Gen. 10.6-8); these are traditional peoples and not indicative of a particular historical era. Exchange is a figurative expression for Cyrus's release of the exiles from Babylon combined with his and his successors' con-quest of the Near East.

Israel is precious, honored and loved (41.8). 'Honored' is *kābēd* and is related to *kābôd*, 'glory' (at 10.3); these are a leitmotif in Isaiah and mean glory, glorious and to glorify (3.8; 6.3; 22.18; 25.3; 40.5; 60.13; 66.5), wealth (10.3), army (8.7), heavy (1.4; 22.24; 47.6), great and important (32.2; 36.2), honored and to honor (22.23; 23.8-9; 29.13; 43.20, 23; 49.5; 58.13). For the play between honor and contempt, see at 16.14 and 22.15-25.

The ingathering of 43.5 was introduced in 11.10-12 (40.11); the four directions allude to the call of Israel (41.9) and of Cyrus (41.2-5, 25; 45.5-6) and are in accord with the global reach of Isaiah's vision. Verses 8-13 are a trial scene that plays upon the calling and gathering of vv. 1-7. All, Israel and the nations, assemble. The dispute concerns prediction (41.21-29; 42.9): 'They' should bring forth witnesses to the truth; 'you' (masculine plural) and 'my chosen servant' (masculine singular) are 'my witnesses'. But there is no time for testimony since the Lord moves immediately to the decision. 'They' will know, believe and understand that 'I am he' (both pronouns are used for maximum impact). 'Believe' and 'true' (v. 9) are both from *'āmēn (at 1.21).

Whereas previous scenes focussed on the other participants, this trial closes with proclamations of the Lord's godhood and power to save. Personal affirmation is stressed; the pronoun 'I' occurs six times. 'Before' and 'after' refer to both time and place; there was and will be no other god and there can be no idol, a formed god, in the Lord's presence. God, and not a strange god (17.10), declared and did. The overlap of vv. 12-13 can be translated 'You are my witnesses but I am God' stressing the Lord's unique godhood. No one can save or rescue from God's power (42.22); God acts and no one can turn it back (14.27).

The divine speech formulas in vv. 1, 10, 14 and 16 remind us who the speaker is but, as before, do not subordinate the divine declarations to the prophet's discourse. Isaiah's vision of the Lord as omnipotent God and God of all is presented as God's own declaration. Verses 14-15 are addressed to Israel. God is Redeemer, Creator, Holy One and King (6.5; 41.21; 44.6). He breaks Babylon and the Chaldeans for Israel's sake (45.1-6); they are symbols of violence, oppression and imprisonment. In Genesis 10–11, Babylon–Babel and Ur of the Chaldeans are scenes of dispersal and leaving. In Isa. 43.16-17, the poet combines that leaving with the Exodus image of a way through the sea, an archetypal image of the Lord's power. Babylon and Egypt merge as the place of captivity; Exodus and return are analogous.

In vv. 18-19 we shift imperceptibly from prophetic to divine speech. Genesis and Exodus contain powerful traditions of the Lord's acts, but Israel is not to remain locked in nostalgia with attention forever on the past. The Lord is doing, *hinᵉnî* with a participle, something new (42.9). It sprouts. This is typical Isaianic vegetal imagery (at 4.2); in 4.2 'branch' is the noun from the verb 'sprout, spring forth'. Attention should be on the new, the present, the future. The way of exodus is the way of return, and the Lord sustains his chosen people in the desert (41.17-20; 42.15-16). Even demonic creatures honor God (13.19-22; ch. 34) and all declare his praise (42.8-10).

Like ch. 42, 43 closes with a denunciation of Israel that contrasts sharply with its context by turning previous terms and themes against Israel. The 'yet' or 'but' of v. 22 is understatement when compared with the might and wonder of the first part of the chapter. Israel does not call on God (vv. 1 and 7); they are weary of him (40.28-31). They, unlike the wild animals in v. 20, do not honor him with sacrifice even though he has honored them (v. 4) and has not burdened them with demands for sacrifice. They, indeed, burden the Lord with their sins. See 1.11-14 and the grotesque parody of sacrifice in 34.5-7. 'To burden' is ironic since this is a form of the verb related to *'ebed* (at 20.3), the servant mentioned in v. 10 and 44.1-2.

The Lord reaffirms, in accord with vv. 10-13, that he is a forgiving God who blots out and does not remember these sins; they are part of the former things to be forgotten (v. 18). In a twist of the trial scene in vv. 8-10, Israel is called to the bar. 'Accuse' is a form of the verb 'to remember', *zākar* (12.4; 26.8); 'proved right' and 'justify' in v. 9 are both from **ṣādaq* (at 1.21). Israel's past, from his 'first ancestor-father'—Abraham? Jacob?—is a story of sin and punishment; 'utter destruction' is the 'doom', the holy war ban, of 34.2.

Chapter Forty-Four

Chapters 42 and 43 end with denunciations of Israel and 43 and 44 open with oracles of salvation introduced by 'but now' and marked by Fear not! 44.1-2 modify previous addresses to Israel. Jacob is servant and chosen (41.8; 42.1; 43.10), and the double affirmation frames the image of God making and forming 'in the womb'. (Previously 'womb' occurred only in 13.18; see 42.14 for the association of God and childbirth.) God the helper first occurs in 41.10-14 (49.8; 50.7-9); he contrasts with Egypt who is of no help (20.6; 41.6). (Jeshurun occurs elsewhere only in Deut. 32.15; 33.5, 26.)

Similar to the vision of transformation in 32.14-20, water and spirit are in parallel; both are poured out and lead to fertility and growth (42.9; 43.19). The servant has the Lord's spirit on him (42.1), but the Lord pours out his anger on Jacob (42.25). Plant and water imagery dominates 44.3-4; water is life-giving (35.1-6; 41.17-20; 43.19-20). Blessing is not a frequent theme in Isaiah; in 19.24-25 Assyria, Egypt and Israel are a blessing of the Lord (51.2; 61.9; 65.23).

Naming (at 35.8) is emphasized in the fourfold repetition in v. 5 which is matched by the Lord's four names in v. 6. To be Israel and Jacob is to belong to the Lord. Verses 6-8 are a crescendo joining themes from the preceding: God's totality, uniqueness and power to predict and to do. ('Do not fear' employs the verb *pāḥad*: 2.10, 19, 21; 12.2; 19.16-17; 33.14; 44.11!; 51.13; 60.5!.) Israel and other humans are the Lord's witnesses; he alone is Rock (17.10; 26.4; 30.29).

Verses 9-20 parody other witnesses, that is, idols and idolmakers. The Lord knows no other rock and the idols 'neither see nor know' (41.20). As I did with 22.15-25, the story of Shebna and Eliakim, I read 44.9-20 on a literal level, a parody of those who worship a physical image, and on a symbolic level, a denunciation of all who put their trust in something or someone who cannot fulfill that trust. The section, on these two levels, denounces Israel, who has trusted in Egypt and intrigue, and the nations who trust in idols and human might. The poet reproves those who fear something that should not inspire fear; vv. 9-20 are, in this view, a restatement of the assurances of vv. 6-8. The detailed description of the idolmaker's activity sets it in contrast to the Lord's creative activity (40.12-14, 21-25; 41.8-10).

The vocabulary and imagery are typically Isaianic. He who fashions and forms Israel is the Lord (43.1, 7, 21); he who fashions an idol is nothing (*tōhû*). Israel delighted in oaks and was ashamed (1.29-30; 41.11; 42.17). The assembly of the idolaters recalls the fiendish gathering in 34.15 and both are a mockery of the (in)gathering of the dispersed (11.12; 40.11). Work with trees mimics images of God as gardener and forester (5.1-7; 10.33-34; 27.2-6; 30.23-26) and carpenter (28.17; 34.11). Trees are symbols of strength and pride (2.13; 9.10; 14.8) and transformation (41.19). Unlike the ironsmith, the Lord is untiring and his arm is mighty (30.30; 40.10-11, 28-31; 51.9-11; 63.5, 12).

'Beauty' is *tip'eret* (v. 13; see at 46.13). The domestic scene of baking and eating in vv. 15-16 contrasts with the absurdity of worshipping the 'remnant' of the wood, 'You are my god'. The Lord says, 'I am god' (41.10; 43.3, 12-13). Only he saves (*nāṣal*: 36.13-20; 42.22; 43.13). The idolaters's ignorance and blindness in v. 19 correspond to that of Israel: 1.3; 6.9-10; 28.7–29.16. Feeding recalls the ambiguous image of flocks in 5.17; 14.30 and 27.10. A fraud is a lie which Israel once trusted in (28.15). The mockery of 44.9-20 is against more than just actual idolmakers and worshippers.

Verses 21-22 intensify the proclamation of salvation and lead into the hymn praising the Lord for his redemption of Jacob. Israel must remember because the Lord will not forget; the Lord fashioned Jacob as his servant (vv. 2, 9-10). 'These things' to be remembered are the warnings of the symbolic narrative in vv. 9-20, the divine assurances of the preceding chapters and the entire book of Isaiah. On the other hand, the Lord does forget and sweep away sins (43.25). The cause and effect pattern is reversed; Israel should return for the Lord has redeemed him (vv. 6, 22, 24). The entirety of creation celebrates the Lord's deed of redemption and glory. Singing is a frequent response to the Lord's saving activity (12.6; 24.14-16; 26.19; 35.2-6; 49.13).

Like 42.10-13, the hymn in 44.23–45.8 is a transition. It is matched by the hymn in 45.8, and the two frame 44.24–45.7 which I divide into 44.24-28 and 45.1-7. 'Thus says the Lord' opens the first section which is composed of a series of eleven participles, most introduced with 'who', identifying the Lord by his ongoing activity. The section ties together Isaianic themes, terms and images. God redeems, forms and creates. He frustrates human power and designs (8.9-10; 14.24-27; chs. 28–29), but confirms the counsel ('prediction', *'ēṣâ*: at 36.5) of his servant and messengers (42.18-20). He proclaims the restoration of Jerusalem and the cities of Judah. Verse 26 opens and closes with the verb *qûm*, to confirm and raise up (at 7.7), positive aspects of being on high. 'Ruins' are low and dry (5.17). (*Ḥāreb* is 'to be dry and waste': 5.17; 19.5-6; 34.10; 48.21; 50.2). Jerusalem is 'wastes' (49.19; 51.3; 61.4; 64.11). The Lord raises up the dry and dries up the deep and rivers (42.15; 44.3).

He declares that Cyrus, named here and in 45.1, is his shepherd. Shepherd alludes to flocks feeding in ruins (5.17; 27.10) and in peace (11.7; 14.30; 30.23), to the Lord (40.11) and to leaders (56.11; 63.11). David was shepherd (1 Sam. 16.11; 2 Sam. 5.2) and Solomon was builder of Jerusalem and the temple (1 Kings 5–8). Cyrus has royal titles and functions, but he is not called king. Kingship is transformed in Isaiah and its functions are available to others, including a foreigner. The Lord's 'purpose' is paralleled in 46.10; 48.14; 53.10 ('will'). 'Purpose' is *ḥēpeṣ* from *ḥāpēṣ*, to delight in (1.11; 13.7) and to be pleased (42.21); I will note subsequent occurrences of the noun and verb in their varied meanings. Cyrus does in v. 28 what the Lord said in v. 26. ('Fulfill' and 'carry out' are *šālēm* which underlies *šālôm*, peace and prosperity; at 9.6-7.) Cyrus is the Lord's servant and messenger; the Lord founds the earth (40.21) and Cyrus founds the temple (28.16). Cyrus is the instrument of the Lord's power.

Chapter Forty-Five

'Thus says the Lord' opens the second part of 44.28–45.7. A series of divine statements follow that tell what God is doing through Cyrus and why. Cyrus is the Lord's anointed, another royal title (61.1; 1 Sam. 2.10; 2 Sam. 23.1; Ps. 2.2). 'Taking by the hand' alludes to divine support for Isaiah (Isa. 8.11), for Israel, the servant and Cyrus (41.13; 42.6) and for Jerusalem (51.18). The support results in victory, levelling (42.16), shattering (43.14-15) and plunder. Cyrus releases prisoners from darkness (42.7) and seizes treasure hidden in darkness (29.14-15).

The Lord does this so that Cyrus will acknowledge that he calls him by name (41.25; 43.1). At the same time, it is for the sake of Jacob his servant that the Lord calls and arms Cyrus, 'though you do not acknowledge me'. He is the only God (44.8); the phrase frames 45.5-6. Thirdly, the Lord acts so that all may acknowledge him as the only God.

In v. 7, the Lord describes his power using five participles. He forms light and creates darkness; he makes peace and creates evil. The verb to create, *bārā'*, refers only to divine activity (4.5); it is therefore surprising that 'the Lord creates darkness and evil'. The verse rounds out 44.24–45.7 by repeating the phrase 'I the Lord do all [these] things' from 44.24; unfortunately, translations obscure the inclusion. NRSV renders 44.24, 'I am the Lord, who made all things'.

Heavens and earth sing the Lord's glory in 44.23; in 45.8 the heavens pour righteousness so that the earth opens and causes salvation to sprout (44.3-4). 'Sprout' is plant imagery that stresses newness (4.2 'branch'; 42.9; 43.19). The hymn closes 44.23–45.8 which emphasizes the Lord's redemption of Israel through his instrument Cyrus. It is fitting that he use a foreigner to save the people since he once called for a far nation, embodied in Assyria and Babylon, to disperse them. Both Assyria and Babylon fail because of their pride, because they refuse to acknowledge that they are divine instruments.

Cyrus, however, is a more shadowy figure; we are never explicitly told of his success or of his ultimate fate. His actual name occurs only twice; his kingdom, Persia, is never named. After ch. 45, he merges with others called by the Lord. Assyria and Babylon appear as personified nations or cities or in the person of their king, named or anonymous. Cyrus has royal epithets and functions ascribed to him, but he is never called king. After ch. 39, only God is called king (41.21; 43.15; 44.6; 52.7), although he may trample kings (41.2; 45.1). Kings are amongst the many who come submissively to the Lord and Jerusalem (49.23; 60.3-16; 62.2). Kingship is transformed and, as a result, human kings, including Cyrus, are reduced.

In two Woe! Oracles (chs. 5; 28–31), the poet challenges those in Israel who question the divine work; v. 9 employs the three verbs *yāṣar*, *'āsâ* and *pā'al* (at 5.1-12; 22.11). Assyrians and Israelites have previously confused the made with the maker (10.15; 29.15-16). The Lord is associated with childbirth, with father and mother (44.2, 24). The divine response to the questioning comes in vv. 11-13. He is Israel's Maker-Potter (*yōṣēr* in 9a, 11) and parent.

The Lord uses the pleonastic pronoun 'I' three times in vv. 12-13 to emphasize his creative power (37.16; 42.5). No one commands him but he commands the heavenly (10.6; 13.3). He arouses Cyrus and levels roads. Cyrus rebuilds Jerusalem (44.28) and frees the exiles (5.13). Verse 14 is addressed to Jerusalem ('you' is female singular). Egypt, Cush and Seba are representative nations first noted in 43.3. They come, serve and pray. Their confession of the one God fulfills the divine motive in v. 6 and, in a chain of allusions, the vision of 2.2-4. I read v. 15 as part of the confession and the speaker—Cyrus?—addresses the hidden yet saving God. Idol makers are ashamed and disgraced (41.11-12; 44.9-11), but Israel is saved by the Lord and never ashamed. The poet introduces the Lord in vv. 18-19 with an elaborate title stressing the order and purpose of creation; the Lord stresses the clarity and trustworthiness of his speech. Although he is a hidden God, he speaks and works openly, not in darkness or chaos (*tōhû*).[1]

Chapter 44.1–45.19 strongly implies a debate that has been going on, at least implicitly, since the start of the book. Isaiah is countering others who are disputing the book's interpretation of Israel's history, present status and future hopes. I comment on the issue as presented in Isaiah; I am not attempting a historical reconstruction. We get only Isaiah's side of the argument and his view of the opposing arguments. Even in 44–45, Isaiah is defending his entire vision of God, Israel and the world. It is not just his portrayal of Cyrus, the foreigner, as savior that is being contested. In the debate Isaiah is employing traditional religious rhetoric about listening to the Lord's word and following his way to foster attention to and acceptance of his interpretation of

---

1.   See Miscall, 'New Heavens'.

Israel's past, present and future. His book is God's word and therefore those who wait for the Lord, who are his servants, should read it and act on it.

In my digression on the servant in ch. 42, I argued that there is not a mission to the nations in Isaiah but that there is an openness to the nations and a willingness to accept them into the vision of God's people who dwell on his holy mountain. Anyone, Israelite or foreigner, can read and act on Isaiah's vision. At points in the commentary I have noted that there are no absolute criteria to distinguish Israel from the nations whether in matters of sin-judgment or salvation-renewal. Israel and the nations join to form 'all humanity' and 'all flesh'; God is Lord of all. Isaiah is using materials reflecting times from the eighth to the sixth–fifth centuries to present a postexilic vision in which he produces a multi-level view of the nations. They are evil and oppressive and are to be destroyed; Babylon and Assyria are the main symbols. They are good and saving; Cyrus, but not Persia by name, is the main symbol. Finally, they are just there whether good or evil, punished or not; they can eventually come to the Lord, but not necessarily to Jerusalem and Israel. Egypt (and Cush and Seba) is the main symbol.

In vv. 20-25 the Lord speaks unannounced and renews his summons of the remnant of the nations to debate. Unlike the nations in v. 14 and like the idolaters in v. 16, they don't know despite the Lord's clear speech (v. 19). Their god is impotent; the Lord saves (vv. 15-17). The argument reprises the Lord's predictive powers (43.9) and his uniqueness. On a rhetorical level, Isaiah is figuratively casting his opponents in the role of the nations and their idols. It is Isaiah's interpretation, his theology, that saves; the opponent's views and proposals are worthless.

Suddenly the Lord (and Isaiah) shifts, in v. 22, from judgment to a call for all to be saved and to worship the God of Israel. The word has gone forth (2.3) and will not turn back (40.8; 55.10-11); if the Lord swears, who can turn it back (14.24-27)? The Lord is righteous and strong (12.2; 26.1). Shame awaits all who oppose him (v. 16; 41.11). The final verse returns to the descendants of Israel (43.5; 44.3). They will triumph (*ṣādēq; at 41.2) in the Lord; they will glory in him (41.16).

Chapter Forty-Six

The poet (or the Lord) has a vision of Babylon. Bel and Nebo are Babylonian Gods being carried in ritual procession. The idols are heavy, and the beasts struggle with the burden. They are weary and go into captivity. (The word for idol also means pain and grief: 14.3; 50.11; 54.6; 63.10.) The Lord calls Jacob to attention (44.1); the remnant of Israel contrasts with the ignorant survivors of the nations (45.20). Although God carries Israel from the womb (44.2, 24) to old age, 'he does not faint or grow weary' (40.28). Idols cannot save but the Lord can.

The Lord's query in v. 5 recalls the questions in 40.18, 25. It is easy to assume that God addresses Israel in vv. 5-13 since they are addressed in vv. 3-4. However, with vv. 1-2 we can also read Babylon and other nations as implied addressees; Israel is not named in vv. 5-13. The detailed description in vv. 6-7 of the idol-maker's futile work and prayers recalls the analogous taunts in 40.19-20; 41.6-7; 44.9-20. They carry it about but it cannot save (45.20).

Through this denunciation of idolaters, Isaiah continues his debate with those who dispute his interpretation. His interpretation is different and those who question and resist it are like idolaters. They cling to past traditions and other proposals for Israel's society and future as though the latter were God himself (43.18-19). But it is God who saves—I am He!—not an interpretation or a tradition. This takes us to the heart of such a debate since the book of Isaiah is an interpretation, a vision of God, the world and Israel. His vision and word are 'counsel and strength' for life that do stand forever, but there is nothing to prevent others from turning the book itself into an idol.

In vv. 8-13 the people are transgressors, rebels (1.2, 28). God implores them to remember the past (44.21) which balances with the future, 'things not yet done'. ('I am God': 43.11; 44.6-8; 45.14, 21-22.) Verses 10-11 highlight God's predictive and performative powers; he speaks and it is. The verses include characteristic terms (14.24-27). 'Do' and 'fulfill' are *ʿāśâ* (three times); 'purpose' is *ʿēṣâ*; 'stand' is *qûm*; 'plan' is *yāṣar* (at 22.11; 43.1; 44.2). 'Intention' is *ḥēpēṣ* which is 'pleasure, delight' (at 44.28; 48.14 'purpose'). He calls one from far away for salvation, no longer punishment (5.26-30; 7.18-20; 13.1-5). 'Listen to me' repeats from v. 3. The people are hard-hearted and far from deliverance (*sᵉdāqâ*: at 1.21 and 41.2; 45.25). From afar God brings the fearsome army, his children (41.8-9; 43.6), 'the bird of prey' and salvation. (For 'near and far', see 29.13-14; 33.13; 54.14; 57.19; note that Cyrus is not named.) 'Not tarrying' recalls the speeding of judgment (5.19; 8.1-4).

Salvation is in Zion; glory (*tip'eret*) in Israel (44.13, 23). 'Glory' is from *pā'ēr, to be beautiful and glorious. Jewels and the 'branch' are beautiful (3.18; 4.2). One can vaunt one's beauty and be arrogant like Assyria (10.15), Babylon (13.19) and Samaria (28.1-4). The Lord is 'a diadem of beauty' for the remnant (28.5) and is glorified in Israel (44.23). An idol can have human beauty (44.13).

Chapter Forty-Seven

Lady Babylon first appeared at the close of ch. 13; her fall was announced in 21.9. This is her final scene; her collapse is proclaimed in 48.14, 20 (Babylon is not mentioned in 52.11-12 and 55.12 which are calls to go forth). As Sawyer notes[1] this is 'the story of the overpowering and humiliation of a woman. Feminine singular forms are used throughout.' There is nothing in the chapter, no gates or walls, to make us think of a city; therefore I speak of Lady Babylon, not the city of Babylon.

Fallen, the lady sits in the dust, a place of death (2.9-21; 5.13-17; 14.3-11). 'Virgin daughter' recalls doomed Sidon (23.12) and exultant Zion (37.22); daughter Zion knows destruction and death (1.8, 21-23; 29.4). Although the chapter mocks Lady Babylon on the manifest level, daughter Zion lingers on the latent level (3.16-4.1). Throughout Isaiah human pride results in destruction and humiliation (2.9-21). Her names—Tender, Delicate and Mistress of Kingdoms—are taken away and, as a sign of annihilation, she is not given a new name (1.26!; 34.12!). The proud queen is reduced to a slave in work and dress. She passes through rivers on her way to enslavement (43.2!). The Lord takes vengeance (1.24; 34.8). 'We'—Israel? nations who now acknowledge the Lord?—interrupt to proclaim 'our redemption' (43.14; 44.6, 23-24; 48.17). Perhaps 'we' are intimidated by the Lord's merciless retribution. The emphasis on the divine name in v. 4 contrasts sharply with the removal of the woman's titles.

Verse 5 parallels v. 1. Silence and darkness symbolize prison, exile and death. Silence, *dûmām*, recalls the oracle on Dumah in 21.11-12 which follows the announcement of Babylon's fall. Analogous to his actions with Assyria in 10.5-15, the Lord, in his anger (34.2; 43.28), gave his people into Babylon's power, but she overstepped her mission. She was merciless and imposed the

1.   'Daughter of Zion', p. 91.

yoke, slavery (9.4), on the old. At times the Lord shows no mercy (9.17; 27.11) and does at other times (14.1; 30.18; 49.10); the Medes, who attacked Babylon, are merciless (13.18). The lines separating God's treatment of his people and of Babylon are not hard and fast; indeed, the lines separating the brutal punishers—God, Assyria, Babylon, Media—are not hard and fast. There is little wonder, then, that some contest Isaiah's vision.

The Lady, as the king in 14.13-14, is quoted. 'I will be mistress forever.' She has not considered that she is part of a larger story in which she is mistress for a limited time (41.20-22; 48.9; 54.7-8). However, Zion is not always characterized by such consideration (22.11). Israel does not understand God's punishment (42.25) and is called to remember the larger story (44.21; 46.8-11). 'But now' (43.1; 44.1) shifts to judgment. The noble women of Israel were complacent and secure (*bāṭaḥ*: 32.9-14; 36.4-10). 'I and no one else' is a claim to near divinity (10.7-14; 14.12-14; 45.21; 46.9). Never to be widowed or bereaved is a claim to unending power. Yet all comes crashing down 'in a moment, in one day' (30.13) despite the great reputation of Babylonian magic; see 19.1-15 and 30.8-14 for analogous declarations against Egypt and Israel.

Verses 10-11 are like a précis of the sin and judgment of Israel in chs. 28–32 with the themes of false trust, hiddenness (29.15), corrupt wisdom and unavoidable disaster. Babylon trusts in evil (wickedness) but evil (disaster) comes upon her. (Compare Israel's covenant with Death in 28.14-19.) She crumbles in ignorance and impotence which are accentuated through the balance and repetition in v. 11. In 12-13, the poet mocks astrology. 'Stand fast' implies resolution, but 'labor' (12, 15) implies weariness (40.28-31); 'perhaps' (used twice) she can save herself. Trust in falsity—magic, Egypt, idols or human power—does not succeed (30.4-5; 44.9-10; 57.12-13); astrologers cannot save or deliver. Unlike the Lord (46.8-10), they cannot predict the future. With characteristic imagery, we see (*hinnēh*) them burn like stubble (5.24; 33.11; 40.24); the flame consumes them (9.18-20); this is not a fire on the hearth (44.14-19). They wander aimlessly (*tā'â*: at 35.8). 'Your Savior does not exist' is a possible translation of the final phrase (43.3!).

Chapter Forty-Eight

The opening is an elaborate name for and an ironic call to Jacob. 'Hear' and 'listen' are the same verb, and this is the fourth in a series of calls to attention: 46.3, 12; 47.8; 48.12, 14; 49.1. The people invoke the Lord and his name (12.4), but not in truth or right (*'āmēn; ṣ^edāqâ) which are high virtues in Isaiah. These are the people named for 'the holy city' (27.13; 52.1) who look to the Lord for support; 'Lord of hosts' recalls one such appeal in 47.4. Their worship is show (29.13-14; 58.1-5).

The Lord speaks without introduction in vv. 3-13 and begins an argument based on his powers of prediction and performance (41.25-29; 43.8-13), but it is Israel, not the nations, who is summoned to the bar for judgment. The Lord declared his action in the past, not to demonstrate his power, but to thwart Israel's claims that an idol did them (45.9-12). This is heavy irony. The people that lean on God have idols and images; it is difficult, if not impossible, to distinguish them from the nations in this regard. Verses 6-8 are the other half of the argument; the people witness against themselves. Hearing and knowing (both four times) are emphasized. The Lord creates new things (42.9-10) so that Israel cannot say 'I already knew them'. Israel may not know, but the Lord knows that Israel is as hard as iron, treacherous (21.2; 24.16) and named Rebel (1.2).

Naming rounds off vv. 1-8 and leads to the declaration in 9-13 which plays upon name and calling. For his name's sake, God holds back his wrath (47.6); he does not cut his people off as a forester would (9.14; 10.33-34; 18.5). Israel has been refined; the image was introduced in 1.24-26 and 4.3-4 (6.5-7). Israel has been profaned (43.28; 47.6), but the Lord won't be. He gives his glory (kābôd) to no other god (42.8; 46.13!).

Jacob is called to hear in v. 12. The Lord accents himself (41.4; 44.6) and his creative power (44.24; 45.18); he uses 'I' four times in vv. 12-13. Earth and heavens stand at attention. In v. 14, someone—prophet? Lord?—summons all, including Israel, to hear. The Lord loves him, Cyrus who goes unnamed, and he loves Israel (41.8; 43.4). Cyrus does the Lord's delight (ḥēpeṣ) against Babylon. God alone, 'I, I', speaks, calls, brings and makes prosper. All approach to hear (33.13; 34.1). He reaffirms his presence and perceptibility (40.21; 41.26; 45.19).

'And now' or 'but now' (43.1; 44.1; 47.8) marks an interruption analogous to the breaks in 45.19 and 47.4. The speaker is confident that 'the Lord has sent me and his spirit'. The Lord's spirit is effective (at 4.4; 28.6; 40.7; 59.21); both the shoot and the servant have it (11.2; 42.1). The speaker in 61.1, who is sent by the Lord, has it. The servant is given by God to effect salvation (49.1-12). Therefore, the speaker of 48.16b is multiple: Cyrus (with vv. 14-15);

Israel as prophet or as servant; or the Lord's word personified. This is an aspect of Cyrus's shadowy figure; unnamed, he can merge with others who are sent by God to do his work.

The Lord harshly criticizes Israel in vv. 17-19. Although he leads Israel in the proper way, he ('you' is masculine singular) had not regarded that way and had suffered exile. If he had, then his prosperity (šālôm; at 9.6-7) would be like the sea and his descendants like the sand on the shore (44.3-4). Ubiquitous water imagery here implies what is immeasurable and uncountable (11.9). Their name would never be cut off, yet such a perpetual name is unconditionally promised in 48.9; 55.13; 56.5.

Babylon is doomed (43.14; 48.14). Israel must leave and proclaim, 'The Lord has redeemed his servant Jacob' (v. 17). The redemption fulfills the hymn in 44.23 (42.10-13). The return from exile is a new Exodus. They do not thirst in the deserts or ruins (44.26) since God makes water gush from the rock (30.23-25; 35.6-7; 43.16-21). However, 'there is no peace [šālôm] for the wicked'. Throughout Isaiah threats of judgment and distinctions between the righteous and the wicked stand in tension with threats of judgment and promises of salvation to the whole people and to the entire world.

Chapter Forty-Nine

49.1-6 (12) is the Second Servant Song (see at 42.1-4 for discussion). I treat vv. 1-13 as a section which closes with a short hymn; it is rich in allusions to its context and other parts of Isaiah. 14–26 are addressed to Zion ('you' is female singular). The summons to the coastlands in v. 1 contrasts with the command to flee in 48.20 and parallels the summons to attend to the Lord's call of 'him' in 48.14-16. The Lord also called and named servant Israel from the womb ('before I was born': 44.2, 24; 46.3; 49.5, 15; 48.8!). Proper naming contrasts with the futility cited in 48.1-2. Unlike the pacifist picture in 42.1-4, yet similar to the shoot in 11.3-4, the servant's mouth is a sword. He is hidden in shadows; 'dark' is here a positive value (4.6; 25.4-5; 32.2; 51.16). The servant is Israel or is another who is here called Israel; this heightens the enigma of an identification for the servant.[1] The Lord is glorified in the servant (pā'ēr: 46.13). However, the servant objects that he has wearied himself for nothing (tōhû). Being hidden and exhausted alludes to God's assurances of support in 40.27-31; the

---

1.   Wilcox and Paton-Williams, 'The Servant Songs'.

situation of vain labor is reversed in 65.23. Israel's cause (*mišpāṭ*: 40.27, 'right') and reward (*pᵉʿullâ*: 40.10, 'work') are with God.

'And now' or 'but now' (48.16) continues or contrasts with the preceding. If the servant is Israel, then how does Israel gather Israel to the Lord? Some posit a distinction between a real and an ideal Israel;[1] others delete 'Israel' in v. 3 so that the servant is not the people;[2] others argue for a change in speaker or subject.[3] I, as with 48.16b, opt for a multiple reading of 'both . . . and'; any servant of the Lord, individual or group, Israelite or foreign, can experience what this servant does. This could include another who is servant and who is now named Israel.

The Lord formed the servant (v. 1; 44.2) to return Jacob, to gather the dispersed; the servant is honored and strong (25.3). This was the servant's past task and it was a comparatively easy one; now the servant, previously in the dark, is 'a light to the nations' (2.2-5; 42.6); the Lord's salvation ('Isaiah') goes 'to the end of the earth' (11.12; 48.20; 5.26!). The Holy One (48.17) speaks to one despised (53.3) and the slave or servant of rulers. ('Despised', *bāzâ*, puns on prey, *bāzaz* 8.1-3; 10.6; 42.22.) This image and the frustration expressed in v. 4 give rise to the phrase The Suffering Servant; his afflictions continue in 50.4-9 and 52.12–53.13. Ultimately the servant is vindicated. Before him kings both rise up and fall down. The Lord is faithful (*ʾāmēn*: 42.3) and has chosen the servant (14.1; 44.1-2).

Humiliation and vindication are a pattern with the servant in 49.1-7; 50.4-9; 52.13–53.12 and with others: Israel, Zion–Jerusalem and all who are oppressed and locked in darkness and who thirst and hunger. The humiliation can be judgment for sin or the result of the violence of the world and of God (especially 13 and 34). Vindication is salvation, restoration and transformation; either it follows upon a return to the Lord, a hearkening to his ways (48.17-19), or it is dramatically declared and then there is return and life (44.21-23).

The Lord speaks in vv. 8-12, although 9b-10 and 12 can be read as comments by the poet. The Lord answers the servant which implies a petition on the servant's part. At one time the Lord does not listen to prayers (1.15); at another he answers

---

1. Whybray, *Second Isaiah*, p. 72.
2. Westermann, *Isaiah 40–66*, p. 209.
3. Muilenburg, 'Isaiah', p. 569; Watts, *Isaiah 34–66*, pp. 182-87.

before he is called (65.24). He answers cries (30.19; 41.17; 58.9), but idols don't (41.28; 46.7). It is 'a time of favor' (*rāṣôn*: 60.10; 61.2); the noun also means 'acceptable' (56.7; 58.5; 60.7). The verb *rāṣâ* occurs in 40.2, 'to be paid, and in 42.1, 'to delight, please'. The notion of a time of favor or vengeance occurs in 34.8; 35.4; 61.2. As in 42.6, the servant is a light and a covenant so that he may establish (*qûm*: 44.26) the land and allot it to the people. Verses 9-10 abound with Isaianic imagery: darkness turning to light; hunger and thirst to satiety; water; protection from the elements (4.5-6; 25.4-5). God has compassion and leads them by a highway over the mountains (40.3-4). In 40.5, the divine glory is seen; in 49.12, the dispersed returning 'from the four corners of the earth' (11.12) are seen. (For MT 'Sinim', see Gen. 10.17.) 'Lo!', *hinnēh*, occurs twice. The Lord's comfort is fulfilled, and all nature celebrates in song. Verse 13 is a hymnic interlude that marks the transition to 14-26 which present Lady Zion and her children. (See 42.10-13; 44.23; 45.8; 48.20 for other interludes.)

Zion. Like Jacob in 40.26, Zion feels abandoned (**'āzab*; at 42.16). 'Forsake' and 'forget', and its corollary 'remember', are leitmotifs in Isaiah. Isa. 49.14–54.17 are characterized by alternating declarations and pictures of desolation, humiliation, and of restoration, vindication, that concern, at different points, Zion–Jerusalem, the servant and the people Israel.

A woman would sooner forget the child in her womb than the Lord, Zion. A depiction, a structural plan, of Zion is on the Lord's hand (44.5; 49.2). In verse 17, 'builders' (*bōnîm*) puns on 'children' (*bānîm*); 'lay waste' is **ḥārēb*, to be dry (at 44.26-27). Verse 18 parallels 12 with the scene of ingathering (11.12; 43.5; 54.7; 56.8; 60.4). The divine oath rounds off 14-18 and connects marriage and childbirth. The theme of innumerable children is developed in 19-21. Zion is now too crowded, too narrow (28.20), but not the narrowness of distress (25.4). Swallowers are far away (6.12); children come from far away (43.6; 60.4, 9). Children born at a time of loss (47.8-9) are troubled because their numbers are too great for crowded Jerusalem. Zion is perplexed at this wondrous event; although barren and alone, she has all 'these' (*'ēlleh*: 3 times) offspring.

Verses 22-26 are two divine speeches divided at 25. The Lord, in a familiar action, raises his hand and signal (5.26; 13.2; 18.3) and the nations participate in the return of Zion's children

(11.10-12). Royalty grovels in the dust before Zion; the high
hand contrasts with the low nobility (v. 7). Zion finally recog-
nizes the Lord (40.21, 28; 41.20) and realizes that those who wait
on the Lord are not ashamed (25.9; 30.18; 33.2; 40.31; 41.11!). A
rhetorical question, similar to the one in v. 15, stresses the miraculous nature of the Lord's intervention. Prey is not taken, but
God rescues Zion from the tyrant. Echoing 41.11-13, he contends
with her contenders; he saves her children (v. 8). In a gruesome
contrast with vv. 9-10, the Lord gives the oppressors flesh and
blood as food and drink. 'And *all flesh* will know' that the Lord
redeems Zion (40.5; 44.6; 45.3-6; 60.16.)

Chapter Fifty
Chapter 49 proclaims the restoration of the servant, the people
and Zion. The Lord uses rhetorical questions to affirm Zion's
salvation and, in 50.1-2, to denounce people and offset the gran-
deur of 49. In ch. 50, salvation and judgment, righteousness and
sin, are not sharply distinguished or ascribed to totally separate
groups. Chapter 49 is explicitly addressed to Israel and Zion; 50
contains no proper names. Verses 1-2 denounce people who
blame their problems on their mother; Israel, the children of
Zion, may be one of these but not the only one. The Lord didn't
divorce the mother (Zion is one example) or sell the people for
his own gain but because of their sin and rebellion (43.24-28).
The mother suffers because of her children's wrong; this is the
same situation we will encounter with the servant in 53 who
suffers because of 'our' sins.

No one helped the Lord (59.16; 63.5). He called and no one
answered; in this silence, Israel is like an idol (41.28; 48.1, 12;
65.1). God can redeem (*pādâ*: 35.10) and deliver (*nāṣal*: 36.13-20;
42.22). Exodus imagery is employed to show the power to save
(4.5-6; 48.20-21) by destroying the enemy (11.15-16; 19.5-10;
43.16-17). He dries up to save and to ruin. (Note the contrasting
meanings in transforming rivers and desert: 35.6-7; 33.20-23;
34.7-10; 41.18; 42.15; 43.19-20; 44.3-4.) The heavens turn dark
(13.10; 24.21-23) and put on sackcloth; this contrasts with the
bride putting on her ornaments (49.18).

The servant speaks in vv. 4-9 and perhaps 10-11. He has a
disciple's tongue so that he can teach—both NRSV meanings,
teacher and one taught, are contained in *limmēd* (2.4; at 8.16-
17; 48.17)—and sustain the weary (35.3; 40.27-31). The Lord
wakens, rouses, him as he did Cyrus (41.2, 25). Unlike so many

others, the servant listens; he is not a rebel who turns back (1.4; 42.17). Not only did he not strike as the servant in 42.1-4, but he was struck and insulted. Now that the Lord helps him (v. 9; 44.2), he is not insulted or ashamed (49.23). A number of verbs and nouns, which I do not distinguish in my commentary, convey the idea of shame, disgrace, insult and humiliation which is a significant image for punishment: 1.29; 4.1; 22.15-25; ch. 23; 30.1-5; 41.11; 45.16-17; 54.4; 61.7.

'To vindicate, acquit' is *ṣādaq and implies a juridical context (at 1.21 and 5.23). (For 'near', see at 46.12-13.) Those who contend with (rîb: 3.14-15) the servant and are his adversaries are summoned into court with the technical phrases 'stand up together' and 'confront'. Since the Lord is there to help, who can convict him (from *rāšaʻ: to be guilty; at 5.23)? (The noun is rāšāʻ, the wicked or guilty: 3.11; 11.4; 14.5; 48.22; 57.20-21.)

The opponents 'wear out like a garment'; the moth eats them. Eating is a ubiquitous image beginning with the aliens in 1.7 and ending with those eating swine in 66.17. The imagery of 50.9 is repeated in 51.6-8. The clothing image occurs in 11.5; 14.19; 49.18; 50.3; transience is signified by chaff (29.5; 40.24), a dream (29.7-8) and mist (44.22); insects occur in 7.17-19; 33.4; 40.22.

'Who?' (v. 10) was used three times in vv. 8-9. Four positive terms—to fear, obey/listen to, trust (12.2) and lean on (10.20; 30.12; 42.17)—frame two negatives—walk in darkness (9.2) and without light (4.5). Trust offsets the dark. 'But all of you' generalizes the castigation of vv. 7-8 and turns it against the people of vv. 1-2. The accusation employs fire imagery: kindlers (64.2) who gird on torches (11.5), walk in the flame (or light) of fire (9.18) and torches. The latter parodies v. 10 and 9.2. The Lord unexpectedly speaks at the close of v. 11. This is their fate 'from my hand': they lie down in pain. ('Pain' puns on 'idol': 46.1.) People lie down in peace (11.6-7; 14.30; 17.2; 27.10) or in death (14.8, 18; 43.17).

Chapter Fifty-One

Verses 1-8 break into three divine speeches, each introduced by 'Listen!' in vv. 1, 4 and 7 (two verbs are used). In 1-2, the Lord returns to the positive classes in 50.10 and adds those who pursue righteousness and seek the Lord (45.19; 65.1). This maintains the distinction between those who seek the Lord and those who are far from him; this is a traditional distinction that Isaiah employs at the same time on another level to separate those who accept his vision from those who don't (see at 45.19 for discussion). The people must look to the rock and quarry from which they come (8.14!; 17.10; 26.4; 30.29; 44.8); these are both the Lord and their ancestors Abraham and Sarah (41.8). God blessed Abraham and he grew from few to many; the same can happen with Zion. In v. 3 the poet comments on the Lord's declaration. He repeats 'for' and brings together themes of comfort (12.1; 40.1; 49.13), transformation of nature (29.17; 41.17-20) and joy (9.3; chs. 12; 35; 44.23). The dry—waste, wilderness and desert—becomes wet and fertile like Eden, the garden of God (at 37.35). The poet goes back to Genesis 2 (see 45.18-19 for Genesis 1).

The two speeches in vv. 4-6 and 7-8 repeat familiar words and themes. Teaching (*tôrâ*) goes forth (1.10; 2.3; 42.2-3); his justice (*mišpāṭ*) is a light to peoples (42.6; 49.6). The roles of teaching, justice and the servant overlap; as I noted in my comments on the servant at 42.1-9, doing God's work is the issue, not the identity of who does it. God brings near deliverance (*ṣedeq*; 46.12-13) and salvation and his arms rule (*šāpaṭ*: at 1.21). Coastlands wait and hope (8.17; 25.9; 33.2; 42.4; 49.23). The people look up and down as heavens and earth vanish (5.30; 8.21-22; 49.18). Smoke is here a symbol for transience, not fire. Like his word, the Lord's salvation is forever. He focusses on those who know righteousness—this can also be 'those who experience deliverance'. 'Fear not!' is the war oracle (at 35.4; 43.1; 44.2). 'Reproach' and 'reviling' characterized the Assyrian defiance in ch. 37; God gave Jacob up to 'reviling' in 43.28. The opponents are transient (50.9), but deliverance and salvation, reversed in order from v. 6, are forever; the repetition rounds off the divine calls and assurances in 4-8 and 1-3.

The poet, in response to the promises, calls the Lord's Arm to rouse and act. (For the power of the 'arm', see v. 5; 30.30; 33.2; 40.10-11; 52.10, 53.1; 59.16; 62.8; 63.5, 12.) 'Arm' and 'you' are female singular and the Lord is addressed as a woman. 'Awake' is the verb 'to rouse, stir up' (13.17; 41.2, 25; 45.13); in 51.17 and 52.1, the command is addressed to another woman, Jerusalem–Zion. The arm puts on strength (12.2) as in the past. It hewed Rahab, the dragon (27.1; 30.7), and dried up sea (44.27; 50.2), the waters of the Deep (Gen. 1.2; Exod. 15.5, 8). The combat myth of creation transmutes into the Exodus, the creation of Israel; the depths of sea become a way for the redeemed (Isa. 35.8-10; 40.3-4). Verse 11 repeats 35.10 with the themes of return and joyous song (51.3).

The Lord reacts, in vv. 12-16, as though the call emanated from fear. He is emphatic, 'I, I comfort' so why fear a mere human (vv. 3, 6-8; 2.22; 40.6-8)? Israel forgets the Lord (17.10) but the Lord doesn't forget Israel (49.14-15); therefore past distress is forgotten (54.4; 65.16). The Lord is Maker of Israel (17.7; 29.16) and Creator of heaven and earth (40.12-26). The oppressor whose wrath Israel fears is not identified and can be both foreigner and Israelite. 'Released' (v. 14) is from 'to open, loosen' which occurs in a variety of contexts of weal and woe: 24.18; 26.2; 35.5; 41.18; 45.1; 58.6; 60.11. Death is going down to the Pit (14.15, 19; 38.17-18); life and death are contrasted in vv. 12-14.

The Lord repeats 'I' in v. 15 to affirm his personal power. (See 5.29-30 and 17.12-14 for the image of the raging sea.) The poet interrupts to proclaim the divine name (47.4; 48.2). God's actions in v. 16a parallel his treatment of the servant (49.2; 50.4) and of Israel (59.21). As creator of the world, he proclaims Zion 'my people'; this is the reverse order of the analogous proclamation in v. 13. This is the only time in Isaiah that Zion is addressed as male; 'you' is masculine singular. Servant, Zion, Israel and others tend to merge since they all are recipients of God's saving acts; the acts are important, not the specific identity of their beneficiary (at vv. 4-6).

The prophet urges Jerusalem to awake. She, in a dark twist on the drinking motif, has drunk deeply from the cup of the Lord's wrath (vv. 13, 17, 20, 22; 42.25). Despite all her children, there is no one to lead her (40.11; 49.10), to take her by the hand (45.1). She grieves alone. Her children are exhausted and, like her, full of her God's wrath and rebuke (50.2). Because of Jerusalem's misery, there is a divine response. The cup is given to her tormentors (49.26). She is wounded, afflicted (*ʿⁿniyyâ*: 54.11); this is the term for the oppressed and divinely protected poor (3.14-15; 10.2; 14.32; 32.7; 41.17; 66.2). She is drunk with wrath, not wine (29.9!); God pleads the people's cause (*rîb*; see 1.17, 23; 50.7-9 for the juridical metaphor.) Her tormentors have walked on her prostrate body (5.25; 10.6; 26.5-6); like the servant, she offers her back (50.6). The image is abject humiliation and filth.

Chapter Fifty-Two

The prophet or God, responding to lowliness, calls Zion to awake and put on strength (51.9, 17). The holy city (48.2) is clothed in beauty (*tip'eret:* at 46.13). As in the Holy Way, there are no unclean in her (35.8-9). She who has been in the dust (29.4; 51.23) rises (*qûm*); the captive opens her chains (51.14).

Verses 3-6 are difficult at best.[1] They do not accord with the style or content of the context and may be a later insertion that encapsulates some of the book's main points. If they are an insertion, this is unusual since I, unlike most other commentators, do not find many, if any, other examples of insertions. The people were sold for nothing and redeemed for nothing (50.1; 55.1-2). ('You' in v. 3 is masculine plural and 'my people' is masculine singular in 4-6.) Oppression in Egypt and Assyria are associated as in 11.15-16 (19.23-25!) but without reference to the way of return. Verse 5 is obscure and translations vary. The Lord's name is a central Isaianic theme; 'Here am I', *hinnēnî*, anticipates the same declaration in 65.1.

Verses 7-10 are a joyous celebration of the Lord's salvation of Zion; the poet gathers many of the positive themes and images of 40–51. The feet of the 'herald of good tidings' (40.9) are beautiful. The beauty resides in action, in announcing peace and salvation. Zion's God reigns (6.7; 24.23; 33.22; 41.21). Unlike other sentinels who see an army advancing (21.1-10), Zion's sentinels sing for joy at the Lord's approach. Ruins rejoice because the Lord comforts and redeems (44.23; 49.13). He bares 'his holy arm' (51.9); 'all the ends of the earth see the salvation of *our* God' (40.5; 41.20; 45.5).

The people and the nations—vv. 11-12 address a plural group—are commanded to depart 'from there', from Babylon itself (48.20-21) and from the bondage symbolized by Babylon. The contrast of unclean and pure allude to v. 1 and anticipate the cultic imagery in 56–66. They depart in calm order, not in panic since God is both advance and rear guard (4.5-6; 58.8). 51.1–52.12 is explicitly concerned with Zion and Israel in contrast to both the preceding (50) and the following.

Isaiah 52.13–53.12. I do not use a title for this section since it would focus on 'the servant' and all the attendant problems of historical identification.[2] I have been influenced by Clines who approaches the poem on its own terms, locates its force in its

1.   See Muilenburg, 'Isaiah', pp. 608-609, and Watts, *Isaiah 34–66*, pp. 214-15, for discussion of details.
2.   Clines, *Isaiah 53*, p. 11.

ambiguity, in its refusal to yield precise information, and argues for open, multiple interpretations (pp. 25-33). In my reading I indicate parallels and ties to other parts of Isaiah to demonstrate the openness, the multiple levels of meaning.

The servant goes from obscurity and denigration to prominence and vindication. This matches the transformation sketched for Jerusalem in 51.17–52.12 and for the woman in 54. The Lord calls attention—*hinnēh*—to his servant who prospers and is wise (the word has both meanings: 41.20; 44.18). In lectures, Frank Cross has argued that this is a name, Yaskil, in accord with Isaiah's penchant for naming. The servant is on high; the three verbs are intensified by 'very'. He is with the Lord (6.1; 33.5-16), not with the proud (2.9-21; 14.9-20).

In vv. 14-15, God draws a distinction between the one and the many (nations and kings) and between a past of humiliation and a present and future of wonder. A precise time frame or chronology is not given; it is transformation over a period of time that is stressed, not a particular historical era for the change. Many were astonished; he didn't even look human. (In MT, 14a is addressed to the servant.) But now many nations (including Israel?) are startled and shocked into silence.[1] They see what had not been related to them and understand (1.4!) what they had not heard. This continues Isaiah's series of complex relationships between hearing-seeing and understanding-knowing: 5.18-19; 6.9-10; 26.7-12; chs. 28–30; 41.20; 43.8-10; 45.1-6; 48.1-8.

Chapter Fifty-Three

'We' speak in contrast to 'him'. 'We' are part of the ambiguity of the poem. Is this Israel or part of Israel as in 1.9; 2.5; 42.24? Is this another mark of a division between 'we' who truly realize the nature of the servant and 'they' who do not, a division that can be related to that between those who do and do not accept Isaiah's vision? (See 42.24; at 45.19). Are 'we' the nations and kings of 52.15 (49.7, 23; 62.2)? However understood, 'we' undergo a transformation in comprehension that is associated with 'his' transformation from humiliation to vindication. How and why 'we' change is not explained.

---

1. See Clines, *Isaiah 53*, pp. 14-15; Watts, *Isaiah 34-66*, pp. 224-30.

'To believe' is the significant root *'āmēn*. The second question is answered in 52.10: he shows his arm to all nations. 'He' began as a sprout, a root in dry ground; plant and dryness imagery are familiar. The opposition of appearance and reality is a major theme in Isaiah. The people confuse good and evil (5.20-22); the shoot does not judge merely by what he sees and hears (the word 'appearance' is in 11.3; 52.14–53.3). The contrast of true and false trust and security and the condemnation of the idols are other aspects of this opposition. At the level of the book, Isaiah is speaking of his vision which appears as worthless to many but which is, in reality, the Lord's vision.

The servant appears to be nothing but is wondrous; an idol appears to be solid but is nothing. The servant is not 'desired' and idols are 'delighted in' (44.9). As in 49.7, 'despised' puns on the word for 'prey'; v. 3 intensifies the image of degradation. The servant's (Israel's) fate in 49.1-12 is similar to that of the servant in 53. 'To hold of no account' is *ḥāšab*, to think and regard; it can refer to confusing appearance and reality (2.22; 29.16; 40.15-17) and to transformation (29.17; 32.15). In 55.7-9, the noun 'thoughts' occurs in a passage emphasizing the essential incompatibility of the divine (reality) and the human (appearance). (See the comments at 40.12-31.) Verse 4 restates the opposition. 'Surely' he carried our infirmities, but 'we'—the pleonastic pronoun occurs— 'thought' that he was afflicted by God (50.1; 51.21). 'But he'—the pronoun accentuates the contrast— was crushed because of our rebellion and sin (50.1). He effected our wholeness (*šālôm*). Sickness and health recall the beaten body of 1.5-6, illness in 10.18 and 17.4 and healing in 19.22; 30.26; 57.18-19. 'We' wander (at 35.8; 47.15). Erring, going one's own way, is a central image for sin. 'And the Lord', he puts our sin on him.

Unlike previous depictions of the, or a, servant, 'he' does not act; 'he' is the passive recipient of human rejection and mockery and of divine affliction and divine exaltation. Afflicted, he is as silent as a lamb led to slaughter; he does not 'open' his mouth. He is taken unjustly and no one gives a thought to his fate. Hezekiah thinks that he is with the dead (38.9-18), and 'he' is treated as though he were dead, 'cut off from the land of the living', in his 'grave' and 'tomb'. (Parallels with the king of Babylon in ch. 14 and Shebna in 22.15-25 emphasize the context of sin and death.) But 'he' has done and said nothing. 'And the Lord', he is delighted (*ḥāpēṣ*: 44.28) to crush him. Somehow in this process (the first part of v. 10 is unclear), he sees his children and lengthens his life. This is analogous to Zion's experience in 49.18-21. The Lord's delight prospers in him as it did in Cyrus (48.15). Verse 11 is unclear although it does contain themes of transformation, bearing the sins of others, and the one and the many.

Divine statements open and close the poem. The Lord lets him split booty with powerful warriors; he shares in the joy of the people (9.3-5). This outcome is not the result of victory but of near fatal humiliation. The poem closes with death, rebellion and sin and thereby taints the servant's vindication and exaltation. This effect anticipates the final verse of the book.

Chapter Fifty-Four

The chapter forms a pair with 52.13–53.12. The latter is about an unnamed man; this, an unnamed woman. Zion-Jerusalem is named in 51–52 but not in 54. The chapter 'is not a story about Jerusalem . . . It is about a woman . . . there is not a single word in it [54.1-10] that refers exclusively to the city'.[1] The grimness of the servant poem is countered and bracketed by joyous song in 52.7-10 and 54.1 (for joy, see at ch. 61). 'The barren who has not born' alludes to Sarah (51.2; Gen. 11.30) just as much as to Jerusalem. The children of the desolate are as many as of the married; the latter term is applied to Jerusalem in Isa. 62.4.

Expansion is the response to crowding (49.19-20); it is a tent, not a city, that is enlarged (4.5-6; 26.15; 33.20). The war oracle, Fear not!, is addressed to a woman as in 40.9. Verse 4 abounds with Isaianic terminology—shame (three verbs); forget; and (not) remember. Widowhood is past (43.18). The woman has a husband, a lord (26.13; 62.4-5), with several names: Maker, Lord of Hosts, Holy One, Redeemer and God of the Entire World. He is called by these names, and he has called her. Like a woman forsaken, forsaken in spirit (the repetition of ʿazûbâ is elided in translation), he comes to her; she was cast off. In v. 7-8, the past harshness is offset by present compassion.

The poet speaks in vv. 1-6; the rest of the chapter is a divine speech.

> God is represented as behaving like a remorseful husband, pleading with his wife to trust him and take him back . . . He

1.   Sawyer, 'Daughter of Zion', p. 94.

sets aside all hardness and pomposity, the frightening manifestations of his power . . . and comes to her, on bended knee as it
were, to plead with her to let bygones be bygones and start again
(Sawyer, 'Daughter of Zion', pp. 95-96).

The notion of a limit to God's anger was anticipated in 6.11-13;
10.25; 40.1-2; 47.6; 48.9 and is repeated in 57.14-19. (See 64.5, 9
for the people's petition for an end to divine wrath.) Compassion,
mercy and pity are a pervasive theme: vv. 8, 10; 14.1; 30.18;
49.10, 13, 16; 55.7; 60.10; 63.7; the absence of mercy is noted in
9.17; 13.18; 27.11; 47.6; 63.15. 'Gather' is the return (11.12; 40.11;
49.18; 56.8). God hides his face for weal (45.15) and woe (8.17;
57.17; 59.2; 64.7). 'Love' is *hesed*: v. 10; 55.3; see at 16.5.

Verses 9-10 are a divine oath analogous to that in Gen. 9.8-17
(See v. 1 and 51.2-3 for other Genesis allusions.) God forswears
his wrath (v. 8) and rebuke (51.2). Mountains and hills may pass
(50.6) but not the Lord's love and covenant of peace (42.6; 49.8;
55.3). The woman is afflicted and not comforted (49.13!; 51.21;
52.9!). Verse 11b is a scene—*hinnēh* with a participle: 'See! I am
setting . . .' The woman gleams with brilliant jewels. Muilenburg
notes that 'pinnacles' is a pun on 'sun' and refers to the 'parts of
a building that gleam in the sun'.[1] Verses 11-12 use the city metaphor to describe the woman: stones and foundations (28.16),
gates and wall; this does not make the woman Jerusalem. ('Precious' is *hēpeṣ*, 'delight, purpose': 48.14; 53.10.) Her children are
taught (48.17; 50.4) and prosperous, a manifestation of the covenant of peace (*šālôm*; at 9.6-7). She is established in righteousness (2.2; 62.7); God establishes both royal authority and the
earth (9.7; 16.5; 45.18). She is far from oppression and terror; see
46.12-13 and 49.19 for the antithesis of near and far. 'Do not
fear' repeats from v. 4. If someone instills fear, it is not the Lord;
and if they do, they fall.

The Lord creates darkness and evil (45.7) in the form of a
smith who works with fire to produce a weapon, not an idol
(40.19; 44.9-20). A weapon has work to do, but an idol has no
purpose. Although God creates the smith and the destroyer (13.5;
14.20; 36.10; 37.12; 51.13), no weapon can succeed (48.15) against
the woman. In v. 17, the Lord shifts from a military to a juridical
metaphor (see at 50.7-9). She will confute or convict any who rise
in court (*mišpāṭ*) to accuse her.

1.   Muilenburg, 'Isaiah', p. 639

The last sentence in 54 stands as a summarizing comment on the preceding and on all of the positive, salvific aspects of 40–54. 'This' contrasts this outcome with that of the torment of the fire-brands in 50.11. The servant transforms into 'the servants, the worshippers, of the Lord'. These, in the rest of Isaiah, are those who hope in the Lord and inherit (*nāḥal*) his holy mountain (57.13). 'Heritage' (*naḥᵃlâ*) refers to the people Israel in 19.25; 47.6; 63.17 and to the land in 49.8 and 58.14. 'Vindication' (*ṣᵉdāqâ*) is 'righteousness' in v. 14 and 'deliverance' in 51.6-8.

Chapter Fifty-Five

This is a transitional chapter looking back to 40–54 (and previous) and anticipating 56–66. The Lord speaks in vv. 1-4 (5) and 8-11; the poet in (5) 6-7; and both in 12-13. The poet accents the themes of newness and transformation with a call, in the center of the chapter, for the wicked to change while there is time. The chapter is inclusive. Israel is addressed only in v. 5; otherwise the people who come to the Lord come from both the nations and Israel.

Transformation is indicated in the first word, Ho! (*hôy*), which is an exclamation and not an introduction to a Woe! Oracle as in 45.9-10 and chs. 28–31. Eating and drinking are common images for salvation (30.23-25; 33.16; 41.17-18; 5.13!; 36.16-17!); buying without money is a new theme although Cyrus saves Israel without reward (45.13). Verse 2 revolves around the distinction of the true and the false (at 53.1-6). The people weary themselves pursuing futile goals (40.28-31); true food, life, is found in listening to the word of the Lord (1.19; 58.13-14). The Lord makes an eternal covenant (54.10; 61.8) which is his old 'steadfast, sure love for David' (*ḥesed*; *'āmēn*: 16.5), now transformed. David was a witness to and leader of peoples; 'you' (masculine singular) call nations that do not know you (see Ps. 18.43-45; Isa. 45.3-6). The Lord glorifies 'you'. *Pā'ēr (at 46.13) implies beauty and brilliance and recalls 'the light of the Lord' in 2.2-5.

All should seek the Lord while he is near (46.12-13); this implies a time of decision, of final judgment, which is developed at greater length in the following chapters, especially 65–66. The wicked, in particular, should leave their way and return to the Lord and his ways. 'Our God' will have mercy on them (54.8-10). The distinction between 'we' (the righteous) and 'they' (the wicked) re-enters (1.27-28; 42.24; 50.11; 54.17). (For 'seek', see 1.17; 9.13; 11.10; 31.1; 58.2; 65.1, 10.)

The wicked (*rāša‘*) are the evil, the guilty, in moral, religious and juridical terms; they are called back to the traditional ways of the Lord. On another level, they are opponents of Isaiah's interpretation of the ways of the Lord. In vv. 8-9, a theological and a rhetorical point are made. Divine ways are not human ways (see at 40.12-13; 53.3); the contrast is strengthened through the familiar antithesis of high and low. Rhetorically, Isaiah tells his audience that his interpretation of divine thoughts and ways is radically different from other interpretations. However, his interpretation and vision are accurate and effective. He, still in the voice of God, compacts the antithesis of heaven and earth. Water comes from and returns to the heavens, but not without soaking the earth and making it produce food (30.23-25). (For 'sprout', see 42.9; 43.19; 45.8.) The simile, 'for as . . . so will', is completed in v. 11. The comparison of food and God's word echoes vv. 1-2 and hearkens back to his word of comfort in 40.1-9 and to the connection of listening and eating in 1.19-20. In the latter 'the mouth of the Lord' speaks (45.23; 48.3; 58.14). The effectiveness and success of the word in its mission, in what it was sent for (6.8; 9.8; 48.16; 61.1), is a central theme and a delayed response to the Rabshakeh's question, 'Indeed, is a word of the lips counsel and strength for war?' (36.5) ('Accomplish' is *‘āśâ*, 'to do'; 'purpose' is 'to delight in', *ḥāpēṣ*; for 'succeed', see 48.15; 54.17!)

The chapter closes with both going out and coming back; mountains and hills celebrate the return (44.23; 49.13; 54.10). Thorns and briers turn to cypress and myrtle (41.19). The transformation is signalled in Hebrew by the changing terms for thorns and briers in 5.6; 7.24-25; 10.17; 32.13 and 33.12; the 'thorn' of v. 12 is also in 7.19 but the 'brier' is only here in Isaiah. In line with my rhetorical reading, 'it (shall be)', in the last half of v. 13, refers to the Lord's word, the book of Isaiah, which stand for and are a sign of the returned and restored people and the transformation of humanity and nature. It is a memorial, a name, and 'an eternal sign that will not be cut off (48.9, 19; 56.5). Although important to this point, name and naming are even more significant in 56–66. Signs occur in 1–39 in connection with Ahaz (7.11-14), Isaiah (8.18; 20.3), Egypt (19.20) and Hezekiah (37.30–38.22); these are signs that may be fulfilled in their time but that can also point beyond themselves to a distant future (8.18), a time of birth (7.14) and life (chs. 37–38).

Chapter Fifty-Six

The formula 'Thus says the Lord' last occurred in 51.22 and 52.3-4. Verses 1-2 are a keynote, a statement of principle; the verbs *šāmar*, to maintain, keep, refrain from, and *'āśâ*, to do, occur three times each and stress action including the positive avoidance of evil. Verse 1 is similar to 55.6 except that justice and right (*ṣᵉdāqâ*) are the object. There is a sense of urgency since the Lord's deliverance (*ṣᵉdāqâ*) is near. (For 'revealed', see 40.5; 53.1.) Happy the mortal (51.12!) who holds to the Lord's way (30.18; 32.20). It is usually the Lord who holds and supports (8.11; 41.9; 45.1); now humans must respond to the divine guidance. In 1.10-15 the prophet depicted the profanation of sabbath and cult; this was where I first discussed Isaiah's use of cultic imagery and terminology. (See chs. 37–38; 43.22-24; 52.11-12 for other examples of such use.)

In 56.3-7, the prophet, speaking for himself and quoting God, presents an inclusive view of the ideal community of Israel; this is a major aspect of Isaiah's view that others are objecting to. Foreigners and eunuchs are two groups representative of those who could be excluded from the community. Foreigners are those already outside who should not be let in under any circumstances (see Ezek. 44.1-14); eunuchs are those on the inside who are excluded for reasons of physical deformity or such (see Deut. 23.1-2). (Note the chiastic presentation of foreigner and eunuch in Isa. 56.3-6.) They can join the community if they keep the sabbath and hold to the covenant. Isaiah is doing a balancing act between a defined community with strict requirements and rules and an undefined community with no limits or borders. Sabbath and covenant represent religious, social and political standards which, however, are not reduced to strict codification.

'Foreigner' is *nēkār* (2.6; 28.21; 60.10); other terms for foreigner and alien are *zār* (1.7; 17.10; 25.2; 28.21; 61.5) and *gēr* (5.17; 14.1). As I have noted at other points, the numerous and varied references to foreigners, the nations, fit with Isaiah's inclusive, universalist thrust. His vision places Israel, the redeemed community, in the context of redeemed and restored nations and nature; the Lord has created the entire world and all its creatures, not just the land and people of Israel. In 14.1 the *gēr* is joined to the people; in 56.3; the *nēkār* is joined to the Lord and fears separation from the people. Being with the Lord is not coterminous with political or national affiliation with Israel. On the other hand, being with the Lord and trusting in him is belonging to the ideal community called 'Israel'.

The eunuch should not consider himself a dry tree, a symbol of infertility and transience (1.29-30; 15.6; 40.6-8, 24). The counter to these worries is the divine word in vv. 4-5. Besides sabbath and covenant, the eunuch should choose (7.15-16) what pleases the Lord (*ḥāpēṣ*, at 44.28; 55.11.) 'House' and 'walls' imply temple and Zion-Jerusalem (54.11-12) which, in their turn, symbolize God's holy mountain, the site where his people gather. A foreigner can be joined to the Lord, can dwell with his people on the holy mountain, without being physically present in the actual city Jerusalem. As I said of the highway image in 40.3-5, literal and actual places and people, Zion and Israel, modulate quickly into symbolic sites occupied by metaphorical travellers who have come to the Lord's holy mountain.

Eunuchs have 'a monument and a name' (*yād wāšēm*) that is better than children; this is a striking promise in view of the constant assurance of children as a sign of salvation (43.5-7; 44.1-5; 48.18-19!; 49.14-22; 54.13). They have an everlasting name (55.13) even without descendants. Foreigners can minister to the Lord (60.7, 10) and love his name. Love includes notions of recognition, acknowledgement and acceptance (41.8; 43.4; 48.14; 63.9; 66.10). The foreigners are among the Lord's servants and worshippers and share in their heritage (54.17).

All of these, foreigners and eunuchs, the Lord brings to his holy mountain (2.2; 11.9; 27.13; 57.13), his house of prayer (37.14-15; 38.20) and his altar (6.6; 19.19-21; 60.7). The latter are metaphors for the ideal community of worshippers. They are joyful and their sacrifices are acceptable (*rāṣôn*: 42.1; at 49.8; 58.5). Verse 7 summarizes 1-2 and 3-6 and proclaims membership in the community in terms of cult and temple. 'For my house, a house of prayer, is called "For All Peoples"' is a possible translation of the end of v. 7 that respects the Hebrew word order and highlights the naming motif and the inclusivity. Verse 8, 'Saying of the Sovereign Lord' (51.22), is a crescendo, a capstone in vv. 1-8. The Lord, the gatherer of the dispersed of Israel (11.12), gathers even more to those gathered (54.7). The ingathering extends beyond Israel and Judah.

However, this vision of the peaceful mountain of the Lord, which accords with the messianic vision of 11.1-9 and 65.17-25, is not a reality. 56.9-12 are best interpreted as an oracle against violent leaders which reflects the division between leaders and oppressed people that is so prevalent in 1–39.[1] These are Israelite leaders and leaders in general; this is the tension of oppressors and oppressed wherever and whenever found. Adapting Watts,[2] I also see this as Isaiah's citation of a possible objection to the vision of an open community; it would be 'easy pickings for raiders and thieves' both from outside and from within the community.

Wild animals, exploiters of all types, devour (*'ākal*) the people (43.20!); this parodies the call to eat (*'ākal*) and drink in 55.1-2. No one stops the violence. The sentinels are blind and ignorant (52.8!). They are silent, indolent dogs who say and do nothing except eat, both food and people. The shepherds (44.28!) are stupid (1.3) and follow their own way. The parallel with sheep in 53.6-7 contrasts these ineffective and rapacious leaders with a servant leader who suffers for his people and walks in God's ways and with the shoot who destroys the violent. Like rulers of long ago, they think only of eating and drinking because tomorrow brings more of the same, not death (22.12-14; 51.21-23!).

Chapter Fifty-Seven

The diatribe continues in vv. 1-13 and becomes more general; the accusations are against any who act corruptly, not just leaders. The Lord is apparently the speaker (vv. 6, 11-13); he addresses a group in 1-6, 'you' is masculine plural, and a woman in 7-13a, 'you' is feminine singular Most of the charges are cast in cultic terms echoing the positive promises of 56.1-8.

While these people are concerned with their own affairs, the righteous and devout perish and no one gives it a thought. (It is debated whether 1b-2 refer to a violent or a peaceful fate for the pious.) Verse 3 begins the direct attack, 'but you'. The polemical style heaps charge on charge: sorcery (2.6), adultery and harlotry, mockery (37.23; 50.6), rebellion and deceit (28.15-17; 44.20). As in 1.29-31 and 17.10-11, there is involvement in a

---

1.   Muilenburg, 'Isaiah', pp. 661-63; Westermann, *Isaiah 40–66*, pp. 316-19.
2.   *Isaiah 34–66*, p. 255.

nature and fertility cult and even in the abominable Canaanite practice of child sacrifice. Previous rulers slaughtered only sheep for their orgies (22.13; 66.3). 'Valleys' and 'clefts of rocks' refer to low and deathly places (2.9-21).

With v. 6, the Lord addresses the woman—Zion? Babylon? Someone else? 'Valley' (*naḥal*) is 'stream, wadi' and puns on 'heritage', *naḥᵃlâ* (54.17). 'Stream' and 'lot' recall the gruesome and demonic land of ch. 34, the site of the Lord's sacrifice. 'Appeased' occurs in 1.24 as 'pour out my wrath' which appeases the Lord; the word is based on 'to comfort' (12.1; 40.1). 'High and lofty' connotes sin, not the elevation of the servant (52.13). 'Bed' intones the sexual imagery of vv. 3-5. Verses 7-8 develop the image of a mountain sanctuary that is also a brothel. The repetition of 'you have set up' draws a parallel between 'bed' and 'symbol' (*zikkārôn*) that is, a sexual, phallic symbol. The term derives from *zākār*, male, and puns on *zākar*, to remember; with this symbol, the woman demonstrates that she doesn't remember the Lord (v. 11). The woman gazes on her lover's phallus (*yād*), a gross parody of 56.5. She lavishes herself on Molech, an Ammonite god, or on the king, some pagan royal deity. She sends far away for lovers; the Lord sent far way for an army (5.26) and to gather the dispersed (11.12; 41.8-9). She makes a pact with Sheol reminiscent of the Israelites's pact (28.14-19). Although wearied, she does not give up or even weaken; this is the reverse of the servant's persistence (49.1-4).

Similar to 51.12-16, the Lord seeks the source of her fear that caused her to lie and not remember him. Is it because he has been silent (54.7-8) that she does not fear him? This parodies the true situation: fear not others but fear the Lord! Verse 12 is ironic: the Lord tells of her goodness but there is nothing to tell. Neither her works nor her idols can help or deliver (44.9; 47.12, 14); they are blown away (40.24). In contrast, those who seek refuge in the Lord (14.32; 25.4) possess (*nāḥal*) 'my holy mountain' (56.7).

To summarise 56.1–57.13, 56.1-2 present the choice and 3-8, the result of the proper choice, the vision of an accessible and peaceful community. 56.9–57.13a juxtapose the violence and sin of society and of the world that block the realization of the vision. 13b, then, repeats, in different terms, the principle of 56.1-2. 56.1–57.13 present us the dream and the nightmare, now more real than mythic, that stand in tension throughout Isaiah. Isaiah's vision, his dream, is a way of life that, if followed, would

bring about the vision. The circularity is captured in play on
*ṣādaq (56.1). If one pursues righteousness, then one is right-
eous (delivered) and experiences righteousness (deliverance:
51.7).

In ch. 57.14-21 as in 48.17-22, God mixes themes of sin, judgment and salvation and draws a distinction between righteous
and wicked; the verses combine the separate parts of 56.1–57.13.
The highway project (62.10) is renewed; this refers both to a
physical road and to a spiritual, moral way. Isaiah works on both
manifest (literal) and latent (metaphorical) levels and at the
same time (see at 56.1-8; 40.3-5). Hope for return from dispersion and for restoration of the people is manifest; roads, ways,
rebuilding, refer to actual movement and action. Metaphorically,
Isaiah refers to spiritual, moral transformation regardless of
where one actually is and of whether one moves to another physical location. One who trusts in the Lord leaves the old way, her
own way, and follows the Lord's way. An 'obstruction' is a 'stumbling block', physical and moral (3.8; 8.15; 40.30; 63.13). Being
high and holy are major divine attributes (6.1-3). 'To inhabit' and
'to dwell' are both šākēn. The Lord dwells on Zion (8.18) and on
high (33.5); the righteous dwell on high (33.16; 65.9). Yet the
High One dwells with the low and the humble. In Hebrew, as in
English, most of these terms have physical and moral, religious
meanings. 'Contrite' means 'crushed' (3.15; 53.5, 10); 'humble in
spirit' means 'broken, low in spirit' (2.11-17). The Lord gives the
lowly life (38.9).

There is a limit to his wrath (54.7-8); if there were not, all
would be beaten and pulverized (28.23-29). It is because of his
sin that he rages against him (43.22-28; 50.1-3); I leave the
antecedent of 'his' and 'him' indefinite. Verses 17-19 describe a
masculine singular character; the wicked in vv. 20-21 are plural. 'Coveting' alludes to the rulers in 56.11; 'hiding', to the Lord
in 45.15; 54.8. Despite the new way built by the Lord, this people keeps going back to its own way. God sees this yet still heals
(30.26; 53.5), leads and repays them (šālēm: at 9.6-7; at 44.26).

'Peace, peace, to the far and near.' Peace, šālôm, puns on
*šālēm; for 'far and near', see at 46.12-13; 54.10. Although God
heals everyone, the wicked rage and roll like the sea (see 5.30;
27.1; 43.16-17 for related images); they are not at peace or rest.
What the Lord said in 48.22, 'my God' now says. There may be
peace, especially for the contrite and lowly, but this quiet and
calm are only achieved at the cost of violence and destruction;

peace for the righteous means judgment, war and death for the wicked. (See 11.1-9; 14.5-9; 18.3-6 for similar pictures.)

Chapter Fifty-Eight

For Isaiah, this is a comparatively extended statement of what it is to walk in the Lord's ways. It is by no means a list or code of proper behavior, but Isaiah usually speaks of righteousness, trust, faithfulness, in general terms without specification. As I remarked in the Introduction, this accords with a vision that pictures the ideal world and community and doesn't attempt to legislate it. More frequently Isaiah speaks of the negatives, sin and rebellion, both in general and in particular.

In v. 1, God calls a prophet to tell the people of their sins. God, using fasting as an example and as a symbol, details their sin, what is acceptable behavior and the results that will flow from choosing the Lord's way. Verses 1-4 address the people as a group; 6-14, as an individual. Calling is a leitmotif in Isaiah. The trumpet signals judgment (18.3) and the ingathering (27.13). Verse 2 plays upon true and false seeking (53.1-6; 55.6) and delighting in the Lord's ways (ḥāpēṣ); a denunciation in the middle of the verse reveals the emptiness of their apparently positive actions. They don't act righteously ('āsâ ṣᵉdāqâ); they forsake justice ('āzab mišpāṭ); yet they ask for 'righteous judgments' (mišpᵉṭê ṣedeq).

The people ask why God does not acknowledge their fasting; to some extent, he already answered in the first chapter (1.15). 'To humble', 'innâ, is the verb related to 'the poor' (3.14-15) and 'the afflicted' (v. 10; 54.11) whom God watches over. The people try to be both poor and humble—note the combination of the physical and the spiritual—by playing a role. God draws attention—Look!—to what they are actually doing. They serve their own pleasure (ḥēpeṣ).[1] While fasting, they viciously fight amongst themselves; because of this they are not heard 'on high' (32.15; 33.5; 57.15).

With the rhetorical questions in vv. 5-6, the Lord explains the fast he chooses (56.4; note the parallel with his choice of Israel: 44.1; 49.7); this recalls Immanuel's need to choose the good and

---

1.   Watts (*Isaiah 34–66*, p. 268) translates the close of the verse, '[you] suppress all your pains' which reflects the Hebrew better than NRSV 'your workers' and balances 'pleasure'.

reject the evil (7.15-16). A time of playing at being poor and humble is not 'an acceptable day' (*yôm rāṣôn*: 49.8; 56.7; 60.7-10). The proper fast involves freeing others and going out from oneself to help others. Lack[1] refers to this as 'The Exodus in Place' in which one does not have to actually move. 'What changes is the relation to things, the manner of being and possessing' (p. 134). The change is expressed in familiar terms and images; divine treatment of the oppressed and miserable should be mirrored in humans' treatment of each other. Major examples are; loosening and opening: 35.5-6; 42.6-7; 49.8-11. Letting go free: 32.20; 45.13. Breaking a yoke: 9.4; 10.27; 14.25; 47.6! Feeding the hungry: 5.13!; 25.6-7; 30.23-25; 33.16; 44.12!; 49.9-10; 55.1-2; 56.11-12!

The prophet commissioned in v. 1 speaks in 8-11; prophet and Lord merge in vv. 12-14. The prophet employs typical light and garden imagery and casts the statement in a clear 'if . . . then' framework. If the people keep the true fast, then light breaks forth as waters break forth (35.6). 'Dawn' and 'spring up' ('sprout': 42.9; 43.19) intone the newness that approaches speedily (51.14). God is again advance and rear guard (52.12). Call is met with answer (19.22; 30.19; 41.17; 49.8; 55.6; 65.24); this is not always the case (1.15; 46.7; 50.2; 65.12; 66.4). God says 'Here I am' (6.8; 52.6; 65.1).

Verses 9b-10a are five more conditions, but there is no mention of fasting. 'Pointing the finger' and 'speaking evil' refer to public derision, defaming (especially in court) and cursing. If they will stop this and care for the needy, then light rises in the dark (8.22–9.2) and gloom is like noon (30.26; 16.3!; 59.9-10!). The Lord guides (57.18) and satisfies (53.11; 55.1-2; 44.16!). The people are like 'a watered garden'; this counters 'the garden without water' of 1.30 and 'the watered [drunk] sword' (34.5) of the demonic land. (See my comment on 'making into a garden' at 37.35.) They are like a spring which does not lie (28.15-17!; 57.11!). In this great day, ruins, 'dry places', are rebuilt and foundations restored (44.26-28; 54.11). A new name is given: Repairer of the Breach; Restorer of Streets to Live in. In the past, hedges and walls were breached (5.5; 22.8-11; 30.13); streets are paths and ways to walk in and live by (42.16; 43.16).

1.   *La Symbolique*, pp. 129-36.

Verses 13-14 are the final set of conditions and results. 'To restore' and 'to refrain from' are forms of the verb *šûb* which means 'to return, repent' (1.27; 44.22; 59.20); the one root ties this entire thematic complex together. The sabbath, the Lord's holy day, is the example as in 56.2-7 (1.10-15), and the concern is to follow God's way, not one's own interests (*hēpēṣ* used twice). The sabbath should be called Delight (55.2) and Honored (43.4; 49.5). If they honor it, then they will have delight. They will ride on heights without crashing down like the king of Babylon (14.12-15); they will feed on Jacob's heritage (54.17; 57.13). 'The mouth of the Lord' fits the feeding image as it does in 1.20.

Chapter Fifty-Nine

The chapter divides into several clear, although intertwined, parts: 1-8; 9-15a; 15b-19; 20-21. In 1-8 a prophet upbraids the people directly ('you' is masculine plural in 1-3) and indirectly 'they' (masculine singular in 4; masculine plural in 5-8). This can relate to a 'we-they' distinction as in 42.24; 'we', that is, 'I' and 'you', are sinful but 'they' are even worse. The verses are a concentration of sin similar to chs. 3 and 5; for example, in vv. 2-4 twelve nouns and phrases for sin are used. 'We', at least, confess our sins in 9-15a. 15b-19(21) are the Lord's violent reaction that ultimately means redemption and covenant for Jacob. Zion and Jacob are named only in the final two verses; otherwise the chapter deals with indefinite and anonymous groups: 'you', 'they' and 'we'. What the Lord does for all, he does for Jacob in particular.

There is nothing wrong with God's hand or ear (50.2) that he has not saved or heard. It is their sins (50.1; 58.1) that have separated them from God (56.3) and hidden his face (57.17). As in 1.4-15 they are a people of sin and blood. Their bodies—hands and fingers (58.9); lips and tongue—are corrupt. (For 'lie', see 28.15; 32.7; 44.20.) Verse 4 contains six short, general statements, all of which have a juridical aspect. 'Justly', 'law' and 'honestly' are based on the three central verbs *ṣādaq*, *šāpaṭ* and *'āmēn* which are also together in v. 14 (at 1.21; 11.4-5; 16.5). The people trust in emptiness (*tōhû*; 30.12; 31.1); conceive and beget iniquity (for similar birth imagery, see 26.18; 33.11). They are snakes and spiders whose eggs bring death and whose webs are useless. 'Hatch' is the same verb as 'break forth' in 58.8; for clothing, see 50.3, 9; 51.6; 58.7; 'works' and 'deeds' are the familiar

ma^{ʿa}śeh and *pōʿal*. Verse 7 expands upon 6b (note 'hands' and
'feet'). They run and hasten (5.18-19; 51.14!; 58.8!) to pour out
blood (42.25). They think (55.7) only of iniquity (vv. 4, 6, 7).
Unlike the Holy Way in 35.8-9 and 57.14-15, highways are filled
with destruction (four separate nouns for 'way' occur in 59.7-8).
There is no peace, justice or knowledge.

'We' confess 'our' sins in 9-15a; 'we' can be 'they', of 4-8, speaking or a separate group. As usual in Isaiah distinctions can be
made but not rigidly or finally; the confession can be read as
spoken by different groups. Like 1-8, the utterance piles up terms
and images to express the sin and futility. Justice is far; righteous, not near (vv. 11, 14; 54.14). Waiting for light or justice but
finding darkness recalls the Lord's 'expecting' ('waiting for') in
the Vineyard Song (5.1-7). Blindness plagues people throughout
Isaiah: 5.12; 6.9-10; 22.11; 29.9-10; 42.18-20; 56.10. The emphasis on gloom and blindness is preparing for their antithesis in
chs. 60–62. The people stumble (57.14!); they growl like bears
and doves (11.7; 38.14). Verse 12 emphasizes 'many' sins by using
four words. Unlike the servant in 50.5, they rebel and turn back;
the servant listens and they speak lies (v. 3). Verses 14-15 are an
impersonal description of the absence of good. Justice and righteousness are far off as in vv. 9, 11; like the people in v. 10, truth
stumbles; uprightness (57.2) cannot enter. Parallel to the accusation in 57.1-2, all who are good are turned to spoil (10.1-4).

The Lord is horrified that there is neither justice nor helper
(50.2), and his arm brings victory, salvation (v. 11). He clothes
himself in righteousness, vengeance and fury. (For 'vengeance',
see 1.24; 34.8; 35.4; 47.3; 61.2; for 'fury, zeal', see 9.7; 26.11;
37.32; 42.13; for wrath, see at 63.3.) He repays his enemies
(*šālēm: 57.18; at 44.26). All, from west to east (43.5; 45.6), fear
his name and glory. He is a flood, as in 8.5-8, driven by a divine
wind (*rûaḥ*).

Verses 20-21 are transitional. They present the effect on
Jacob—named only here in the chapter—of the Lord's coming
and pave the way for 60. The Lord is Redeemer (54.5, 8) for those
who repent (at 58.12-13; 48.18-19). God has a covenant which is
his spirit (*rûaḥ*) on Jacob and his words in his mouth; the words
will never depart from his mouth or that of his descendants. The
passage alludes to the shoot (11.1-2), the servant (42.1; 50.4-6),
an anonymous speaker (48.16), the people (51.16; 55.3) and the
woman (54.10). What the Lord does for Jacob in particular, he
does for all.

Chapter Sixty

Chapters 60–62. They form a section that is framed by the descriptions of the Lord's wrath in 59.15b-19 and 63.1-6 and by the first person, singular and plural, prayers in 59.1-15a and 63.7–64.12.[1] The chapters are a vision of restoration, a vision of brilliance, salvation and abundance of people and wealth; the restored people and city are both a crown and a garden. The chapters are a crescendo, the high point and climax of Isaiah's vision of restored Jerusalem; they weave together all the major Isaianic positive terms, themes and images. To note all the parallels to these chapters would simply be a citation of the book of Isaiah. 60 addresses a woman ('you' is feminine singular); 62, the woman Zion-Jerusalem; and 61, a people ('you' is masculine plural). Although transformed Zion caps the section in 62, I do not therefore limit 60–61 to Zion and the people Israel. This is a vision of transformation and restoration of a woman and of a people. All who are miserable and lowly, including Lady Babylon, can be restored; Zion and Israel are Isaiah's main example and focus but this does not make them the exclusive addressees of 60–61.

Chapter 60. A prophet calls to the woman in 1-3. She rises from lowliness and dust; a new dawn breaks; the Lord's glory arises. The call plays upon high-low and light-dark antitheses (26.14, 19; 51.17; 52.2; 58.8, 10). Her brilliance is accentuated by the darkness over all about her; the gloom of 59.9, and of 5.30 and 8.22–9.2, are reversed. The Lord's glory is seen and nations are drawn to her light; she is a beacon, a signal (2.2-4; 11.10; 40.5).

Similar to Zion in 49.18, the woman looks out upon the ingathering of her many children coming from afar. She is raised on high and bathed in light, and is therefore able to see the return. Sight is connected with radiance, joy and transformation. Transformation is marked on the verbal level. In v. 5, 'radiant' is *nāhar (see Jer. 31.12; Ps. 34.6) which means 'flow' in 2.2; 'river', nāhar, is the noun (59.19). Water turns to light; the people pass through rivers and fire safely (43.2). 'Thrill' is pāḥad which elsewhere denotes abject fear (33.14; 44.11; 51.13). 'Abundance' is the tumult of an attacking army (13.4; 17.12; 29.5-8); it does have

1. See *La symbolique*, pp. 125-28.

a positive connotation in 31.4; 33.3. 'Sea' is threatening in 5.30; 17.12; 'wealth' is an army in 36.2; 43.17.

What were invading and overrunning multitudes now come for the woman's benefit. She is covered with camels and wealth, not darkness (30.6!). Characteristic of chs. 40–66 and different from the specific and historical names in 1–39, the named nations are all traditional and appear first in Genesis, either in the Table of Nations in Genesis 10 or in Abraham's descendants in Gen. 25.1-18. Isaiah's vision is a recapitulation of the promises and hopes of Genesis but expanded to all nations, not just Israel.

Gold and frankincense are acceptable (*rāṣôn*) offerings given with praise (42.8-12; 43.23!; 56.7). Flocks, symbolizing the nations, minister to her (56.6). The restored site is God's altar (56.7) and glorious house (**pā'ēr* is used twice; it occurs six times in all in the chapter: 60.7, 9, 13, 19, 21). The vision is proclaimed in cultic terms which connote wealth, abundance and return. The rhetorical question in v. 8 recalls that in 49.21; doves now symbolize speed of flight, not moaning (59.11). Coastlands wait (51.5; 59.9!) so that they can return the children from far away (v. 4); the children trade places with their previous invaders (49.19). Silver and gold are for wealth, not idols (2.7; 30.22; 40.19; 46.6); the latter were thrown out 'in that day' (2.20; 31.7). Transformation continues as negatives become positive and as 'that day' is realized.

God glorifies the woman as he glorified his house (*pā'ēr*). Foreigners can now join the community and minister; this is anticipated in 56.3-6. The woman is figured as a city in vv. 10-18 (54.11-12). The moment of wrath is over (54.8-9; 57.17) and replaced by favor and mercy (*rāṣôn*; 47.6!). She is not imaged as a fortified and closed city like the city of chaos in 24.11-13; 25.1-3; 26.5-6 and like Jerusalem so often in 1–39. Her gates are open (26.2; 45.1!); 'open' implies sight and release (35.5; 42.6-7; 51.14). Wealth, nations and kings are ubiquitous in Isaiah, although here they appear in a strictly positive sense. Verse 12 is a nationalistic note similar to those in 45.14 and 51.22-23; those who will not serve (55.4-5) are waste (*ḥārēb*).

Lebanon and trees are a mark of glory (35.1-2; 41.19), not of haughty arrogance and pride (2.12-16; 10.18-19). God beautifies and glorifies his sanctuary (43.28!; 63.18!) and foot rest (66.1). Oppressors, afflicters (**'innâ*), bow and grovel. The fact that it is their descendants indicates passage of time; the vision is for the future. The woman, the city, is renamed City of the Lord, Zion of the Holy One of Israel. The woman, symbol of the oppressed and the desolate, becomes Zion, the Lord's holy mountain where all those saved by the Lord dwell. Zion is both the actual city of Jerusalem and the symbolic site for those who take refuge in the Lord.

Transformation is explicitly thematized in v. 15. Abandoned, hated and impassable describes Zion, Babylon (13.19-22) and a host of other cities visited by the Lord's wrath. But this is past; now they are majestic and joyous (at 61.3). ('Majestic' can be glory [2.10; 4.2] or pride [13.11, 19; 14.11]; for the imagery of milk and nursing, see v. 4; 49.23; 55.1.) This is a strange image; the woman is an infant sucking at the breasts of kings! Verse 16 closes with an elaborate title of the Lord that emphasizes knowledge in accord with the proclamations in 11.9 and 49.26.

Transformation is marked in v. 17 by the replacement of the lesser with the greater. Bronze and iron are good (45.2!; 48.4!) but silver and gold are better (v. 9). In 9.10, a similar process of replacement characterized the Israelites's arrogance. But this is not a harsh city. She is ruled by Peace and Righteousness, not the brutal rulers so much in evidence in Isaiah ('taskmaster' is the same root as 'oppress' in 58.3). The violence of war—the negative trio is cited in 59.6-7—is no longer heard (2.4) and the woman calls her walls and gates Salvation and Praise (vv. 6-16). The city is symbolic, not real; it is the Lord's holy mountain and sanctuary that is open to all; it is a glorious site for the saved who joyously praise the Lord. It is hoped that actual Jerusalem can be an embodiment of the symbol and Israel, of the saved.

In vv. 19-20 the prophet returns to the light imagery of vv. 1-3 and alludes to the sun and moon passages of 24.23 and 30.26 (13.10!). The Lord as light and glory (*tip'eret*) shines day and night and never sets (for 'everlasting', see 55.3, 13; 56.5; 59.21). The time of mourning (57.18) is past, fulfilled (*šālēm*: at 9.6-7; 44.26-28; 57.18). Verses 21-22 depict the righteous people who possess the land (57.13). The prophet shifts from light to garden imagery. The people are the Lord's shoot (11.1) that he planted (61.3); Jacob's children are 'the work of his hands' (64.8) as, however, are the Assyrians (19.25) and all creation (45.11). The vision is focussed but not restrictive or exclusive. God is glorified (*pā'ēr*) with the brilliance and beauty of jewels and flowers. The chapter concludes with transformation as the least and smallest become large and mighty; this alludes to Israel's growth in Egypt. 'My ancestor went down into Egypt and lived there . . . few in number, and there he became a great nation, mighty and

populous' (Deut. 26.5). 'Its time' can be a day of salvation or
judgment (13.22); 'quickly, hastening' connotes the same ambiguity (5.19; 8.1-3; 28.16).

Chapter Sixty-One

One who is enspirited, anointed and sent by the Lord speaks in
vv. 1-4 and perhaps in 5-7. The question is not, who is the speaker?;
rather it is, what does it mean to be so endowed and commissioned? (See my discussions of the prophet at 40.6 and of the
servant at 42.1-9 for similar remarks.) Within Isaiah, divine
word, prophetic book, prophet, king, people, shoot, city, woman
and man, foreigner and Israelite, one and many have all filled
this role, or part of it, at different points. According to 61.1-4, to
be so endowed is to proclaim and thereby to effect liberty and
restoration; the book of Isaiah proclaims just this. Whether anything is thereby effected is up to us and to other readers of the
book.

Verses 1-4 are a concentration of Isaianic terminology and
imagery for deliverance; I note some parallels in the order of the
verses. Zion and a messenger bring good news (40.9; 52.7; 60.6
'proclaim'). The oppressed are the afflicted, the poor (3.14-15;
58.7; 60.14); the Lord binds and heals (30.26). The broken-hearted
are analogous to the crushed at heart in 57.15; there are both
physical and spiritual senses in the phrases. 'Release' is 'to open'
(37.17; 60.11). There are two verbs for 'to open' in Isaiah; they
occur together in 35.5. The year of favor and of vengeance is both
judgment and salvation (34.8; 49.8; 63.4). 'Comfort' and 'mourn'
are themes that punctuate the book (3.26; 12.1; 24.4; 33.9; 40.1;
57.18). A garland (*p⁽ᵉ⁾ēr*: 44.13) replaces ashes (*'ēper*: 44.20) as a
'literal' symbol of transformation (60.17).

Gladness, *śāśôn*, occurs in 12.3; 22.13!; 35.10; 51.3, 11; it is
from *śûś, to be glad, rejoice (35.1; 61.10; 62.5; 65.18-19). A second noun, *māśôś*, joy and gladness, is in 24.8; 32.13-14; 60.15;
62.5; 66.10. The one root ties together many of the passages of
joy or absence of joy; I note several other roots in the following
comments.

The Righteous Oaks glorify the Lord (60.21). This is a new
name (1.29!) for the people who have received the proclamations
and experienced liberation. They, the liberated, build 'the ancient
ruins', fulfilling 44.26-28 and 58.12, and 'the devastations'. For
the image of devastation and desolation, see 1.7; 5.9; 13.9; 33.8;
49.8, 19; 54.1; 62.4. As in 60.10, foreigners care for flocks and

vines while 'you' (masculine plural) are named priests and min-
isters (56.6; 66.21) and enjoy the wealth (*kābôd*) of nations (60.5).
The people's shame and disgrace (at 50.6-7; 54.4) were double;
therefore, they possess (60.21) double the land and the joy. Joy is
*śāmaḥ: 9.3; 14.8!; 22.13!; 25.9; 35.10; 51.3, 11; 55.12; 65.13;
66.10.

The Lord speaks in vv. 8-9. Love implies close association
(56.6) and hate, total separation (1.14; 60.15). 3.13-15 and 10.1-4
reflect the incompatibility of justice (*mišpāṭ*) and robbery. Faithfulness is a divine attribute, although not always a human one
(48.1). 'The everlasting covenant' was broken in 24.5 and established in 55.3; 59.21. The fact that 'their descendants' will be
known by all reflects the same awareness of a passage of time as
in 60.14. 'Bless', on the other hand, is not a frequent term,
although it does occur in significant contexts: 8.2 (Jeberechiah);
19.25; 51.2; 65.16.

The one sent rejoices (*śûś*) and exults because the Lord clothes
him in salvation (59.17) as a bridegroom and bride deck themselves (*pā'ēr*). (See 54.1-6 for marriage imagery.) 'Exult' is *gîl,
another word for joy: 9.3; 25.9; 29.19; 35.1-2; 41.16; 49.13; 65.18-
19; 66.10. Verse 11 presents a simile, 'as . . .', and the compared
action, 'he causes . . .', in the reverse order of v. 10. The two com-
parisons in vv. 10-11 therefore begin and end with divine action.
Plant and garden imagery repeat from v. 3 (60.21); 'shoot' and
'spring up' are from *ṣāmaḥ: 4.2; 42.9; 43.19; 45.8; 58.8; 55.10.
(Note the pun with *śāmaḥ, to rejoice.) Righteousness and praise
grow in the sight of all nations which parallels the recognition
described in v. 9.

Chapter Sixty-Two

The one commissioned by the Lord carries out the general and
inclusive commission by unceasingly proclaiming the particular
salvation and restoration of Zion. Verses 1-5 continue the imagery
of brilliance, beauty and marriage. Being silent is a divine attribute
elsewhere: 42.14; 57.11; 64.12; 65.6; resting is human: 7.4; 30.15;
32.17; 57.20; and divine: 18.4. In a familiar image, vindication
(*ṣedeq*: 61.11) and salvation blaze brightly so that all nations see
Zion's glory (*kābôd*: 60.1-2, 13, 19; 61.6). A new name symbolizes
transformation. (See 58.14 for 'mouth of the Lord'.)

Samaria was anything but a beautiful crown (*tip'eret*: 28.1-4).
Zion is like the Lord in 28.5, a true crown, and is in the Lord's
hand (49.16), not on the Lord's head. Royalty is transformed into

an institution of care and protection, not of power and severity (49.7, 23). Zion is no longer Forsaken (*ªzûbâ* 49.14; 60.15) and Desolate (*šªmāmâ* 49.19; 61.4), but My Delight is in Her (*ḥepṣî-bâ*: at 44.28) and Married (*bª'ûlâ*: 54.5). Verse 5 is comprised of two similes comparing Zion's builders-sons (at 49.17) and God to the joy (*śûś*) of a newly married couple.

The prophet has posted watchmen on Jerusalem's walls (60.11, 18); like the prophet, they are never silent. They are not there to warn the city of trouble as the sentinels in 21.6-12 are, but to remind the Lord that he has promised to establish Jerusalem (2.2; 54.14) and to make her a term of praise (61.3, 11). They allow no rest or silence. The divine oath in v. 8 is paralleled in 14.24; 45.23; 54.9. 'His mighty arm' occurs in 41.10; 45.1; 48.13-14; 51.9-11; 59.16. The provision of food recalls 60.16; 61.5 and anticipates 65.21-22 when people enjoy the fruits of their labor. The harvesters praise the Lord. The Lord's 'holy courts' (1.12!) is another cultic phrase designating the place or state of being with the Lord (56.7; 57.13; 60.13).

The chapter, and all of 60–62, close with a summons for those in Jerusalem to go out through the open gates (60.11, 18) to 'prepare the way of the people' as others 'prepared the way of the Lord' (40.3). The highway project is underway. Clearing the stones, however, recalls the preparation of the vineyard in 5.2 which had a disastrous outcome. Even in its most joyous and glorious parts, the vision is troubled by the memory and reality of evil and judgment. Raising a standard, a signal, is also double in its signification of judgment (5.26; 13.2) and salvation (11.10-12; 49.22). Verse 11 presents a scene; *hinnēh* occurs three times. See, he declares without limit (48.20) that Zion's salvation approaches; see, his recompense is with him (49.4; 11c repeats 40.10b). The people are transformed and renamed, Holy, as forecast in 4.3 (63.18). They are redeemed (35.9; 51.10). She who seeks the Lord is now Sought Out (55.6); she who once felt forsaken is now Not Forsaken (v. 4; 49.14).

Chapter Sixty-Three

The watchmen for the Lord (62.6) are surprised when they see a powerful and blood-stained warrior coming from Edom, the site of a bloody slaughter (34.5-7), but it is the Lord with deliverance and salvation. His robes are red because he has trodden the wine-press (*'ādōm*, red, puns on *ªdôm*, Edom; see Gen. 25.29-34). Tread-ing and trampling are familiar actions (see at Isa. 10.6) that allude to the vineyard (5.1-7), Assyria (10.6) and the wise farmer (28.23-29). In verse 3c, 'stained' (*'eg'āltî*) puns on redeemed (*g^e'ûlâ*). As in 59.15-18, God acts alone in his wrath (the word occurs three times; 34.2). The 'time of vengeance' was noted at 61.2 (see 49.8). Although he has no helper (50.7-9!), his own arm (62.8) saves him. This alludes to the powerful arm of the Lord in 51.9-11. 'To crush' is translated 'to make drunk' in 51.21; 'to pour out' is 'to bring to earth', that is, to the netherworld as in 14.11, 15.

An unidentified speaker, or the people as speaker, praises the Lord in vv. 7-14 for his salvation of Israel in days of old despite their sin. This is the praise forecast in 62.9. The praise is the basis for a communal petition and confession to the Lord that begins in v. 15 and extends through ch. 64; note the shorter confessional counterpoint in 59.9-15a. To praise someone is to tell of their greatness or great deeds. 'To recount' is a causative form of the verb 'to remember' (see 12.4; 26.13; 49.1; 62.6); to praise is to bring to mind. 'Gracious deeds' and 'steadfast love' are both forms of *hesed* (at 16.5; 54.8, 10; 55.3) which bracket the list of divine goodness in v. 7.

Back then he thought that his people, his children, would not lie (57.4!; 59.13!); he, his very presence, saved them from distress because of his love and pity. He carried them in those past times (40.11, 31; Exod. 19.4). 'But they', in sharp contrast, tormented 'his holy spirit' (vv. 11, 14) and he, in response, warred against them. This, in brief, is a summary of the times of exodus, wandering and conquest. While at war with the Lord, they remembered (v. 7; 46.8-9) the times of Moses, times of freedom and divine care, and wondered, where is God now? In vv. 11b-14, they recall the God who brought them out of Egypt, through the sea, and settled them in the land. He brought them through the sea, through divided waters and depths (43.2, 16; 51.9-11). The shepherds in v. 11 are not the rapacious shepherds of 56.11. He enspirited the people and led them with 'his glorious [*tip'eret*] arm'. They did not stumble then as they do now; then they rested, now they grope and growl; then they were like sure-footed horses and cattle, now like bears and doves (59.9-15a). He led them, as in 49.10, to make himself a glorious name (*šēm tip'eret*) to match his everlasting name in v. 12 (*šēm 'ôlām*).

In 63.15–64.12, the community, 'we', lament their misery, confess their sin and ask God to look and to act (18.4). This, in general, repeats the structure of vv. 7-14, which itself contains the repetitive structure: a past time of divine graciousness is negated by human sin and the resultant divine punishment; the broken people recall the past and ask God to act graciously towards them again.

At one time, God looked and there was no one to help (63.5). His dwelling on high is holy and glorious (*tip 'eret*: vv. 12, 14). Where? occurs for the third time (v. 11). Divine zeal (9.7; 42.13; 59.17), martial might (11.2; 28.6; 42.13), yearning and compassion are no longer manifest. God is their father, 'Our Redeemer from times past'. Neither Abraham nor Israel recognize them (51.2), although all peoples should (61.9). This again reflects the division and debate about the book of Isaiah; his vision is so novel and different that it is not acknowledged as legitimate by others who consider themselves Israel, the true children of Abraham. Isaiah, in response, clothes his argument in traditional discourse and imagery. His vision of the Lord is the Lord of exodus and conquest; if people accept and act on the vision, then they will re-experience divine deliverance from their desolation and will be brought to the Lord's holy mountain.

Where? is followed by Why? in v. 17. The Lord has caused them to wander (*tā'â*: 3.12; 35.8-10!; 47.15; 53.6) from his ways; they don't fear him as they should (25.3; 33.6; 59.19). God must return (*šûb*) for his servants (54.17; 56.6), his tribes (49.6); this is a twist on the usual theme of the people's need to return (1.27; 44.22; 59.20). The people had possession (57.13) for a short time but now enemies trample (v. 6) the sanctuary (43.28; 60.13!). The people are treated like those with another God (26.13) and those called by another name. A different name is now a symbol of judgment, not restoration.

Chapter Sixty-Four

The chapter is 'our' request that the Lord intervene in this scene of sin and desolation. The petition is mixed with praise and confession. 'O [*lû*] that you would . . .' is matched by the Lord's 'O [*lû*] that you had . . .' to Israel (48.18). The Lord spreads the heavens (40.22; 44.24); now he should rend them and come down from his high and lofty place (57.15). 'Quaking mountains' recall 'trembling mountains' (5.25; 13.13). The double simile in v. 2 combines fire and water (30.14; 43.2; 60.5). The intervention is so that the enemies may know God's name (45.3-6; 63.12-19) and that the nations may tremble.

Once God performed fearsome deeds that 'we' hadn't expected ('waited for': 59.9-11; 5.1-7). Verse 4 is the people's reiteration of

the Lord's self-affirmations (43.11-13; 45.5, 21-22; 46.9). He acts
for those who wait for him (8.17; 30.18), those who remember his
ways (63.7). 'But you' changed and so did 'we'. You were angry
and we sinned; any causal relation between divine anger and
human sin is left open (the meaning of 5d is uncertain).

Verses 5-7 are the people's lament of their sin and desolation.
They are unclean (6.5; 35.8!; 52.1, 11!). They fade like a leaf
(1.30; 34.4) and their sins blow them away (40.24; 41.16). None
of them call on the divine name (48.1-2!; 63.19) or cling to God
('take his hand': 45.1; 56.2-6). The hidden God is a motif encountered at 8.17; 45.15; 57.17; 59.2. God, 'our father', echoes 63.16
(45.10). The contrast between 'we', the people, and 'you', God, is
accentuated in Hebrew by the repeated use of the pronouns.
People had the relation between clay and potter backwards in
29.16 and 45.9. (Clay is not just formed but also trodden on: 10.6;
41.25; 63.3.) The play on work and worker recalls 17.7-8; 29.16;
44.2; 51.13; 54.5; 60.21.

Verses 9 and 12 are petitions framing a description of a burned
and desolate land (1.7); the frame is marked by the repetition of
the adverbial phrase *'ad me'ōd* translated 'exceedingly' and 'so
severely'. God's anger (v. 5) and punishment should have limits
as he has promised (6.11-13; 47.6; 48.9; 54.7-9; 57.16-18). 'Now
consider' (*hēn habbēṭ*) matches 'Look' (*habbēṭ*) in 63.15; both sections are petitions. 'We are your people' balances 'you are our
father'; this is the heart of the relationship between the Lord
and his people: 'I am your God and you are my people' (at 43.5).

All is destroyed—cities, Zion-Jerusalem, house-temple and
pleasant places. Listing and contrasts emphasize the destruction: wilderness (51.3!; 63.13!); desolation (1.7; 6.11); burned
(1.7; 9.5; 33.12; 47.14); and ruins (44.26). But all of these places
have been holy, beautiful (*tip'eret*) and sites of praise (60.6, 18;
63.7). Faced with the ruin of his holy places, can God still hold
himself back (42.14; 63.15), keep quiet (57.11; 62.1; 65.6) and
continue to afflict (*'innâ*) them exceedingly (v. 9)?

Chapter Sixty-Five

Although chs. 65–66 bring Isaiah to a conclusion, they do not
resolve its tensions and problems. The vision is still of an open
and inclusive community; the Lord is God of all yet God of his
servants in a special way; there is a distinction between the
righteous and the wicked but the distinction does not correspond to identifiable social or national groups; finally, there

are still those who question and reject Isaiah's vision. The righteous and the wicked are those who follow the Lord's ways and those who choose their own ways. A final separation of the two groups, and the destruction of the latter, is hoped for, but it is not a reality.

The Lord speaks in 65.1-7; a speech formula occurs only in v. 7. God is available to those who do not seek him. Neither Ahaz nor the people ask for the Lord's counsel (7.11-12; 30.20); if they do seek it, it is under false pretenses (58.2). God is present ('Here I am': 52.6; 58.9), but the nation does not call (48.1-2; 64.7). (For seeking and finding, see 51.1 and 55.6.)

His hands are spread out (1.15!) to rebels (1.23; 30.1) whose way is not good (1.17). ('Devices' are 'thoughts' in 55.7-9.) Verses 2-5a are composed of a series of participles and related imperfect forms describing the people. Worship in gardens is condemned in 1.29-30 (17.10-11); such worship perverts the restored garden of 61.11, the new Garden of Eden (51.3). 'Incense is an abomination' (1.13; 41.24; 44.19). Verses 3-4 describe particular pagan cultic practices. 5a is bitterly sarcastic. The people are holy, not the Lord, and want him to stay away from them; in Hebrew 'keep to yourself' is 'be near to yourself' (55.6!).

Indeed, vv. 5-7 are ironic since several of the terms and images occur elsewhere with positive connotations. Their incense is not a fragrant offering but noxious smoke to the Lord. Fire is a pervasive image and anticipates the unquenchable fire of 66.24 (1.31). 'See [hinnēh], it is written', that is, read and reread Isaiah. In a twist of the people's petition in 64.12 and of the prophet's and sentinels's resolve in 62.1, 6-7, the Lord affirms that he will not keep silent. However, his action will be the punishment that they want removed. 'To repay' is *šālēm (at 9.6-7; 44.26-28; 57.18; 59.18). They revile God although he destroyed those who reviled them (51.7). 'Payment' is pᵉullâ which is positive 'reward, recompense' in 40.10; 49.4; 61.8; 62.11.

In his speeches in vv. 8-12 and 13-16 the Lord distinguishes sharply between 'my servants' and 'you who forsake the Lord'. He begins with a simile. Because wine is found in a grape cluster, it is not destroyed (51.13; 54.16); 'there is a blessing in it'. Indirectly this recalls the vineyard which is overrun (5.1-7); directly, 'the blessing in the midst of the earth' which are Israel, Egypt and Assyria (19.23-25). Using the latter in the simile, the earth will not be destroyed because of these three nations. The simile anticipates the blessings in vv. 16 and 23 (66.3!). The impact of the simile is not simple or obvious. At first glance, the comparison seems to refer to judgment that leaves a (righteous) remnant, figured as the wine, the blessing. This is the point of smelting and refining in 1.21-26 and 4.2-4 and of threshing in 27.12-13. But it is the grape cluster as a whole that is not destroyed; the image is not one in which juice is produced and the refuse of the grape thrown away. The point God draws at the close of v. 8 is analogous; for his servants's sake, he will not destroy the whole. What and how much is to be destroyed is not addressed. Threshing, as described in 28.23-29 and not in 27.12-13, is a related image and process. A harvester beats the grain but not forever; he crushes it but does not pulverize or annihilate it. Not everything is destroyed, but the passage does not explicitly describe what is left.

In v. 9 the Lord shifts slightly and employs the remnant image. He leaves a descendant, an inheritor, a chosen one, his servants. Servants can be a fourth category or a summary category inclusive of the first three which are all singular. At points all of these terms, including servant, are used of Jacob, of God's people, without a distinction between righteous and wicked. Most of the parallels that I note to vv. 10-16 indicate that these verses are anchored in Isaiah and that it is impossible to equate the 'wicked' with any one social or national group. Similar to the many identifications of the 'righteous' or of 'the one sent', sections such as these define what it is to be against the Lord, to choose things that do not please him (see at 42.1-9 and 61.1-4). 'To inherit' is *yāraš, 'to possess': 57.13; 60.21; 61.7; 63.18! ('Wine', tîrôš, puns on the term.) Jacob–Israel is the chosen in 42.1; 43.20; 45.4.

Sharon in the west and Achor in the east are a merism for the entire land. However, 'pasture' and 'place to lie down' symbolize both peace (11.6-7; 32.18; 35.7) and devastation (13.20-21; 17.2; 27.10; 34.13). Isaianic images do not have one single meaning and are not used in only one type of context. The renewal is for the benefit of 'my people who seek me' (v. 1). The distinction between 'righteous' and 'wicked' is developed with a vengeance in vv. 11-16. 'But you' (masculine plural) presents the contrasting group, the ones addressed directly. They forget the Lord (51.13; 58.2) and engage in blatant pagan cultic practices worshipping Gad (Fortune) and Meni (Destiny), deities of fate.[1]

---

1. Muilenburg, 'Isaiah', pp. 751-52.

God destines (*mānîtî* puns on *m*ᵉ*nî*) them to sword (1.20; 3.25; 13.15; 34.5-6) and slaughter (34.2, 6). They did not answer when he called them; instead they did evil and chose what did not please (*ḥāpēṣ*) God (56.4!). 'Therefore', which looks both back and forward (at 5.24), introduces a second divine utterance that pointedly plays 'you' and 'my servants' off against each other. Verses 13-14 contain four contrasts marked by *hinnēh* (see RSV: 'behold') and 'but you' (v. 11); the contrasts are typical: eat-be hungry; drink-be thirsty; and rejoice-be ashamed. The shame (at 50.6-7) is expanded upon at the expense of 'you' since one good is offset by two evils: 'gladness of heart', by 'pain of heart' and 'anguish of spirit'; 'sing', by 'cry out' and 'wail'.

'Your name' will be used as an oath; this does not have to be a curse. (For to swear, see v. 16; 14.24; 45.23; 54.9.) Although there are grammatical problems with the reading, 'May the Lord God kill you' is a possible translation of 15b and could be the oath, in content a curse;[1] 'you' is masculine singular in contrast to the masculine plural of the context.

The context speaks of ongoing suffering, not the finality of death.[2]

'Another name' and 'a different name' are both adequate translations of the end of v. 15. The first emphasizes the servants's transformation (62.2); the second, their distinction. Verse 16 stresses blessing and oath, perhaps implying the use of the servants's new name. 'Of faithfulness' is *'āmēn*, Amen![3] 'Forgetting' and 'being hidden' are positive when it is a matter of 'former troubles or distress' (43.18; 46.9!; 49.2).

Verse 17 shifts to a scene: *kî hinᵉnî* with a participle. 'See, I am creating a new heavens and a new earth.' This echoes the book's opening call and all the book's depictions of the violence and corruption on the earth, despite that fact that former things are not remembered (44.21!). New creation is accompanied by joy (*śûś*; *gîl*: 42.8-12; at ch. 61). 18b is a second scene: *kî hinᵉnî* with a participle. 'See, I am creating Jerusalem a joy [*gîlâ*], her people, gladness [*māśôś*].' 'Her people' are 'my people' (51.16; 64.8); there is no crying in her (v. 14!; 30.19).

1. Muilenburg, 'Isaiah', p. 753.
2. Westermann, *Isaiah 40–66*, p. 406.
3. Muilenburg, 'Isaiah', p. 754.

Long life (ch. 38) is highlighted by the four members of v. 20 and the simile 'like the days of a tree' (6.13) in v. 22. The devastation of the land (5.8-10), figured as cutting down a forest in ch. 10, is overcome by building and planting, by eating and drinking; the people enjoy the fruits of their labor, 'the work of their hands' (49.4!; 62.8-9). They are blessed (v. 8). Previously others, whether conquerors or corrupt leaders, have consumed their produce (3.13-15; 56.9-12). The vision of restored Jerusalem in chs. 60–62 is a major part of the new creation. In the new order, the Lord responds before people even call out, an advance over 30.19 and 58.9 (65.12!). The close of the scene invokes the peaceful vision of 11.6-9, of creation restored to its state at the end of Genesis 1. The attributes and work of the shoot in Isa. 11.1-5 have been transferred to the servant(s), the chosen, the one(s) called and sent, the people as prophet, priest and king. 'My holy mountain' is the new creation, the new heavens and earth, the place where all flesh trusts in the Lord and walks in his paths.

Chapter Sixty-Six

The book of Isaiah closes with a chapter comprised of statements and scenes of sin and judgment, joy and abundance, and life and death. It is a fitting ending for the book because of its variety and because of its refusal to tie everything together, to leave no loose ends.

Since the Lord dwells in heaven and on earth and everything in them is his creation, he asks, what is this ('ê zeh), a house? Human works, whether altars, temples or idols, are not God. Nor can a human building contain God. The question, and all of Isaiah by implication, does not reject a temple or sanctuary in itself; it rejects the theology and ideology that would in any way restrict God's presence in the world to a particular building or site. This is consonant with Isaiah's vision of an open community to which all can come (2.2-4); the dwelling place of the community is a pavilion, a tent (4.2-6; 33.20; 54.2), not a fortified and closed city. The latter are destroyed (24.10-13), and this place's walls and gates are Salvation and Praise (60.18).

Membership in the community, residence on the Lord's holy mountain, derives from a person's response to and attitude towards God, walking in the Lord's paths, and not from genealogy or political affiliation. 'But on this one' (we'el zeh) I look (63.15; 64.9), 'the humble and contrite in spirit'; the latter has both religious and physical connotations (see at 57.14-15). To this point 'trembling' has been negative (10.29; 19.16; 32.11; 41.5); now it is akin to the positive fear of the Lord (8.13; 11.2-3).

In vv. 3-4, God denounces those who choose and delight in their own ways (56.4!; 65.2-3). Verse 3 begins with a series of seven participial phrases that are simply juxtaposed; there is no 'like' or other connective term in Hebrew. The relationship between the members, whether comparison or equivalence, is left open. Slaughterer, killer, sacrificer and neck-breaker, are listed as the attributes of each member of this group. 'Yes they choose . . .' and 'yes I choose . . .', both employing *gam* with the pronoun, stress the poetic justice. The last portion of v. 4 repeats the last part of 65.12 and continues the sharp distinction between the Lord's enemies and the Lord's worshippers.

Verse 5 stands separate as a summons to the Lord's servants. They are hated and spurned by their own people ('your brothers') because they are called by the Lord's name (60.9; 63.19!). Being hated associates them with the majestic, but hated, woman of 60.15). The mockery of their foes links the people's joy and God's glory, thereby underlining the relationship between people and God; both joy and glory contrast with the foes's shame. Verse 6 also stands separate. It recalls the cosmic army of ch. 13. 'Listen' and 'voice' are both *qôl* (13.4; 40.3, 6!); an uproar is heard. In 66, the din is from the city, the temple (44.28), and not the mountains. The temple is a scene of retribution (*šālēm: 65.6), not worship.

Verses 7-14a, in three sections (7-9; 10-11; 12-14a), abruptly switch from judgment and speak of Zion-Jerusalem's vindication and abundance; 7-9 are spoken in general and end with address to Zion, 'Your [feminine singular] God'. Wondrously she gives birth before the onset of labor and its pain (13.8!; 42.14!; 49.19-21). Verses 8-9 accentuate the unprecedented event with six rhetorical questions. No one has seen or heard the like (48.3-8!); a land and nation are not born overnight, but Zion delivered her children in a moment. God both opens and delivers; he does not close. This refers to the womb and childbirth here and alludes to other closed entities—eyes, cities, prisons—that can be opened.

Verses 10-11 address a masculine plural group who love Jerusalem (56.6; 61.8). They rejoice with her; all three verbs for joy occur in v. 10 (at 61.3, 7, 10; 65.18-19). Mourning for Zion is at an end (60.20; 61.2-3). The imagery of nursing, carrying and feeding in v. 12 is paralleled in 40.11; 49.23; 55.2; 60.4-5, 16; comfort and

consolation, both from the same verb, are highlighted (v. 13). 12-
14a are a divine speech in which the Lord presents a scene: *hinᵉnî*
with a participle (65.17-18). The prosperity (*šālôm*) and wealth
(*kābôd*) of nations (60.5) are like a flood in their abundance, not
in their destructiveness (8.5-8; 30.27-28; 48.18-19). With the simile of mother and child, God highlights comfort by using the term
three times. See, rejoice and flourish combine light and plant
imagery; 14a rounds off 10-14a by repeating the theme of joy.

In 14b-16(17), the poet returns to vv. 1-6 with the theme of
retribution and the separation of God's servants and enemies.
The Lord's fury (10.5; 13.5; 30.27) is against his foes; he comes in
fire, like a whirlwind (5.28; 29.6), with anger, rage and rebuke
(50.2; 51.17, 20; 54.9); the result is judgment, the sword and
corpses (3.25-26; 14.18-19; 34.3). The brutality stands in stark
opposition to the preceding glory. Verse 17 is a comment, an
aside, in the vein of 58.1-5; 65.3-5, 11; 66.3, on those who, in a
perverse manner, ritually prepare themselves to go into gardens
to eat abominations.

(In v. 18 I accept the textual emendations noted in NRSV, but
the reference of the first part of the verse is still not clear.[1]) God
comes to gather all so that all flesh may see his glory (40.5). He
puts a sign in the midst of all the nations; a sign echoes signs of
judgment (7.10-17; 8.18; ch. 20) and salvation (37.30-32; 38.7, 22;
55.13). Survivors (4.2; 10.20; 37.31-32) go to the nations (note the
'survivors of the nations' in 45.20). The nations named in v. 19
represent the Table of Nations in Genesis 10 (60.6-7). Those who
are so far away that they have not yet heard of or seen the Lord's
glory will be told of his glory by these survivors.

They, survivors and nations, bring your kin ('your brothers'
who hate you [v. 5]?) as a gift to the Lord; they come by every
means possible just as the Israelites bring gifts to the Lord's
house. This is analogous to the cultic metaphors in 52.11-12;
56.1-8; ch. 58. Some of them, returnees, survivors and nations,
will be like priests and Levites who minister to the Lord; they
can be foreigners (56.6-7).

Verses 22-23 are two divine statements. The first is a simile
comparing the endurance of the new heavens and earth, 'that I
am making', to the endurance of 'your' (masculine plural)
descendants and name. This looks back to the promises of name

1. See Conrad, *Isaiah*, pp. 92-97.

and posterity in 55.13 and 56.3-5 and into the future since it is
'your descendants' and not 'you' (60.14; 61.9). They endure forever and, in the same everlasting future, all flesh worships the
Lord; nations and peoples come to the mountain of the house of
the Lord. The particularity of this people and their descendants
is placed in the context of worldwide recognition and acceptance
of the Lord and of his teaching and his ways.

The book of Isaiah closes on a chilling note. They—their specific identity is left indefinite—worship the Lord in his presence,
in his house, in his city, on his holy mountain Jerusalem—I could
continue the metaphors—and then 'they go out' and see the
corpses of the rebels. (The people Israel are rebels at the book's
opening: 1.2, 28.) Their worm (14.11) is immortal and their fire
unquenchable (1.31). They are 'an abhorrence to all flesh'. Abhorrence, dērā'ôn, occurs elsewhere in the Hebrew Bible only in
Dan. 12.2 which is probably alluding to this passage in Isaiah.
The term may have been coined by Isaiah to denote the unique
disgust with the rebels. The verse is chilling and, at the same
time, visionary. Surveying Isaiah as a whole, we cannot distinguish and separate 'those within' from 'those without' in terms of
actual social, religious or national groups. The final verse, and
the pointed distinctions in 65–66 which prepare for it, reflect a
hope, a trust, that there is such a distinction and that the Lord
will ultimately put it into effect. It is a hope that humans should
try to bring about by trusting in the Lord, by walking in his ways
and by dwelling on his holy mountain, not by consigning other
humans to the pit outside the redeemed city.

Bibliography

Ackerman, S., 'Isaiah', in *The Women's Bible Commentary* (ed. CA. Newsom and S.H. Ringe; Louisville: Westminster Press, 1992), pp. 161-68.

Ackroyd, P.R., *Studies in the Religious Tradition of the Old Testament* (London: SCM Press, 1987).

Alonso Schökel, L., 'Isaiah', in *The Literary Guide to The Bible* (ed. F. Kermode and R. Alter; Cambridge: Harvard University Press, 1987), pp. 165-83.

Alter, R., *The Art of Biblical Poetry* (New York: Basic Books, 1985).

Auld, A.G., 'Poetry, Prophecy, Hermeneutic: Recent Studies in Isaiah', *SJT* 33 (1980), pp. 567-81.

Berlin, A., *The Dynamics of Biblical Parallelism* (Bloomington: University of Indiana Press, 1985).

—'Motif and Creativity in Biblical Poetry', *Prooftexts* 3 (1983), pp. 231-41.

Brueggemann, W., 'Unity and Dynamic in the Isaiah Tradition', *JSOT* 29 (1984), pp. 89-107.

Clements, R.E., 'Beyond Tradition-History: Deutero-Isaianic Development of First Isaiah's Themes', *JSOT* 31 (1985), pp. 95-113.

—*Isaiah 1–39* (New Century Bible Commentary [RSV]; Grand Rapids: Eerdmans, 1980).

—'The Unity of the Book of Isaiah', *Int* 36 (1982), pp. 117-29.

Clifford, R.J., *Fair Spoken and Persuading: An Interpretation of Second Isaiah* (Theological Inquiries; Ramsey, NJ: Paulist Press, 1984).

Clines, D.J.A., *I, He, We, and They: A Literary Approach to Isaiah 53* (JSOTSup, 1; Sheffield: JSOT Press, 1976).

Conrad, E.W., *Reading Isaiah* (Overtures to Biblical Theology; Minneapolis: Fortress Press, 1991).

Coogan, M.D. (trans. and ed.), *Stories from Ancient Canaan* (Philadelphia: Westminster Press, 1978).

Darr, K.P., 'Like Warrior, Like Woman: Destruction and Deliverance in Isaiah 42.10-17', *CBQ* 49 (1987), pp. 560-71.

Dick, M., 'Prophetic *Poiesis* and the Verbal Icon', *CBQ* 46 (1984), pp. 226-46.

Dumbrell, W.J., 'The Purpose of the Book of Isaiah', *TynBul* 36 (1985), pp. 111-28.

Erlandsson, S., *The Burden of Babylon: A Study of Isaiah 13.2–14.23* (Lund: Gleerup, 1970).

Exum, J.C., 'Of Broken Pots, Fluttering Birds, and Visions in the Night: Extended Simile and Poetic Technique in Isaiah', *CBQ* 43 (1981), pp. 331-52.

—' "Whom Will he Teach Knowledge?": A Literary Approach to Isaiah 28', in Clines, Gunn and Hauser (eds.), *Art and Meaning: Rhetoric in Biblical Literature* (Sheffield: JSOT Press, 1982), pp. 108-39.

Fewell, D.N., 'Sennacherib's Defeat: Words at War in 2 Kings 18.13–19.37', *JSOT* 34 (1986), pp. 79-90.

Fishelov, D., 'The Prophet as Satirist', *Prooftexts 9* (1989), pp. 195-211.

Frye, N., *The Great Code: The Bible and Literature* (New York: Harcourt Brace Jovanovich, 1982).

Geller, S.A., 'A Poetic Analysis of Isaiah 40.1-2', *HTR* 77 (1984), pp. 413-20.

—'Were The Prophets Poets?', *Prooftexts* 3 (1983), pp. 211-21.

Grønbaek, J.H., 'Baal's Battle with Yam—A Canaanite Creation Fight', *JSOT* 33 (1985), pp. 27-44.

Gruber, M.I., 'The Motherhood of God in Second Isaiah', *RB* 90 (1983), pp. 351-59.

Gunn, D.M., 'Deutero-Isaiah and The Flood', *JBL* 94 (1975), pp. 493-508.

Hayes, J.H. and Irvine, S.A., *Isaiah: The Eighth-Century Prophet: His Times & his Preaching* (Nashville: Abingdon Press, 1987).

Irwin, W.H., *Isaiah 28–33: Translation with Philological Notes* (BibOr, 30; Rome: Biblical Institute Press, 1977).

Jensen, J., 'The Age of Immanuel', *CBQ* 41 (1979), pp. 220-39.

Johnson, D.G., *From Chaos to Restoration: An Integrative Reading of Isaiah 24–27* (JSOTSup, 61; Sheffield: JSOT Press, 1988).

Kaiser, O., *Isaiah 1–12* (2nd edn, completely rewritten, trans. J. Bowden; OTL; Philadelphia: Westminster Press, 1983).

—*Isaiah 13–39* (trans. R. Wilson; OTL; Philadelphia: Westminster Press, 1974).

Lack, R., *La symbolique du livre d'Isaïe* (AnBib, 59; Rome: Biblical Institute Press, 1973).

Magonet, J., 'Isaiah's Mountain or the Shape of Things to Come', *Prooftexts* 11 (1991), pp. 175-81.

March, W.E., '*Lākēn*: Its Functions and Meanings', in J.J.Jackson and M. Kessler (eds.) *Rhetorical Criticism: Essays in Honor of James Muilenburg* (Pittsburgh Theological Monograph Series, 1; Pittsburgh: Pickwick Press, 1974), pp. 256-84.

Millar, W.R., *Isaiah 24–27 and the Origin of Apocalyptic* (Harvard Semitic Monographs, 11; Missoula, MT: Scholars Press, 1976).

Miscall, P.D., 'Isaiah: New Heavens, New Earth, New Book', in D.N. Fewell (ed.), *Reading Between Texts* (Louisville: Westminster Press, 1992), pp. 41-56.

—'Isaiah: The Labyrinth of Images', *Sem 54* (1991), pp. 103-21.

Muilenburg, J., 'The Book of Isaiah, Chapters 40–66', in *The Interpreter's Bible,* V (Nashville: Abingdon Press, 1956), pp. 381-773.

Murray, D.F., 'The Rhetoric of Disputation: Re-examination of a Prophetic Genre', *JSOT* 38 (1987), pp. 95-121.

Rice, G., 'A Neglected Interpretation of the Immanuel Prophecy', *ZAW* 90 (1978), pp. 220-27.

Roberts, J.J.M., 'Yahweh's Foundations in Zion (Isa. 28.16)', *JBL* 106 (1987), pp. 27-45.

Sawyer, J.F.A., 'Daughter of Zion and Servant of the Lord in Isaiah: A Comparison', *JSOT* 44 (1989), pp. 89-107.

Schoors, A., *I Am God Your Saviour: A Form-Critical Study of the Main Genres in Is. XL–LV* (VTSup, 25; Leiden: Brill, 1973).

Scott, R.B.Y., 'The Book of Isaiah, Chapters 1–39', in *The Interpreter's Bible*, V (Nashville: Abingdon Press, 1956), pp. 149-381.

Seitz, C.R. (ed.), *Reading and Preaching the Book of Isaiah* (Philadelphia: Fortress Press, 1988).

—'The Divine Council: Temporal Transition and New Prophecy in the Book of Isaiah', *JBL* 109 (1990), pp. 229-47.

Tromp, N.J., *Primitive Conceptions of Death and the Nether World in the Old Testament* (BibOr, 21; Rome: Biblical Institute Press, 1969).

Tsumura, D.T., '*Tōhû* in Isaiah XIV 19', *VT* 38 (1988), pp. 361-64.

Watson, W.G.E., 'Further Examples of Semantic-Sonant Chiasmus', *CBQ* 46 (1984), pp. 31-33.

—'Gender-Matched Synonymous Parallelism in the Old Testament', *JBL* 99 (1980), pp. 321-41.

Watts, J.D.W., *Isaiah 1–33* (WBC, 24; Waco, TX: Word Books, 1985).

—*Isaiah 34–66* (WBC, 25; Waco, TX: Word Books, 1987).

Webb, B.G., 'Zion in Transformation: A Literary Approach to Isaiah', in D.J.A. Clines, S.E. Fowl and S.E. Porter (eds.), *The Bible in Three Dimensions* (JSOTSup, 87; Sheffield: JSOT Press, 1990), pp. 65-84.

Webster, E.C., 'A Rhetorical Study of Isaiah 66', *JSOT* 34 (1986), pp. 93-108.

—'The Rhetoric of Isaiah 63–65', *JSOT* 47 (1990), pp. 89-102.

Westermann, C., *Isaiah 40–66: A Commentary* (OTL; Philadelphia: Westminster Press, 1969).

Wilcox, P. and D. Paton-Williams, 'The Servant Songs in Deutero-
        Isaiah', *JSOT* 42 (1988), pp. 79-102.
Wilshire, L.E., 'The Servant City: A New Interpretation of the "Servant
        of The Lord" in the Servant Songs of Deutero-Isaiah', *JBL*
        94 (1975), pp. 356-67.
Whybray, R.N., *The Second Isaiah* (OT Guides; Sheffield: JSOT Press,
        1983).
—*Thanksgiving for a Liberated Prophet: An Interpretation of Isaiah
        Chapter 53* (JSOTSup, 4; Sheffield: JSOT Press, 1978).
Yee, G.A., 'The Anatomy of Biblical Parody: The Dirge Form in 2 Sam-
        uel 1 and Isaiah 14', *CBQ* 50 (1988), pp. 565-86.
—'The Form-Critical Study of Isaiah 5.1-7 as a Song and a Juridical
        Parable', *CBQ* 43 (1981), pp. 30-40.

Index of Authors

Printed in the United Kingdom
by Lightning Source UK Ltd.
120643UK00001B/740